DANGER OF HINDUTVA TO SECULAR INDIA

DANGER OF HINDUTVA TO SECULAR INDIA

DANGER OF HINDUTVA TO SECULAR INDIA

R R Choudhary

MD PUBLICATIONS PVT LTD
NEW DELHI
www.mdppl.com

Published by :

MD Publications Pvt Ltd
"MD House", 11, Darya Ganj,
New Delhi - 110 002
Phone : +91-11-45355555
E-mail : contact@mdppl.com
Website: www.mdppl.com

ISBN: 978-81-7533-284-3

Published and Printed by Mr. Pranav Gupta on behalf of **MD Publications Pvt Ltd** at Mohit Enterprises, Delhi.

PREFACE

The term "Hindutva" is derived from the two terms "Hindu Tattva", which literally mean "Hindu Principles". Now the question is what Hindu Principles are and what comprises the "Hindutva" Outlook? Hindutva a word coined by Vinayak Damodar Savarkar is the term used to describe movements advocating Hindu nationalism. Hindutva is commonly identified as the guiding ideology of the Sangh Parivar, a family of Hindu Nationalist organizations, and of the Rashtriya Swayamsevak Sangh in particular. In general, *Hindutvavaadis* (followers of Hindutva) believe that they represent the well-being of Hinduism, Sikhism, Buddhism, Ayyavazhi, Jainism and all other religions prominent in India.

While the 1990s saw the beginning of the confrontation between the Hindutva and the secular, pluralist forces in Indian polity and society, much of the ground was prepared by the creation of a 'Hindu' public through religious serials on TV. While the book under review traces the connection between religious and market fundamentalism, it fails in its understanding of the Nehruvian model of development.

During the 1990s, Indian society, polity, culture and economy experienced a break with the past 40 years of post-Independence India, because all secular, modern and moral principles underlying the pluralist and secular constitutional democracy were in pieces before the forces of Hindutva.

In India, an umbrella organization called the Sangh Parivar champions the concept of Hindutva. The Sangh comprises organizations such as the RSS, Bharatiya Janata Party, Bajrang Dal, and the Vishwa Hindu Parishad. This ideology has existed since the early 20th century, forged by Veer Savarkar, but came to prominence in Indian politics in the late 1980s, when two events attracted a large number of mainstream Hindus to the movement. The first of these events was the Rajiv Gandhi government's use of its large Parliamentary Majority to overturn a Supreme Court verdict granting alimony to an old woman that had angered many Muslims. The second was the dispute over the 16th century Mughal Babri Mosque in Ayodhya - built by Babur after his first major victory in India. The Supreme Court of India refused to take up the case in the early 1990s, leading to a huge outcry. Tempers soon flared, and a huge number of nationalist Hindus from all parts of India razed the mosque in late 1992, causing nationwide communal riots. The razing of the mosque and subsequent conflict arguably lifted the BJP and Hindutva to international prominence.

I am very grateful to Mr. Pranav Gupta, Director of MD Publications Pvt Ltd, New Delhi, for his kind cooperation and support for this book.

R R Choudhary

Contents

	Preface	*v*
1.	Hindu Revivalism and the Hindutva Movement	1
2.	At the Mercy of Hindu Nationalism	25
3.	Hindutva and Multiculturalism	45
4.	Gandhian and Secularist Critique of Hindutva	87
5.	Hindutva and Cultural Nationalism	113
6.	Hindutva: The Brahman Conspiracy	133
7.	Hindu Nationalism: Origins, Ideologies and Modern Myths	155
8.	The Concept of Hindu Nation	173
9.	The Notion of "Hindu Fascism"	195
10.	The Emergence of Hindu Nationalism in India	281
	Bibliography	289
	Index	293

1

Hindu Revivalism and the Hindutva Movement

Hindutva is the term used to describe movements advocating Hindu nationalism. In India, an umbrella organization called the Sangh Parivar champions the concept of Hindutva. The sangh comprises organizations such as the RSS, Bharatiya Janata Party, Bajrang Dal, and the Vishwa Hindu Parishad. This ideology has existed since the early 20th century, forged by Veer Savarkar, but came to prominence in Indian politics in the late 1980s, when two events attracted a large number of mainstream Hindus to the movement. The first of these events was the Rajiv Gandhi government's use of its large Parliamentary Majority to overturn a Supreme Court verdict granting alimony to an old woman that had angered many Muslims.

The second was the dispute over the 16th century Mughal Babri Mosque in Ayodhya— built by Babur after his first major victory in India. The Supreme Court of India refused to take up the case in the early 1990s, leading to a huge outcry. Tempers soon flared, and a huge number of nationalist Hindus from all parts of India razed the mosque in late 1992, causing nationwide communal riots. The razing of the mosque and subsequent conflict arguably lifted the BJP and Hindutva to international prominence. According to Savarkar, Hindutva is meant to denote the Hindu characteristic, or Hinduness.

In a judgment the Supreme Court of India ruled that "no precise meaning can be ascribed to the terms 'Hindu',

'Hindutva' and 'Hinduism'; and no meaning in the abstract can confine it to the narrow limits of religion alone, excluding the content of Indian culture and heritage." The Court also ruled that "Ordinarily, Hindutva is understood as a way of life or a state of mind and is not to be equated with or understood as religious Hindu fundamentalism. A Hindu may embrace a non-Hindu religion without ceasing to be a Hindu and since the Hindu is disposed to think synthetically and to regard other forms of worship, strange gods and divergent doctrines as inadequate rather than wrong or objectionable, he tends to believe that the highest divine powers complement each other for the well-being of the world and mankind."

It believes in an "integral" and "holistic" approach to create a harmonious society. It does not accept the Western political philosophies as a blueprint for the Indian society, because of their "preoccupation" with materialism [citation required], and their overall over-looking of the social well-being of the individual. Both capitalism and socialism are seen as inadequate - stimulating as they do from greed, class antagonisms, exploitation and social anarchy.

CULTURAL NATIONALISM

According to this, the natives of India share a common culture, history and ancestry. M S Golwalkar, one of the main proponents of Hindutva believed that India's diversity in terms of customs, traditions and ways of worship was its uniqueness and that this diversity was not without the strong underlying cultural basis which was essentially native. He believed that the Hindu natives with all their diversity, shared among other things "the same philosophy of life", "the same values" and "the same aspirations" which formed a strong cultural and a civilizational basis for a nation.

Savarkar similarly believed that the Indian subcontinent (which includes the area south of the Himalaya and the Hindu Kush or Akhand Bharat is the homeland of the Hindus. He considered "Hindus" as those who consider India to be their motherland (*matrubhumi*), fatherland as well as their holy land, hence describing it purely in cultural terms. RSS, one of the main votaries of Hindutva has stated that it believes in a cultural connotation of the term Hindu. "The term Hindu in the conviction as well as in the constitution of the RSS is a cultural and civilizational concept and not a political or religious dogma.

"The term as a cultural concept will include and did always include all including Sikhs, Buddhists, Jains, Muslims, Christians and Parsis. The cultural nationality of India, in the conviction of the RSS, is Hindu and it was inclusive of all who are born and who have adopted Bharat as their Motherland, including Muslims, Christians and Parsis. The answering association submit that it is not just a matter of RSS conviction, but a fact borne out by history that the Muslims, Christians and Parsis too are Hindus by culture although as religions they are not so."

SOCIAL JUSTICE

The acceptance that Hindu social structure "is ridden with castes and communities", and that this has led to "barriers and segregation" and condemnation of "obnoxious vice of social inequality" and "untouchability".The supporters of Hindutva have a positive outlook towards the *Dalit* community, which they aim to bring to leadership positions in their organizations.

UNIFORM CIVIL CODE

Leaders subscribing to Hindutva have been known for their demands for a Uniform Civil Code for all the citizens of India. They believe that differential laws based on religion are violative of Article 44 of Indian Constitution and have sowed the seeds of divisiveness between different religious communities. The advocates of Hindutva often use the term pseudo-secularism to refer to policies which they believe are unduly favorable towards the Muslims and Christians. They oppose what they see as a 'separate-but-equal' system; some supporters of Hindutva see it as the Indian National Congress party's effort to woo the sizable minority vote bank at the expense of true equality.

The subject of a Uniform Civil Code, which would remove special religion-based provisions for different religions (Hindus, Muslims, Christians, etc.) from the Indian Constitution, is thus one of the main agendas of Hindutva organizations. The Uniform Civil Code is opposed by Muslims and political parties like the Indian National Congress and The Communist Party of India (Marxist). Followers of Hindutva have questioned differential religious laws in India which allows polygamy and triple talaq among Muslims and thereby compromises on the status of Muslim women and "marginalizes" them.

The passing of the Muslim Women (Protection of Rights on Divorce) Act, 1986 by Rajiv Gandhi government to dilute the secular judgment of Supreme Court under pressure from the conservative Muslims was opposed by Hindutva organisations. The new act, in tune with the Shariat, denied even utterly destitute Muslim divorcees the right to alimony from their former husbands.

PROTECTION OF HINDU INTERESTS

The followers of Hindutva are known for their criticism of the Indian government as too passive with regard to the ethnic cleansing of Kashmiri Hindus by Kashmiri Muslim separatists and advocates of Hindutva wish a harder stance in Jammu and Kashmir. They have called for the protection of native Hindu traditions holy structures, rivers and the cow (which is considered holy by Hindus). Hindu nationalists have the stated aim of uniting the Hindu society which is plagued by casteism, regionalism, and passive religion.

VIEWS ON OTHER FAITHS

The votaries of Hindutva believe that the way Muslims and Hindus have treated each other in the past is a one-way compromise and they intend on making society more balanced and fair towards the majority Hindu population. The BJP has also invited Muslims to be a part of this new society and work with the Hindus, Buddhists, Jains and Sikhs for a better India. Even more militant parties such as the Shiv Sena have invited Muslims to join and the party leader declared after the Babri

Mosque incident, "We must look after the Muslims and treat them as part of us." Hindutva groups are supportive of the Jewish State of Israel, including Savarkar himself, who supported Israel during its formation. The RSS is politically pro-Israel and actively praised the efforts of Ariel Sharon when he visited India. R.S.S spokesperson Ram Madhav recently expressed support for Israel.

VIEWS ON INDIAN HISTORY

The Hindu organisations like the RSS, believe that the history of India was written by the the Birtish with a condescending attitude towards the native people and their culture. M S Golwalkar writes that the history of ancient India was summed up as "Tanglewood Tales". Similar concerns were raised by Nobel Laureate Rabindranath Tagore in his essay, "The History of Bharatvarsha", way back in 1903. He calls the history books "nightmarish account of India". He writes "while the lands of the aliens existed, there also exists the indigenous country" meaning the latter was grossly being neglected. He adds that the British accounts of Indian history "throw a beam of artificial light on such a spot that in our own eyes the very profile of our country is made dark".

M S Golwalkar argues that it was a delibrate Imperialist strategy to teach Indians a wrong version of history. In this context, writings of Lord Macaulay,"the brain behind the system of English education", are referred to as an indication of this. Lord Macaulay had stated "We must at present do our best to form a class who may be interpreters between us and millions whom we govern - a class of persons Indian in blood and colour, but English in tastes, in opinions, in morals and in intellect." He had also written "No Hindu who has received an English education ever remains sincerely attached to his religion. It is my firm belief that if our plans of education are followed up, there will not be a single idolater among the respected classes 30 years hence."

Senior RSS leader H V Sheshadri refers to this attitude of "White man's burden" which he believes shaped the English education system in India and British version of Indian history.

The RSS is opposed to the theory of Indo-Aryan migration to India, a number believing in the alternative Out of India theory. While largely uncontroversial in academia, the "Aryan Invasion theory" debate in India, involving e.g. Sita Ram Goel, Romila Thapar, Irfan Habib and Arun Shourie, is also a matter of politics. Further information: Indigenous Aryans and Aryan Invasion Theory (history and controversies).

ORGANIZATIONS

Hindutva is commonly identified as the guiding ideology of the Sangh Parivar, a family of Hindu Nationalist organizations, and of the Rashtriya Swayamsevak Sangh in particular. In general, Hindutvavaadis (followers of Hindutva) believe that they represent the well-being of Hinduism, Sikhism, Buddhism, Ayyavazhi, Jainism and all other religions prominent in India. Most nationalists are organized into political, cultural and social organizations. The first Hindutva organisation formed was the Rashtriya Swayamsevak Sangh, founded in 1925. A prominent Indian political party, the Bharatiya Janata Party (BJP) is closely associated with a group of organisations that advocate Hindutva.

They collectively refer to themselves as the "Sangh Parivar" or family of associations, and include the Rashtriya Swayamsevak Sangh (RSS), Bajrang Dal and the Vishva Hindu Parishad. Other organisations include:

- Hindu Swayamsevak Sangh - Overseas branch of the RSS
- Bharatiya Mazdoor Sangh - Worker's Union
- Akhil Bharatiya Vidyarthi Parishad - A Student's Union
- Bharatiya Kisan Sangh - A Farmers' organisation

The major political wing is the BJP which was in power in India's Central Government for six years from 1998 to 2004 and is now the main opposition party. It is also in power in the states of Gujarat, Madhya Pradesh, Chhattisgarh, Karnataka, and Uttaranchal. It is an alliance partner in the states of Orissa, Punjab, and Bihar. Political parties pertaining to the Hindutva ideology are not limited to the Sangh Parivar. Examples of political parties' independent from the Sangh's influence include Praful Goradia's Akhil Bharatiya Jana Sangh and Uma Bharti's Bharatiya Janshakti Party. The influence of these groups is relatively limited.

The controversial Maharashtrian political party, the Shiv Sena, converted its ideology to the Hindutva one in recent times. It has been very influential in the Indian state of Maharashtra. The party is not part of the Sangh Parivar but is associated with the Bharatiya Janata Party. Similar is the Shiromani Akali Dal, which is a Sikh religious party but maintains ties with Hindutva organizations, as they also represent Sikhism.

CRITICISM AND SUPPORT

The opponents of Hinduvta philosophy consider Hindutva ideology as a euphemistic effort to conceal communal beliefs and practices. Many Indian Marxist sociologues have described the Hindutva movement as fascist in classical sense, in its ideology and class support specially targeting the concept of homogenised majority and cultural hegemony. The Hindutva movement on the other hand terms such description as coming from the far left. More moderate critics of Hindutva do not base their criticism on allegations of "fascism", but raise issues with regards to their sometimes-vacillating attitudes towards non-Hindus and secularism.

The epithet of "fascism" is also used to evoke double standards against Hindus in political and academic discourse. The academia and polity have been accused of engaging in a form of anti-Hindu McCarthyism against Hindu political expression by leveling the accusation of "fascism" against anyone who expresses sympathy for Hindus. Marxist critics have used the political epithets of "Indian fascism" and "Hindu fascism" to describe the ideology of the Sangh Parivar. For example, Marxist social scientist Prabhat Patnaik has written that the Hindutva movement as it has emerged is "classically fascist in class support, methods and programme."

Patniak bases this argument on the following "ingredients" of classical fascism present in Hindutva: the attempt to create a unified homogenous majority under the concept of 'the Hindus'; a sense of grievance against past injustice; a sense of cultural superiority; an interpretation of history according to this grievance and superiority; a rejection of rational arguments against this interpretation; and an appeal to the majority based on race and masculinity.

Views on Hindutva and fascism include those of the Christian convert to the RSS viewpoint, Anthony Elenjimittan, who based his views on RSS's symbolism of the Bhagva (the banner of lord Shiva), Dharma Chakra [the Wheel of Faith] and Satyameva Jayate [Truth alone triumphs] (one must note that these symbols are normative in Hinduism and bear no relation to Hindutva and the latter is the national motto of a secular democratic India). The description of Hindutva as fascist has been condemned by pro-Hindutva authors such as Koenraad Elst who claim that the ideology of Hindutva meets none of the characteristics of fascist ideologies.

Claims that Hindutva social service organisations such as the Rashtriya Swayamsevak Sangh are "fascist" have been disputed by academics such as Vincent Kundukulam. Academics Chetan Bhatt and Parita Mukta reject the identification of Hindutva with fascism, because of *Hindutva*'s embrace of cultural rather than racial nationalism, because of its "distinctively Indian" character, and because of "the RSS's disavowal of the seizure of state power in preference for long-term cultural labour in civil society". They instead describe Hindutva as a form of "revolutionary conservatism" or "ethnic absolutism".

Nobel Laureate VS Naipaul also rejects these allegations and views the rise of Hindutva as a welcome, broader civilizational resurgence of India. The members of RSS (Rashtriya Swayamsevak Sangh) whom I met in Calcutta in early March gathered in their yard every morning just at sunrise. They recitated Gita and sang patriotic songs. After the devotion they concentrated on physical exercises.

Each branch of the RSS ('Hindu home troops') organization acts in the same way throughout India. The Hindu communalism movement consists of the RSS, the VHP (Vishwa Hindu Parishad, 'Hindu World Council') and the BJP (Bharatiya Janata Party, 'Hindu People's Party'). The BJP is nowadays the largest party in the parliament of India. In the Indian context communalism means belief that Hindus, Muslims, Christians and Sikhs form different and distinct communities, so that they constitute separate homogeneous and cohesive communities.

The communalists also believe that in every religion the social and cultural identity is different, because religion forms the foundation for the basic social identity and is the determinant of the basic social relationships. According to the world view of Hindu or Muslim communalists, this means that a 'real' Hindu or Muslim can belong to only one party in the community and all Hindus and Muslims must think alike in politics because they are Hindus or Muslims.

Hindu communalists carried out their old threat on December 6, 1992 and destroyed in Ayodhya. According to tradition, Rama, the incarnation of Vishnu, was born in the holy city of Ayodhya in the Treta Yuga, which would make it thousands of years before the Kali Yuga, sometimes calculated to begin in 3102 BC. Hindu organizations have claimed that Babri Mosque was built in 1528 by the Moghul ruler Babur on the very spot where Ramajanmasthan (the birth temple of Rama) was located. In their world view Rama is the most important god among other Hindu gods, and Ayodhya is the holiest city among other Hindu holy cities. That is why Babri-masjid had to be demolished - in their vocabulary 'to be released'. We can interpret this as an eschatological process compared to the attitudes of Christians and Jews towards the holy city of Jerusalem. Ayodhya had to be released, because it was one of the most important signs that 'Rama Rajya' (the kingdom of Rama) could be realized in the near future. When the BJP won the last assembly election in Maharashtra and Gujarat, their principal newspaper (Organiser) wrote that they celebrated the victory as being as meaningful a historical issue as was the release of the Ramajanmasthan temple.

They argued that this means the beginning of a brand new era for Hindus: the Hindus will take their fate into their own hands, first in Maharashtra and Gujarat and then throughout in the country. In South Asia, religious revivalism has taken many forms in this century, reflecting the multicultural and multireligious complexity of the whole subcontinent. Revivalist movements have also represented a wide spectrum of ideologies, ranging from defences of traditional orthodoxy to completely new formulations of traditional norms and practices.

REVIVALISM IN THE NATIONALIST MOVEMENT

The Indian nationalist movement arose in the second half of the 19th century, basically to meet the challenge of foreign domination. In December 1885 the Indian National Congress was born. Under its leadership Indians started a prolonged struggle for independence. National political consciousness concentrated on the National Congress, and from the beginning it was dominated by upper caste Hindus. Until very late in the 19th century, most leading nationalists were willing to collaborate with the British colonial administration.

A shift from collaboration to criticism came right at the end of last century. Two broad movements emerged among Hindus as a reaction to colonial rule: modernists and revivalists. The former movement adopted basically Western models for political and social change in India while the latter looked back to the roots, to Hindu antiquity. It is obvious that within both groups the ideological sphere was wide. Revivalism included those who wanted to preserve the traditional social order as well as Hindu reforms, whose basic aim was to strengthen Hindu solidarity. Hindu revivalists argued that the national identity could be recovered only by seeking the fundamental religious and cultural truths again. They idealized the past, and demanded a return to the older and purer forms of Hindu culture that had degenerated under foreign rule.

The revivalists preferred a more aggressive, 'kshatriya' (warrior) world view than the modernists. Research by

Western orientalists confirmed the faith of the revivalists in the achievements of Hindu civilization. According to many leading revivalists, Hindu society had degenerated, because Hindus no longer followed *'dharma'*. They claimed that India could not regenerate itself unless dharma was properly observed. For example Aurobindo Ghose emphasized that 'all great awakenings in India, all her periods of mightiest and most varied vigour have drawn their vitality from the fountainhead of some deep religious awakening'. Aurobindo Ghose and other revivalists shared the view that a good society can exist only when it is based on the correct principles of dharma.

Like the millennial movements in Europe, the political character of Indian revivalism derived much of its strength from the importance of preparing for salvation. The 'Dharma-karma' concept was adjusted for political purposes mainly by three persons: Swami Vivekananda (1863-1902), Aurobindo Ghose (1872-1950) and Bal Gangadhar Tilak (1856-1920). They all legitimated their religious and political ideas by the 'Bhagavad Gita'. According to Aurobindo Ghose, the nation was a divine expression of God. That is why he could emphasize that 'nationalism is a religion that has come from God'.

According to Girilal Jain (1994: 45), there are three notable points in Swami Vivekananda's 'religion of patriotism': firstly his identification of Mother India with the supreme God, secondly his attempt to reintroduce the Kshatriya element in the Hindu psyche, and thirdly his conviction that India was destined to be a teacher of the human race in the spiritual reality. On his return to India from the meeting of the Parliament of Religions held in Chicago in 1893, he declared that the indebtedness of the universe to India knew no bounds. While civilizations had come and gone, the civilization of India was 'indestructible and eternal'. And the message of this civilization had to be spread throughout the world.

The Indian National Congress was in the hands of modernists until 1916, although it also included many revivalists, who advocated a more militant style of protest and greater contact with the masses. In 1916 the political power passed to a group, whose leader was the Maharashtrian revivalist B.G. Tilak. Four years later Mohandas Karamchand Gandhi got the leadership of the Congress. At the beginning Gandhi received widespread support from the revivalists when he appeared in India after World War I.

Actually many revivalists believed him to be one of them. But quite soon many of them came to oppose him as they became better acquainted with his basic ideas. The revivalists felt that Gandhi's views were both contradictory to their ideology and what was worse; his ideas were in practice inefficient. They rejected his ascetic non-kshatriya style of leadership, his definition of dharma as the nonviolent pursuit of truth as well as his idea about the Indian nation as a brotherhood of different communities. They preferred 'himsa' (violence) to 'ahimsa', as they connected 'himsa' with Tilak's idea of 'energism' and the militancy needed to drive the British troops from the Indian subcontinent. Moreover, some revivalists claimed that the conception of ahimsa was Christian and not Aryan.

The last straw for the revivalists was the riots between Hindus and Muslims which swept across India in the early 1920s. They felt that Gandhi was wrong. His noncooperation movement did not prevent the riots; on the contrary, it aroused and created communal rioting. Many revivalists believed that it was because of the 'weakness' of the Hindu community, and it could be overcome only if Hindus strengthened their community bonds and adopted a Kshatriya outlook. In this atmosphere in 1915 a new Hindu organization called *Hindu Mahasabha* was founded. It emphasized such Hindu interests as cow protection, Hindi in Devanagari script and caste reforms.

The leaders of Hindu Mahasabha were alarmed by the entry of Muslim 'ulema' into politics, for some Muslim leaders had expressed the need for a holy war and general pan-Islamic aims. The Hindu revivalists felt that they had to create an effective organization if they wanted to struggle against militant Islam. Hindu Mahasabha continued the revivalist tradition, which got its first expressions in Bengal in 1867. The Hindu Mela organization was then formed to revive pride in Hindu civilization. Vinyak Damodar Savarkar founded the Mitra Mela in 1899 in Bombay. It was later known as the *Abhinava Bharat Society (Young India Society)*. It advocated armed struggle to throw off the shackles of foreign rule. But the most famous of these revivalist organizations was the Arya Samaj. It was formed in 1875 by S. D. Sarasvati.

Arya Samaj was a reformist movement which was popular in Northern India, especially in Punjab. It tried to change some basic elements in Hindu religion, for example the hereditary aspect of the caste system, the ritual supremacy of Brahmins, child marriage, and idol worship. The organization also advocated strict monotheism and simplified ritual. It borrowed many organizational techniques from Christian missionaries. Keshav Baliram Hedgewar founded RSS in Nagpur in 1925. From the beginning the organization was connected with the epic story of Ramayana. According to his biographer, he 'chose the sacred day of Vijaya Dashami for the historic occasion'.

That day of Vijaya Dashami when RSS was founded traditionally symbolized the conquest of good over evil, Rama's victory over the demon king Ravana. The rest of the most important festivals are also celebrated on the sacred dates connected with the life of Rama. Hedgewar emphasized the need to develop members of the RSS both physically and spiritually. 'All of us must train ourselves physically, intellectually and in every way so as to be capable of achieving our cherished goal,' he declared in 1925. Wearing uniform (khaki shorts) during parades soon became obligatory for the Swayamsevaks.

A special training programme for selected members was begun in 1927. The object of the programme was to equip the Swayamsevakas to enable them to carry on the RSS activities on their own, wherever they might go. The first training camp in the same year included physical exercises from 5 to 9 in the morning and again in the evening. The afternoon hours were spent in discussion and writing. The traditional Hindu gymnasium is closely associated with the ksahtriya life style all over India. These training camps have continued right up to the present day. The daily activities could start with the following kind of prayer:

> Salutations to the Motherland where I was born
> Salutations to the Hindu Land where I was brought up
> Salutations to the Land of Dharma for which may my body fall
> To Her, I salute again and again.

In the RSS organization the basic units are called 'shakhas' (branches). The membership of each shakha varies between 50 and 100 male participants. Nowadays it is estimated that there are around 300 000 shakhas all over the country. Each shakha is further divided into four age groups: 6-10, 10-14, 14-28 and over 28 years. The age groups are further divided into 'gatas' (groups), which are composed of a common age group, and the members tend to live in a particular locality.

Above the shakha in the pyramid of RSS is the 'mandal committee' (formed from participants from three or four *shakhas*). And then representatives from 10 to 12 mandals form 'a nagar' (city) committee. Above the city committees there may be 'zilla' (district) and 'vibhag' (regional) committees, but most of the daily work takes place at the city level. There are also the 'prantiya pratindhi sabhas' (state assemblies) and the 'Akhil-Bharatiya pratinidhi sabha' (central assembly), but they have no real power.

At the top of the organization is the 'sarsanghchalak'. In their constitution he is called the 'guide and philosopher'. Sometimes he is also called 'guru' or even 'avatar' (the incarnation of Vishnu). M. S. Golwalkar was chosen to this position by Hegdewar in 1940, and B. Deoras was chosen by Golwalkar only a few days before his death in 1973. They claim that a competitive election would be considered a disruptive catalyst, resulting in the disunity of the organization. In the nationalist movement the RSS remained rather nonpolitical until India's independence in 1947.

For example V. D. Savarkar, who was elected president of the Hindu Mahasabha, frequently denounced the RSS for its 'purely cultural' orientation. In 1948 the organization was banned, because the government suspected that the RSS and the Hindu Mahasabha had both been involved in a conspiracy to assassinate Mahatma Gandhi. The assasinator Nathuram Godse had previously been a member of the RSS, but had left the organization because he felt it was not radical enough. At the time of the assassination Godse belonged to the paramilitary Hindu Rashtra Dal organization, which he had formed in 1943. He was also at that time an editor of a pro-Hindu Mahasabha newspaper in Pune.

After the ban RSS was more actively involved in day-to-day politics. They also began organizing various social welfare activities in order to give a new and less paramilitary orientation to the RSS. The results of the new political orientation were seen in the early 1960s. The RSS got more public respect, most dramatically demonstrated by the government's decision to permit its participation in the 26 January Republic Day parade in 1963. The organization clearly benefited from the upsurge in nationalism during the Sino-Indian war in 1962.

By the mid-1970s, when a state of emergency was declared by Prime Minister Indira Gandhi, the RSS was banned a second time among other political parties. During the Emergency years 1975-77, the RSS and the whole Hindutva movement adopted a more liberal interpretation of Hindu nationalism. This also meant that the mutual suspicions of the RSS and its political opponents were reduced significantly. The organization took at least partial credit for the defeat of Prime Minister Gandhi in 1977. The Janata party then won 298 out of the 542 seats. The share of the Jana Sangh party was 93 seats in the Janata alliance.

The Jana Sangh party was formed in 1951 to act as a political wing of the RSS. Some leaders felt that 'though the RSS had mass following, it had no political voice'. But the new party was also strongly opposed by some senior RSS leaders.

The Bharatiya Janata Party (BJP) replaced Jana Sangh in 1980. Before the Jana Sangh party the Hindutva movement was enlarged by a student organization 'the Akhil Bharatiya Vidyarthi Parishad' in 1948. And again in 1955 the Hindu 'family' got a new member: they decided to form a new labour movement, 'the Bharatiya Mazdoor Sangh'.

The trinity of the Hindutva movement was complete when Vishwa Hindu Parishad (VHP) was formed in 1964. The RSS was banned a third time after the demolishing of Babri Mosque in Ayodhya. The national government also declared the VHP an illegal organization. Actually the demolishing was basically organized by the VHP. It organized the worshipping and consecration of bricks in every village with a population of over 2000. These bricks were subsequently to be sent to Ayodhya for the construction of the temple. In this way a large number of Hindus were politically mobilized.

THE CONCEPT OF NATURAL ORDER

The concept of dharma is one of the most important concepts in Hindu world view. Its meaning differs slightly from one religious or philosophical tradition to another, but all interpretations share the view that it means something like 'natural order' or 'innate law' in a special individual, society and in the universe. The Hindu communalists also emphasize the concept of dharma. The second leader of the RSS, M.S. Golwalkar, defined dharma as the innate and fundamental law of the universe and human nature.

According to him, this very law of dharma is the standard for deciding the propriety of behaviour in various situations. He argued that "if we carry this concept of Dharma even further, not only the State and the Nation, but the nature of entire mankind will have to be considered. In other words, the constitution of a nation cannot be contrary to the natural laws". And he emphasizes that since dharma is the supreme law, their ideal of the state must be 'Dharma-Rajya'. The rulers ought to follow those innate laws. Hence even omnipotent God "who can do everything cannot act contrary to Dharma".

In practice this has meant that the Hindu communalists have tried to define the natural inhabitants of Hindustan and the natural borders of the country as well as the natural order in the society. In 1915 V. D. Savarkar wrote a book called '*Hindutva*'. The book deeply influenced the ideas of the RSS founder Keshav Hedgewar. It was precisely the question of who was a Hindu that Savarkar tried to resolve in Hindutva. He declared that the problem came into being because of the loose and eclectic usage of the terms Hindu, Hinduism and Hindutva. Savarkar begins his book with a long discourse on the importance of a name, because "the thing gets mystically entwined with the word that signifies it, the name seems to matter as much as the thing itself".

Savarkar tried to adjust to political sphere the idea of mystical unity of 'word' and 'thing', the idea which is similar to Sufi tradition and certain Hindu bhakti practices. Firstly he tried to choose the proper name for the country. He considered the names applied to India:

Aryavarta, Brahmavarta, Dakshinapath, Bharatvarsha and Hindustan. He chose the last one which was, in his reading, the original, the authentic and most sacred name of this sacred land. In Hindutva Savarkar accepted the common argument that the terms 'Hindu' and 'Hindustan' were derived in the distant past from 'Sindhu', which was given by Aryans to the river Indus and, later, to all rivers and seas in the subcontinent.

Savarkar writes that "it is quite probable that the great Indus was known as Hindu to the original inhabitants of our land and owing to the vocal peculiarity of the Aryans (the easy conversion of the sound 'h' to 's', and vice versa) it got changed into Sindhu. Thus Hindu would be the name that this land and the people that inhabited it bore from time so immmemorial that even the Vedic name Sindhu is but a later and secondary form of it". According to Savarkar the term Hindutva does not mean only the religion Hinduism; it covers the complete Hindu civilization and history. Hinduism is only a fraction of the civilization called Hindutva.

That is why he used the term Hindu to refer to the collectivity of the people of India - Hindus, Muslims, Christians, Sikhs, Parsis, etc. In the rising nationalist movement at the end of last century there are some examples proving that this kind of 'loose' vocabulary was accepted among different religious groups. For example, the Muslim nationalist leader Sir Syed Ahmad Khan (1817-1898) used the term Hindu to mean 'the inhabitants of Hindustan'. The most important thing is that 'real' Hindus accept natural and thus right attitudes towards their land. Savarkar emphasizes that "a Hindu means a person who regards this land of Bharatvarsha, from Indus to the seas as his Fatherland as well as his Holyland that is the cradle land of his religion".

Since Savarkar the RSS leader M. S. Golwalkar has stressed the importance of defining the natural borders of Hindustan. In his most famous book called 'We or our nationhood defined' (1939) Golwalkar means by India or Hindustan the 'lands from sea to sea'. In fact, the map on the cover of the book gives the outline of his geographic limitations of India, which stretches from Afghanistan to Burma and also includes Sri Lanka.

In the caste system of India it has been a very common expression to argue that 'everybody had to follow his/her caste dharma'. If you did not respect your caste duties, then you were acting against the natural order. According to *varnasharam dharma* ideology, mankind is divided into four categories, varnas, which are ranked according to their religious purity. In Hindu literature and in popular Hinduism there are numerous examples which try to legalize and naturalize the caste system by using anatomical and zoological metaphors. Like other animals or species of animals, men have different and unequally important capabilities and potentialities. The popular metaphors may express this: 'you cannot train a tiger to nibble grass, or you cannot train a goat to hunt'. In the same way people belonging to Vaishya Varna are the best generators of wealth because they are naturally acquisitive. And Shudras are the best servants because they are naturally servile.

RAMA-RAJYA

Both individuals and society have to follow their dharmas. The ideal society acts according to the natural order. In the vocabulary of the Hindutva movement the ideal society is called Rama-Rajya or Dharma-Rajya. They believe that the kingdom of Rama really existed once. They describe the Rama-Rajya in a way that is common to numerous descriptions of earthly paradises or the golden ages of mankind. Their mythic story of history used to begin with the pre-Muslim period. It was an age when India was studded with temples. It was a time of growth and development, a time of progress, of high levels of cultural and intellectual achievements. But then came the Muslims, the golden age was over. India declined from the age of civilization to the age of barbarism. The Muslim era meant death and destruction as well as cruelty, forced conversations, religious repression and economic collapse.

The destruction of the temples epitomized this cultural decline. Now the only way out of this cultural collapse was through a return to the origins of the Hindu culture, a recovery of the original glory. That is why Rama's birth temple had to be 'released', because it meant that the Hindus had taken the first steps towards Rama-Rajya, towards the culture where they can again feel pride in their origin and cultural achievements. Their mythic history concentrating on the struggle between heroes and villains represents the deeper conflict between the forces of truth and falsehood, justice and injustice, dharma and adharma, order and disorder. Muslim rulers are transformed into archetypal villains, and Hindus who fought the Muslim rulers become the heroes.

The story of *Ramjanmabhumi* revolves around several myths: the myth of ancient Ayodhya, the myth of its loss and rediscovery, and the myth of the miraculous appearance of Rama's idol. Rama was born in the Treta Yuga in Ayodhya, where he spent his childhood. When King Rama moved his capital to Saketa, Ayodhya went into decline. But the Rama's temple, Ramjanmabhumi, survived in anonymity, although its location was lost. Then a man called Vikramaditya miraculously rediscovered Ayodhya, and built a temple at the Janmasthan. After him Ayodhya again went into decline but the temple and the place at the Janmasthan survived. According to the story, when Babur came to India he pillaged and plundered like all Muslims. He destroyed the temple at the Janmasthan and built a masjid. In the Muslim era and under British rule Hindus made repeated efforts to recover control over the Janmasthan, but the temple could not be liberated. In 1949 Rama himself appeared there to remind the Hindus of the sacred history of the place and their duty to liberate it. According to them, the city of Ayodhya is more sacred than all other sacred places in India. Ayodhya is the source of origin of all the worlds: Brahmalok, Indralok, Vishnulok, and Golok. It was the original nature from which the human world was created. To create the cosmos, Manu needed a place to work. That is why Manu brought Ayodhya from heaven and placed it on earth. The city of Ayodhya is also sacred, because it is located on the right bank of the river Ghagra, as it is called within the sacred precincts, on latitude 26 48' north and longitude 82 13' east. It has been argued that the Hindutva movement has placed one sacred book, *Ramayana,* above the other sacred scripts. The story of Ramayana is well known and popular all over India.

When Indian television began to show a serial based on the Ramayana story in 1987, the serial became maybe the most popular programmr ever shown on Indian television. It has been said that never before had such a large percentage of South Asia's population been united in a single activity. Observers estimated that over eighty million people watched the serial every week. In a land where most people do not own televisions and electricity is in short supply, many watched the programme at the homes of relatives or at tea shops, or entire villages joined together to rent a television set. I once arrived in Delhi on a Sunday, the day the serial was shown, but unfortunately people could not follow the programme on that Sunday because of the shortage of electricity. Some people got so angry that they blew up a local electric plant out of revenge. Despite the fact that the goverment network had only contracted with the producer for one year's episodes, the audience demanded more. For example sanitation workers in Jalanhar went on strike because the serial was due to end without depicting the events of the final book of the Ramayana. The strike spread to sanitation workers in many major cities in North India. And the government was forced to sponsor the desired episodes in order to prevent a major health hazard. Many people became so religiously involved in the story of Rama that they used to bathe before watching, garlanded the set like a shrine, and considered the complete viewing to be a religious experience.

The Rama cult originates from the fifth and sixth centuries AD. According to Hans Bakker, the myth of Vishnu's incarnation as Rama became popular in the Gupta age. But the cult in which Rama was worshipped as the supreme form and main manifestation of Vishnu did not rise until the eleventh and twelfth centuries. It began to emerge in the latest period of independent Hindu rule in North India and before Muslim power was firmly established. The spread of devotion to Rama within Hinduism was a gradual process which evolved over a period of several centuries. The widening process was concurrent with the spread over North India of an emotional type of devotion. One important factor of the religious life during those centuries (13th-16th) was the rise of the cult of the name: the practice of repeating the name of god (Rama), conceived of as a sadhana, a way to release. And in the 15th-16th centuries Rama had become the most common word to denote 'God'. The deification of Rama started gaining acceptance in the 13th century. The importance of the festival of Rama's birth was duly recognised by Hemadri, who wrote his book on Hindu dharma between 1260 and 1270. After the 16th century, the story of Rama became so popular that it wove its way inexctricably into the fabric of rural culture and religion. Rama came to be worshipped as the ideal man, hero king, and an avatar of Vishnu. It is interesting to note in what way the Hindutva movement has changed the traditional iconography of Rama. According to popular Hinduism, icons are believed to represent the essential features of a deity. The body, posture, gestures, face, and even costume are styled so as to transmit the meanings of the godhead. Traditional icons tended to represent Rama, Janaki, and Laksman standing shoulder to shoulder, gazing outward, smiling serenely. Hanuman was in profile, sitting at their feet. It was usual for Rama to have a bow but unusual to be shown using it. Quite evidently the figures represented compassion and benevolence, 'the shanta rasa'. We may consider, for example, two popular posters, the traditional one and the modified one. In the first poster Rama, Sita and Lakshman are facing us frontally. Frontality is crucial to the relationship between the devotee and the icon. Hanuman is in profile, kneeling at the feet of the trio. Rama and his companions quite obviously represent grace, benevolence and serenity.

In the modified posters that have emerged directly out of the Ayodhya controversy the mood of the pictures is anything but tranquil. Rama is often heavily armed, ready for war, and alone. Rama is crusading for a temple against all evil forces. Traditional posters represented Rama almost with an androgynous, unmuscled, somewhat disengaged body. Now the popular posters in the Hindutva movement represent Rama as an angry, aggressive, and masculine figure. In the second poster Rama is shown alone. His several weapons bring to mind a warrior. His 'dhoti' is flying, his chest and legs are bared, hair unrolling in the wind. He is determined, a crusader who is ready to punish. Now he is not fighting against Ravana but against Muslims. The stormy weather is a symbol of the contemporary cultural crisis in India. The nation and the Hindu culture are in danger. The practical message of the poster is obvious: every Hindu male has to follow the example of Rama, and fight with arms if necessary against the evil, the Muslims.

It has often been argued that Hinduism is getting Semitic features at the hands of the Hindutva movement. There is one god, Rama, and one holy script above the others, Ramajana. And one holy place, Ayodhya, where the complete cosmos and the Hindu civilization were created. According to Hans Bakker (1991: 84-88), the concept of holy war was inconsistent with the early Hinduism before the 13th century. The concept of truth in Hinduism was diffuse and inclusive, contrary to the two-fold exclusive truth concept. This kind of world view cannot include the powerful duality between good and evil. The individual Hindus basically tried to release their individual souls. That is why the cohesive religious community did not have the same meaning as in Semitic religions.

In the Muslim and British era the situation gradually changed, however. In Northern India especially there evolved a new Hindu identity formed basically on Rama's devotion. That is to say that in this process and particularly in the 20th century, the importance of the religious community increased. The *'holy war'* of the Hindus culminated in the release of the Ramajanmasthan in Ayodhya. The process can be compared to the Christian crusades in the Middle Ages, one of their basic goals being the release of Jerusalem. Since the early 1980s there has been a new phase in Hindu communalism. They have, for example, organized Hindu Samajotsavs (Hindu Unity Conferences) and different 'rath-yatras', as Vishal Hindi Aikya Yatras, Rama Ratha Yatras, and Ekatmata Yatras. In these political rituals they have tried to reach new bonds of unity through such sacred symbols as earth (consecrated bricks), water (ganga-jal), fire (torch-lights), blood, and ashes of the dead.

The last Ekatmata Yatra began in September 1995. It lasted 25 days and ended at Nagpur, where the RSS headquarters are located. This Ekatmata Yatra or actually yatras because it consists of nine yatras, followed the same pattern as the previous yatras with their slogans raising religious and social issues with political overtones. According to VHP leaders, the aim of the Yatra was essentially to create public awareness of 'anti-national activities such as cow-slaughter, proselytisation by Muslim and Christian missionaries'. The Ekatmata Yatra was obviously a beginning of the pre-election campaign. The parliamentary elections will be held next March. One of the main themes of the Yatra was also a demand to construct the Rama temple in Ayodhya and to liberate the temples at Kashi (Varanasi) and Mathura (Krishna temple). During the past few decades the Hindu communalists have repeated once again that Hinduism is in danger. They have argued that experiments in modernism have failed in India: such western concepts as rationalism, secularism, materialism and consumerism have led to a civilizational crisis in India. According to Richard Fox (1990: 73-76), the changes in social structure have created the foundation for Hindu nationalism. The traditional rural elites have lost their economic and social positions since the 1960s, especially in Northern India. Members of the rural elites have claimed that agricultural and caste policy has essentially favoured the middle classes ('the Other Backward Classes'). The rural elites have traditionally consisted of upper caste people. And the upper castes have mostly supported the politics of the Bharatiya Janata Party.

The modernization process in India also breaks the basic social elements, such as the traditional extended families and the economic structure of villages. It has caused a rapid urbanization process. Migrants are easily alienated in big cities. This social uncertainty favours the Hindutva Movement, which at least on grassroot level emphasizes antimodern practices and values. In summary, we can say that Hinduism gradually changed in the middle Ages. The resistance to the new Muslim rulers posed challenges for the Hindus in Northern India, and the importance of the more cohesive religious community became obvious in this process. The cult of Rama arose in those centuries. Late in the 19th century the revivalist movement idealized the past, and demanded a return to purer forms of Hindu culture.

The RSS and the whole Hindutva movement continued this revivalist tradition in the early 1920s. The cult of Rama became the central element in their modified and political Hinduism. They emphasized the natural order in society. The ideal society has to be based on the laws of dharma, just as individuals have to follow their dharmas. From this point of view they have tried to define the natural inhabitants of India and the natural borders of the country. During the past few decades the number of communal riots has increased alarmingly. The contemporary rise of Hindu communalism can be seen as a reaction to modern society.

2

At the Mercy of Hindu Nationalism

One of the most important developments across the world over the last thirty years has been the rise of nationalist/ religious identity movements. Whether in Israel, the Arab world, the former Soviet Union, or a host of other sites, nationalist/religious identity movements have become a significant political force. Nowhere is this trend more evident than in India, where Hindu nationalist parties have become the dominant political force in the nation. In contrast to the secular parties that founded India, Hindu nationalist parties, like nationalist parties across the globe, have taken extremely strong positions on issues relating to national and religious identity. On several occasions, Hindu nationalists have participated in violence against the Islamic minority in India, most notably in the destruction of the Babri mosque, which has been labeled as the "pivotal" event in the rise of Hindu nationalist parties to power.

As Pankaj Mishra (2002) noted, "India changed fast after that moment of Hindu nationalist rage" while "for most of the 50 years since independence [Hindu nationalists] had been on the political sidelines," after Babri mosque that changed rapidly and they "now hold top positions in the Indian government". The importance of radical Hindu nationalists was also evident in violence that erupted early in 2002 when nationalist groups took steps toward building a temple on the site of the former mosque. What is particularly surprising is that these acts have been taken on behalf of a religious tradition fundamentally antithetical to crude sectarian violence.

There is a strong consensus among scholars and political leaders that Hindu civilization is basically tolerant. The eminent scholar of Indian history, A.L. Basham, writes in The Wonder that was India that Hinduism encourages kindliness and tolerance in human relations. In his opinion, all Hindu texts teach mercy, compassion, and benevolence. Shashi Tharoor recently noted that Hindu nationalists who use violence "are profoundly disloyal to the religion they claim to espouse, which stands out as... an eclectic embodiment of tolerance". Tharoor (2002) concluded that the "true Hindu seeks no revenge". Given Hindu belief structures, many find the growth and radicalism of the movement shocking. In this essay, we argue that at least a portion of the answer to the riddle of how a religious tradition associated with peace, mercy, and compassion, which has been perverted into an extremist movement, can be found in a mythic narrative at the heart of Hindu nationalist rhetoric.

Nationalist sentiment serves as the motive, but myth forms the engine for the movement. We build this argument by noting that Hindu nationalist rhetors draw on a rhetorical pattern quite similar to that identified by Kenneth Burke (1973) in his analysis of Nazi rhetoric in "The Rhetoric of Hitler's Battle." This pattern is not imitative of Hitler, nor are we saying that Hindu rhetoric is Nazi-like. Rather, the pattern is tied to a distinctive mythic narrative of nationalist and religious re-definition and re-birth through return.

Our argument is that the discourse of identity movements, either in a nationalist or religious form, is tied to a mythic story, which tells of great actions by the heroes of the movement against great evil committed by those who oppose the nation or religion. Mythic redefinition is a response to the exigency posed by lost identity. Such redefinition requires a return to origins, the (re)establishment of dignity and identity, and the claim of sacred space. In turn, such redefinition leads to the demonization of the other. In the conclusion, we argue that this mythic structure is tied to the broad rhetorical situation facing any nationalist/religious identity movement that is outside the mainstream power structure in a society.

The conclusion that nationalist/religious identity discourse tends by its very nature toward narratives of mythic return is quite important both for understanding the rise of such movements and also for clarifying the way that contemporary myths of return function. We also argue more broadly that there are a limited number of narrative patterns that are often called for by a restricted set of rhetorical situations. In this way, we propose a relationship between some types of narrative and generic theory and also suggest a means of expanding the applicability of generic criticism.

A CASE-STUDY OF THE RHETORIC OF HINDU NATIONALISM

The Hindu nationalist movement in India is not a completely new phenomenon. Its beginnings can be traced to the late nineteenth and early twentieth century, when both Hindus and Muslims exploited religion to mobilize their communities. The religious antagonism between Hindus and Muslims was exploited by the British rulers, which culminated in the partition of India and the formation of Pakistan in 1947. While it might seem that the proximate cause of the rise of Hindu nationalism in India was the partition of the subcontinent, in fact, Hindu-Muslim communal conflict within India was relatively limited in the first several decades after the birth of the nation, in part because of the commitment of the Indian government to a secular society that protected the rights of both Hindus and Muslims.

As late as 1993, William Pfaff (1993) argued that "the conflict between Hindus and Moslems in India" was not an issue "of nationalism." While not denying the "passions" of the conflict, he argued that it was not based on nationalism, which is the "expression of a form of group identity attached to an existing state". At the very time that Pfaff's book was being published, however, what had been a relatively minor conflict was being transformed into a major one based on nationalist/religious identity. One of the most important incidents in the development of Hindu nationalism occurred on December 6, 1992, when more than 300,000 Hindu militants converged on the Hindu pilgrimage town of Ayodhya located in the northern state of Uttar Pradesh in India.

That afternoon, under the leadership of several Hindu nationalist parties, a vanguard of Hindu demonstrators broke through the police barricades and stormed the Babri mosque. This mosque was built in 1528 by Babar, the Muslim ruler who founded the Mughal dynasty in India. The Hindu activists demolished the mosque because they believed that the Hindu god, Lord Rama, was born at that site and that a Hindu temple located there had been destroyed by Babar. The supporters of the Hindu nationalist movement justified the demolition of the mosque in Ayodhya as an act aimed at liberating Hindu sacred space. The Indian Muslim community, on the other hand, perceived the destruction by Hindu activists as an overt act of violence against them. The demolition of the Babri mosque led to a major crisis, in which the Indian nation was engulfed in communal violence between Hindus and Muslims that lasted from December 1992 until January 1993. The riots, which took about 2,000 lives and provoked widespread destruction of property across much of India including the cosmopolitan city of Bombay, located on the West coast of India.

Bombay [renamed Mumbai] experienced the worst Hindu-Muslim conflagration the city has ever known, which Sharma (1995) describes as "one of the darkest periods in the city's contemporary history". During the riots in Bombay, it is estimated that over a thousand people were killed and several thousand wounded (Human Rights Watch, 1995; Masselos, 1996). The riots in Bombay took place in two phases. In the first phase, the news of the demolition of the Babri mosque provoked hundreds of Muslims to go on a rampage, attacking government property and police, resulting in the deaths of many Indians.

The second phase of the riots resulted in still greater violence when the Bombay-based nationalist political party, Shiv Sena, under the leadership of Bal Thackeray, incited its Hindu followers into attacking Muslims in their homes and business establishments. By relying on the ideology of "Hindutva" and an anti-Muslim rhetoric, Thackeray provoked the Shiv Sena members and others to assail the Bombay Muslim community. In particular, Thackeray and the Shiv Sena party relied on their party newspapers Saamna and Marmik to fan the communal embers. During the riots, both Shiv Sena newspapers contained "open vitriol against the Muslims".

Sardesai has noted the key role played by the Shiv Sena party in the Bombay riots in 1992-93. By targeting Muslims in India as the enemy of the state, the Shiv Sena party secured the role of "protector of the Hindus" and the "flag bearer of militant Hinduism". The Washington Post compared the cult of violence and intimidation of the Shiv Sena party and its chief, Bal Thackeray, to that of Al Capone. While the analogy may be accurate in some ways, there is a central difference.

Capone was a thug who was dangerous because he was willing to use violence for his own ends. Thackeray and Shiv Sena operate within a myth-based Hindu nationalist movement that is willing to use violence to activate their sense of identity and destroy conflicting identities. By recasting the gentle and benign image of the Hindu god, Lord Rama, and projecting him as a warrior who never fails to achieve his objectives, the Shiv Sena party provides its followers with a sense of heroic identity and an enemy to be confronted, namely the Muslim population of India.

In this essay, we use the rhetoric of Bal Thackeray and his party as a case study of Hindu Nationalist discourse. The focus on Thackeray and Shiv Sena is appropriate given the central role that Thackery and Shiv Sena played in inciting violence between the two communities in 1992-1993. The recent crisis between India and Pakistan, in which the Hindu Nationalist government of India massed hundreds of thousands of troops on the border with Pakistan and spoke openly of the possibility of waging a war, points to the importance of explaining the rhetorical characteristics of Hindu nationalism. Thousands of people have lost their lives in the numerous religious wars that have marked India's history; murderous conflicts have broken out time and again between the Hindu majority and the Muslim minority. But this time, the Gujarat massacre goes beyond interreligious squabbling: it gives indications of a new government-condoned strategy based on ethnic cleansing.

RISE OF THE FAR RIGHT

The Hindu nationalist Bharatiya Janata Party (BJP) has controlled the governing coalition in New Delhi since 1998, and also leads the Gujarat state government. The BJP is imbued with a far-right ideology that has its roots in the fascism of the 1930s. Trumpeting the slogan "one nation, one people, one culture," the party promotes Hindutva or "Hindu identity," a concept based on Hindu racial purity. The Muslims, India's largest religious minority, have been the main victims of this recrudescence of right-wing violence.

That the government condones the carnage in Gujarat has been clearly shown. For example, the Chief Minister of Gujarat ordered the police not to intervene to stop the violence. All high-ranking BJP members in the federal government, including Prime Minister Vajpayee, have stood by him. Rumours are circulating to the effect that the riots had been in the planning for a long time. Clearly, the interreligious massacres in Gujarat are more than an outburst of sectarian violence related to Hindutva: they are a tool serving the political interests of the BJP. Since January, the BJP has watched its popularity drop precipitously, losing seats in the Indian Parliament. The events in Gujarat are directly connected to the attempted imposition of Hindutva, and observers suggest that the BJP is trying to shore up its sagging position by exploiting them.

SHIFTING POLITICAL WINDS

The carnage in recent months revealed not only the rise of Hindu nationalism but also the weakening of India as a nation-state. The Indian National Congress Party, which held power prior to the BJP, had promoted secularity for India as the founding vision of the country. For four decades, from independence in 1947 until the 1990s, the Congress Party had managed to maintain a degree of national cohesion despite the country's great cultural diversity.

During its initial years in power, the Congress Party was able to build on the foundation laid by the unified national movement that had fought for India's independence. But over the years, national sentiment faded, scandals and corruption came to light, and public confidence in the Congress Party eroded - as did its strong governing majority. As a member of a coalition, it could not maintain the national cohesion necessary or the country's political stability. India no longer had a shared political project around which all citizens could rally.

Capitalizing on the discredit into which the Congress Party had fallen, the Hindu nationalists gained ground. The BJP's rise filled a political void; Hindutva was its blueprint for society. Arriving in power, the BJP substituted an essentially Hindu Indian state for the secular one. As Romain Maitra, a journalist based in Calcutta, explains in Le Monde diplo-matique, "The manoeuver was clear: to replace constitutional democratic nationalism with nationalism based on race and pedigree."

What happened in Gujarat did not come out of nowhere. It is the direct consequence of the political shift taking place in Indian society. The events exposed an ideological undercurrent which had been repressed by the Congress Party, but is now being exploited by the BJP. But Gujarat is not India. Alternative regional political movements are building steam, and could soon provide a counterweight to the BJP, putting a damper on its plans for Hindutva.

In February 1998 India's Hindu nationalist Bhartiya Janata Party (BJP) rose to power on a platform of hard-line Hindu nationalism. The BJP's election slogan was 'One People, One Nation, and One Culture' (i.e. Hindu culture). Systematic, violent persecution of Christians escalated nationwide under

BJP rule. Anti-conversion laws were enacted; 're-conversion' ceremonies (to Hinduism) were promoted; Indian history was 'saffronised' (rewritten); and in 2002, up to 2000 Muslims were massacred in Gujarat in a BJP-incited pogrom. The BJP governed also through India's economic boom years, so when they lost power in the April-May 2004 elections, it was a huge shock to the world's political analysts who had not counted on the disaffection of the impoverished, persecuted, left-behind masses.

There was a lot of prayer through the election period in which voting was conducted in four stages. With the BJP leading after the second stage, requests for urgent prayer rang out. By the time the voting was over, the BJP had lost power. Christians praised God for what they saw as a divine mercy in answer to the prayers of many. A year of squabbling, blame shifting and policy revision followed in the BJP. Then the 'sangh parivar' - the umbrella body dedicated to the advancement of Hindutva (Hindu supremacy) - emerged, committed to restoring the BJP to power. By the beginning of 2006 the BJP was back, both with a vengeance and a strategy.

For decades Hindu nationalists have been working at converting India's animist tribal masses to Hinduism. They tell tribal Indians that their ancestors were actually Hindus and that their animist religion is in fact a corrupted form of Hinduism. The sangh parivar adopted this strategy and added a motivating element: fear! They tell the tribals that India's security and sovereignty are under threat from foreign forces and that Christian missionaries are agents of the CIA working to divide India with communal strife ahead of invasion and occupation. They say the only way to save India is for the tribals to join the Hindu 'mainstream', vote BJP and join a Hindu militia. The religious conversion of the tribals - who traditionally vote for the Congress Party - is far less important to the Hindu nationalists than their political conversion. In this way Hindu nationalism has been revived amongst the masses and persecution of Christians has escalated all across the nation. The Congress-led United Progressive Alliance (UPA) government of PM Dr Manmohan Singh has so far failed to address either the issue of intolerant Hindutva or its immediate consequence: violent religious persecution. The BJP is currently demanding a confidence vote in the parliament because the ruling UPA may have lost its majority when leftists withdrew from the UPA over the government's nuclear deal with the US.

The UPA losing that vote would pave the way for an early election. After defeating Congress in the Karnataka state polls in May, the BJP is confident they and Hindutva have returned. "Everybody's got a plan until they get hit," so said, Mike Tyson some years ago in the most brilliant statement of political realism since Thucydides. Bharat Mata, or "Mother India," the birthplace of the glorious *Upanishads* as well as Prince Siddhartha, has been sucker punched by 21st century monsters.

The blood from the innocent victims was barely dry when journalists published articles, not about the vicious killers, but about the dangers of a "rightward tilt" in India. The rise of Hindu nationalism however began as a response to a perceived lack of "manliness" in the Hindu warrior the result of which was an open door to centuries of foreign persecution and terror in India. When explaining the "root" causes of the massacre in Mumbai we will hear plenty in the coming weeks about disaffected Muslims living in India, or about the menacing American war on terror, or about the situation in Kashmir.

What the literati in the media will probably miss however is a profound and paradoxical thread stitched into the very fabric of Hindu culture: what does it means to be a "man?" In other words, is the true "male" the *Kshatriya* caste warrior or the *Brahmin* caste renunciant? Was it the Hindu patriot and warrior-hero Shivaji Bhosle, the 17th century equivalent to Scotland's William Wallace, who organized the first successful guerilla campaign against Muslim rule in India? Or is the "real man" the gentle, transnational and priestly archetype embodied in figures such as Mohandas Gandhi, who renounces violence in the name of universal love? Simply put, Hinduism's masculinity crisis is deeply embedded in its social structure, in its ancient texts, and in the language of modern Hindu nationalists such as Swami Vivekenanda and Lala Lajpat Rai. Both men would have identified the complexities of caste as the "root cause" of over 800 years of Muslim and then British rule in India. That is, when searching for the reasons why Hindus have been traditionally defenseless in the face of foreign invaders Hindu nationalists tend to see their own culture and traditions as the culprit. Beginning with British rule in the early 18th century, Hindu nationalists began some serious soul searching concerning their inability to protect Mother India from subjugation.

Lala Lajpat Rai spoke for many Hindus when he speculated back in 1907:

"A question that has often haunted us, asleep or awake, as to why is it that notwithstanding the presence among us of great, vigorous, and elevating truths, and of the very highest conception of morality, we Hindus have been a subject race, held down for so many centuries by sets of people who were neither physically nor spiritually nor even intellectually so superior to us as to demand our subjugation."

Trying to explain why a handful of foreigners coming from six thousand miles away in England could become India's masters became the focus of an intense amount of scholarly activity among Hindu intellectuals. Profound thinkers like Aurobindo Ghose, India's greatest 20th century philosopher, argued that the "ascetic ideal" etched into Hindu identity became oppressively "top heavy" in India and smothered the more warlike themes in Hindu tradition and culture. In his *Foundations of Indian Culture* Aurobindo claimed:

"Still it is true that the ascetic ideal, which in the ancient vigor of our culture was the fine spire of life mounting into the eternal existence, became latterly its top-heavy dome and tended under the weight of its bare and imposing sublimity to crush the rest of the edifice."

Although Aurobindo's vision was of a harmonious and peaceful international community inspired by Hinduism's spiritual grace and maturity, he was quite impatient with what he called the "fanatics of pacifism" whose myopia threatened this lofty goal. Aurobindo understood, as pacifists like Gandhi did not, that the international community was still a menacing state of nature. Aggressive national actors were always ready to fill, as Thucydides said in Greece over 2 millennia ago, any potential vacuum including the one in India. Therefore, for the Hindu warrior warfare could be an elevating experience if the conflict safeguarded the "principle of right, justice, and law which shall be the basis of the harmony towards which the struggle ends."

Nationalists like Aurobindo, in other words, were not foolish enough to believe that Islamic armies, or armies from the West for that matter, wouldn't continue to take advantage of India's "top-heavy" orientation toward gentle, non-violent renunciation. A "handful" of British occupiers for example managed to turn much of India's Northern provinces into an opium industry. From here British entrepreneurs derived the powerful narcotic that British troops eventually helped to cram into the veins of helpless Chinese addicts during the Opium Wars of the 1840s. Aurobindo argued that pacifism can do nothing to root out the causes of war or oppression. Indeed, he said, the non-violent approach may be responsible for extending the shelf-life of international conflict:

"It is not enough that our own hands should remain clean and our souls unstained for the law of strife and destruction to die out of the world; that which is at its root must first disappear out of humanity. Much less will mere immobility and inertia unwilling to use or incapable of using any kind of resistance to evil abrogate the law."

Aurobindo and other nationalists recognized that traditions of renunciation in India together with the gentle wisdom contained in Buddhism, Jainism, and the inward-searching *Upanishads* had conditioned Hindu men to meet foreign aggression with passive resistance. This "top-heavy dome" of the spirit in other words had smothered the more aggressive and warlike features of the Hindu edifice. In fact, the roughly 4th century B.C. *Bhagavad-Gita* - considered to be the "Hindu bible" - highlights the spiritual adventures of Hinduism's greatest *warrior* in history, Arjuna. (Arjuna is something like a combination of Achilles and Socrates - on steroids).

In the *Bhagavad-Gita*, or "Song of God," Krishna - an incarnation of God - persuades Arjuna, through the lush philosophy characteristic of Hinduism's greatest thinkers that he should choose to *fight* when threatened by subjugation and injustice. In one famous passage Krishna tells Arjuna:

"Happy are the *Kshatriyas* (warriors) O Arjuna, for whom such a war comes of its own accord as an open door to heaven."

Indeed, of the four traditional castes in Hindu culture, the warrior caste, or *Kshatryia*, was created by God to be the "arms" or protectors of society. Their courageous protection and sacrifice allowed members of the other castes such as the *Shudras* (servants), *Vaishyas* (merchants), and *Brahmins* (priests) to accrue spiritual merit in the successive lives that would eventually result in the rediscovery of God as the ground of each person's entire being. God is telling Arjuna that to fulfill his caste obligations he should *not* shrink from battle.

To be overrun by enemies would be to threaten the entire soul-making process at the heart of every individual Hindu's journey back to God. The problem many modern Hindu nationalists noticed however is that those with the highest spiritual discipline and merit, the *Brahmin* priests, fulfilled their caste obligations by *renouncing* the same ties to nation and family that provided the bulwark against foreign invaders. By renouncing all earthly attachments - including violence and anger - in the pursuit of God those at the top of the Hindu hierarchy provided an example that was troublesome to the warrior's maintenance of national integrity.

Simply put, it meant that the very existence of nationhood was an impediment to rediscovering God. This left India at the mercy of Western and Islamic civilizations, both of which had no problems combining religion and statecraft in the pursuit of their national interests. Another way to look at this is to ask yourself the following: how often were Hindu armies leaving India to ransack and colonize non-Hindu civilizations? Why were Muslims in Delhi instead of Hindus in Mecca? When was the last time a Hindu tried to convert you on your front porch or at the leading edge of a sword?

Muslim and British conquerors met little resistance in a culture that had become, in Aurobindo's words, so spiritually top-heavy as to make any kind of violence a nauseating prospect. Noticing the weak resistance they encountered, both British and Muslim occupiers openly called Hindu men "effeminate." In some cases the Muslim occupiers refused to allow their children to mingle with Hindu boys for fear of being contaminated by the Hindu male's "effete" qualities. This cavalier dismissal of Hindu male identity penetrated the Hindu male psyche like a hot knife through butter.

Gifted Hindu nationalist writers and orators over the last century and a half like Swami Vivekenanda were stung by these Western and Islamic criticisms. Vivekenanda's project was to reinvigorate the essence of manhood in the Hindu *Kshatryia* warrior. The Swami's poignant pleas to his creator spoke for many Hindu men when he cried out in anguish:

"O Thou Mother of the Universe vouchsafes manliness unto me! O thou mother of strength, take away my weakness, take away my unmanliness, and - Make me a Man!"

It was Vivekenanda who famously said that Hindu men needed an intense regimen of "beef, biceps, and the *Bhagavad-Gita*." Weightlifting and wrestling became popular in India. "No more weeping, but stand on your own feet and be men" said Vivekenanda. "It is a man-making religion that we want. It is man-making theories we want. I want the strength, manhood, *kshatravirya*, or the virility of a warrior." Posters of Hindu guerrilla fighters like Shivaji Bhosle began to adorn the walls of gyms. Vivekenanda recognized that without a tough warrior caste *Brahmin* priests would be helpless in the face of international aggressors:

"The *Kshatriya* [warrior] said, "But for the power of my sword, where would you be O *Brahmin* [priest], with all your power of lore? You would in no time be wiped off the face of the earth." The sad truth is that for much of its history since the late medieval period Hindus have been the victims of proselytizing, aggressive, and often violent foreign powers who swept into the vacuum created by a Hindu culture that values internal, not external spiritual conquest. It's no wonder that today in Mumbai Hindu nationalists are again on the rise. The "progressive" Western press disparages these warriors as dangerous right wingers, thus betraying their bottomless naiveté concerning India's aggressive Muslim neighbors, past and present.

Nationalists like Aurobindo and Vivekenanda reminded Hindus however to evaluate for themselves the efficacy of pacifism. Weakness only invites invasion. Warrior energy, or *rajas* as the Hindus call it, is a normal and natural part of cultural survival. During the 19th century flurry of intellectual activity in India journalist Walter Bagehot, 6,000 miles away in England, made a rather cryptic remark about the Darwinian struggle for survival among nation states:

"History is strewn with the wrecks of nations which have gained a little progressiveness at the cost of a great deal of hard manliness, and have thus prepared themselves for destruction as soon as the movements of the world gave a chance for it."

When will "movements of the world" like Islam for example stop menacing neighbors and filling vacuums? Well, according to the brilliant French philosopher Blaise Pascal as soon as they recognize that conquest and invasion are byproducts of discontent at home - not some mission ordained by God:

"I have discovered that all the unhappiness of men arises from one single fact, that they cannot stay quiet in their own chamber. A man, who has enough to live on, if he knew how to stay with pleasure at home, would not leave it to go to sea or to besiege a town."

For Aurobindo, until that day arrives - the day when we're all content enough to "stay with pleasure at home" - a nation would be foolish to let its guard down in the name of "progress."

The primary objective and aim of the Hindu nationalist movement is the unification of all Hindus into a single community that would serve as a foundation of a strong Hindu *rashtra* and that would ensure social cohesion in India. The Indian state, civil society and social formations should be according to this ideology "reorganized in a holistic and organic way along exclusively 'Hindu' precepts". The ideal of Hindutva is thus one of assimilation, one that aspires to dissolve all religious pluralism and constitute India as a religiously homogenous Hindu nation.

This means for the Hindu nationalist movement overcoming of all the innumerable divisions of the Indian society (caste divisions which remain the strongest, family, gender, territory, rural-urban divisions etc.) and integrating all the marginal groups, such as untouchables and other backward classes, into the body of the Hindu society and simultaneously reinforcing and strengthening the division between non-Hindus, especially Muslims, and Hindus themselves. Muslims are being constructed as the Other, as invaders, foreign transplants and as a great threat to Hindus. Muslims and secularism are recognized as the two main enemies.

We can thus identify four basic premises underlying the claims of the right-wing Hindu nationalists: for the first the 'Hindu' identity is constructed as the privileged, exclusive identity, encompassing all other types of identities which are considered as subordinate; for the second the bearers of the above mentioned identity are presupposed to share a distinct 'Hindu' culture, which is perceived as a source of common interests; for the third " 'Hinduism' is a phenomenon which can be understood largely *sui generis*, and in isolation from political and economic processes and conflicts" and for the fourth 'Hinduism' is primarily considered as a culture that is associated with a particular group of people and with a particular country ("one nation, one people, one culture").

Though the Hindu nationalist movement is often labeled as "fundamentalist", I would rather use the more fitting label borrowed from Nikki R. Keddie and consider the Hindu nationalist movement as a part of the New Religious Politics (from now on *religiopolitics*), which is characterized by several distinctive features which are all part of the Hindu nationalist politics:

These features include, first, an appeal to a reinterpreted, homogenized religious tradition, seen as solving problems exacerbated by various forms of secular, communal or foreign power. Second, these are populist movements that aim at gaining political power in order to transform governments on the basis of their religiopolitical program. Third, they are not led by liberals or leftists and have predominantly conservative social views. This definition has the advantage of being broader and including not only religiously fundamentalist aspects of Hindu nationalism and omitting all the connotations the word "fundamentalist" without question has.

THE HINDU NATIONALISM AND THE SANGH PARIVAR

The origin of the idea of the Hindu Rashtra lies in the mid to late nineteenth century, in the British colonial period and is connected with the names of Vivekananda, Dayanand Saraswati and Aurobindo Ghose. But it must be noted that it is highly problematic to trace the historical origins of Hindu nationalism since Hindu nationalism itself claims legitimacy in the writings of this period. Vivekananda has thus for example become a crucial icon of the Hindu nationalist discourse, though the Ramakrishna Mission he founded has distanced itself from the Hindu nationalism.

But the birth of Hindutva itself can be dated from 1920s when the founding text of Hindu nationalism and a definition of Hindutva – Vinayak Damodar Savarkars *Hindutva – or who is a Hindu*? (1923) – was written. Hindutva can be translated as 'Hinduness', i.e. *the essence of being Hindu*. "Hindutva is fundamentally an empty signifier that has become extraordinarily politically potent" and serves as a great example of the invention of a primordial tradition that is supposed to stand at the core of the contemporary identity politics.

Hindutva is associated with common blood resp. 'race', jati, Vedic-Aryan forefathers, and makes use of different ethnic, religious, 'racial' and nationalist motives, but does not use any of these exclusively – its nature is thus fundamentally eclectic. In 1924 the most important male nationalistic organization – the Rashtriya Swayamsevak Sangh (RSS) – was founded by Keshav Baliram Hedgewar, while Golwalkar is considered as the ideological father, the great "guruji".

This organization is still at the core of organizations that are allied to Hindutva ideology (the so called *Sangh Parivar*); it is a highly centralized semi-paramilitary organization devoted to recruitment and training of young men for service to the Hindu Nation. Later numerous offshoot organizations were created, the most important ones were: the Jana Sangh in 1951, which was the precursor of the current Bharatiya Janata Party (BJP) and the Vishwa Hindu Parishad (VHP) in 1964. This 'family' of organizations which RSS created is often labeled as Sangh Parivar, and these organizations are the largest body of organizations in Indian civil society. The BJP formed in 1998 its first shaky coalition government which was followed by another coalition government in 1999 which was in power until 2004.

DEMONIZING THE MUSLIM OTHER

The *Muslim Other* plays in the Hindutva ideology a crucial role in defining, delineating and creating a boundary around the Hindu community; the Muslim Other is usually portrayed as the absolute opposite of the Hindu, where the Hindu is the educated, civilized, tolerant, rational, modern, caring etc. This polarization is also present in the distinction between Semitic and non-Semitic religions which is being continually emphasized. The well-known case of the Ayodhya, the recovery of Ram's birthplace from the hands of its Muslim "occupants" and the building of a new temple became another strong and potent symbol of the restoration of the Hindu nation and its pride and of demonizing the Other.

Muslims are also presented as a "pampered" minority with special reservations and since the era of the 'Mandalisation' of politics, when special reservations were assigned to different groups of the Indian society – which was apprehended as dividing the Hindus – the Muslims began to be perceived as greater a threat to the Hindu nation; the stereotypes and prejudices were strengthened. Secularism is in this context conceived of as overriding Hindu rights (and labeled as 'pseudo-secularism') since it is connected with appeasement of minority claims and favoring of Muslims, secularism is thus "portrayed as a source of national weakness".

Another way how to create and strengthen the boundary between Hindus and Muslims is the strategy of using Hindu women's bodies and portraying Muslim men as violators of the Hindu women and thus the evil and threat to the Hindu nation. The nuclearization of India serves as another mighty symbol and an agent of Othering between India and Pakistan.

IDEALIZED MEN AND WOMEN AS PORTRAYED

Men and female bodies hand in hand with cultural representations of femininity and masculinity serve as powerful symbols and metaphors for depicting a nation. In the discourse of Hindu nationalism two images of manliness and masculinity are especially highly celebrated - i.e. the image of Hindu soldier and warrior monk - and have great impact also on women, who are trying to respond properly to the call of nationalism that glorifies muscular strength, moral fortitude, readiness to go to the battle and defend the nation against the enemy, the Other.

Women can thus within the frame of this ideology play either roles of heroic mothers, chaste wives or celibate warriors. The gendered power imbalances as such are not challenged and the patriarchal Hindu family remains in the ideology of Hindutva the primal reference point.

HINDU RELIGIOPOLITICS AND PUBLIC RITUALS

Since the primary aim of the Hindu Religiopolitics is to unite all Hindus and overcome all possible divisions within the Indian society, the ever-present polytheism and hierarchichal differentiation within Hinduism is necessarily perceived as a great problem that must be dealt with. It is highly problematic to translate all the multiple - regional, caste, family - gods and goddesses, beliefs and practices into symbols of unity, when these signify belonging to a definite group or category. The Hindu nationalist leaders are perfectly conscious of this situation and have therefore chosen several deities that appeal to as great number of people as possible and that symbolize best the pan-Hindu unity.

The pantheon of the 'celestial nationalists' thus consists of Rama, Ganesha, the 'epic' Krishna, Durga and others. The Hindu unity is promoted in public rituals and worships of these gods and in diverse festivals, which also serve as a manifestation of Hindu strength and physical control. "Converting private devotion into demonstrative public worship has been a consistent strategy of Hindu nationalists, whose broader aim is to transform the polity and civil society, and the public sphere as a whole."

As we have seen from the brief sketch of the ideological background, symbolism and metaphors employed by Hindu nationalists, the arena where Hindu nationalists operate is very broad and can not be reduced to either the religious or the political field. The Hindu nationalism emerges in the sphere of the public and thus attacks directly and in different ways the representation and recognition of individuals and the creation and institutionalization of diverse communities.

highly problematic to translate all the multiple – regional, caste, tribal – gods and goddesses, beliefs and practices into symbols of unity, when these mainly belong to a definite group or category. The Hindu nationalist ideologues are perfectly conscious of this situation and have therefore chosen several deities that appeal to as great number of people as possible and that symbolise best the pan-Hindu unity.

The pantheon of the 'coloured' nationalists thus consists of Rama, Ganesha, the cow, Krishna, Durga and others. The Hindu unity is promoted by public rituals and worship of these gods and in diverse processions, which also serve as a manifestation of Hindu strength and physical control. "Converting private devotion into demonstrative public worship has been a consistent strategy of Hindu nationalists whose broader aim is to Hindu-ise the polity and civil society and the public sphere as a whole."

As we have seen from the brief sketch of the ideological background, symbolism and metaphors employed by Hindu nationalists, the arena where Hindu nationalists operate is very broad and can not be reduced to either the religious or the political field. The Hindu nationalism emerges in the sphere of the public and thus attacks directly and in different ways the representation and recognition of Indic image and the creation and institutionalisation of diverse communities.

3

Hindutva and Multiculturalism

In India the term "minorities" refers to religious communities present in much smaller numbers than Hindus - Muslims, Christians, Buddhists, Jains, Sikhs, and Parsis/ Zoroastrians. According to a 1991 census of India, out of the total Indian population of 846 million, there are 687.6 million Hindus of various sects, 101.6 million Muslims, 19.6 million Christians, 6.3 million Buddhists, 3.3 million Jains and 3.1 million adherents of other traditions. Christians are thus less than 3 percent of the total population whereas Hindus number about 83 percent. "Minorities" may also allude to those communities that have traditionally been kept outside the Hindu-based caste system - *Dalits* and *Adivasis* (or Tribals).

Dalits number between 180 and 200 million and *Adivasis* number between 85 and 90 million in a population that has now crossed the one billion mark. While they are now included into the general category of Hinduism, these groups have been treated with overt hostility and repression, and have been the target of concerted and calculated attacks from the majority community. Christianity is also targeted violently and systematically in contemporary India, especially Christians who have been identified as Dalits and Adivasis.

An analysis of the ideology and agenda of Hindu nationalism in an historical perspective will reveal the way in which the Dalits and Adivasis are perceived to present a threat to the fulfillment of this nationalist agenda. The Hinduization of India manifests itself with a propensity to eradicate all forms of variant plurality. Indian society is divided into three communities - caste, outcaste (*Dalit*), and indigenous (*Adivasi*). First, the caste community consists of four castes that are hierarchically ordered) The Brahmins (priests) are the preservers and protectors of the eternal laws of the Universe (Dharma); the Ksatriyas (rulers and warriors) are the defenders and the guarantors of the safety and security of the community; the Vaisyas (business persons) are the conservers and distributors of wealth; and the Sudras (the laborers) are the working majority involved in the production of essential commodities.

Although there is a clear separation between the first three castes, which are ritually pure and socioeconomically dominant (referred to as the twice-born), and the fourth laboring caste, which is ritually suspect and socioeconomically dominated (referred to as the once-born), together they form the Hindu human community. Second, related to, but outside of, these four segments of the Indian human society there exists a fifth outcaste community. Even though this populace consists of about 15-20 percent of the Indian community it is considered sub- or nonhuman; thus it is not included in the community's composition.

This large group has been ejected from the contours of Hindu society; it still lives outside the gates under the labels "outcaste," "untouchable," "exterior caste," "depressed class," and "Dalit." I use the term "Dalit" in this paper for three reasons. First, this term has become an expression of self-representation, which *Dalit* activists and writers have chosen both in recovering their past identity and in projecting themselves as a collective whole? Second, "Dalit" comes from the root dal meaning "oppressed," "broken," and "crushed," which realistically describes the lives of members of this community. The Human Rights Watch report has the following to say on the situation of the Dalits:

More than one-sixth of India's population, some 160 million people, live a precarious existence, shunned by much of society because of their rank as "untouchables" or *Dalits* - literally meaning "broken" people - at the bottom of India's caste system. Dalits are discriminated against, denied access to land, forced to work in degrading conditions, and routinely abused at the hands or the police and of higher-caste groups that enjoy the State's protection.... In what has been called "hidden apartheid" entire villages in many Indian states remain completely segregated by caste.

Finally, "Dalit" incorporates elements of a positive expression of pride and a resistive surge for combating oppression. The third community includes many more or less homogeneous indigenous communities, which are not obligated to the Indian caste system yet are marginalized by caste communities. These have been grouped under the term "Adivasis," and they are also referred to as Tribals or Schedule Tribes (ST). India has the largest concentration of such indigenous and tribal people. "India has 427 'scheduled' tribes - each unique in its own right.

As many as 400 tribes exist in India... "They ostensibly are a major segment of the Indian social fabric with a legitimate share in the subcontinent's unmatched pluralities." The numerous Adivasis of India can be classified under three major racial and linguistic groups, which are spread over the mountainous and the plateau regions of the country: the Austric Munda language family group; the Dravidian group; and the Tibeto-Burman Mongoloid group. "Adivasis" (meaning the ancient or original dwellers of the land) is utilized here to retain an awareness of their claim to being the original people of the land and to point to their cultural and religious relatedness to things of the earth.

Further, according to a recent article entitled "Call us Adivasis, Please," Gail Omvedt suggests that this is the term by which they want to be known. The Adivasis "generally have lived through exploitative, oppressive and suppressive social and political structures in India." Mostly, they have been alienated from their land both by "greedy" caste communities and by overzealous governments, which take away tribal land for mining and big industries." Thus, poverty and estrangement from the means of their livelihood (the land) threaten *Adivasi* communities in India. Along with this, there is a serious threat to their traditional culture and worldview from the forces of modernization and Hinduization.

THE MINORITIES VIEWPOINT

Hindu nationalism, which is alive and well in India today, is concertedly engaged in the assignment of absorbing minorities into its ideology, Driven by the ideology of Hindutva - a term coined by V. D. Sarvarkar which has always advocated a comprehensive project involving the coming together of culture, society, and politics, it seeks to fuse all the distinct particularities and differences of religious minorities (Muslims and Christians) and ethnocultural minorities (Dalits and Adivasis) into its Brahmanic construction of an Indian nation. Thus, Hindutva threatens all minorities in the Indian nation who assert features of their distinct variance from this imagined homogeneous identity. Historically, the emergence of Hindu nationalism with its founding credo of Hindutva must be seen within the context of colonialism.

The Indian reaction to the psychosocial and politico-economic trauma of the long and complex process of colonial rule was paradoxical. On the one hand, it reproduced the myth that colonialism constructed: India is one unitary and homogeneous entity held together by its essential religiosity, which can be captured under the label Hinduism. Thus, the colonized other claimed for itself some integral features which the colonial Self ascribed to it. On the other hand, it rejected the tendencies in colonial policy to divide the Indian community into numerous divisions according to the colonialist's own whims and fancies.

The divide-and-rule tactic of British colonialism almost succeeded in making Indians believe that they were merely a disparate conglomeration of human tribes loosely held together. Thus, "torn, broken up and confined in watertight compartments, the Hindus themselves had come to doubt if they were a homogenous power at all." As a counter movement to this splintering of India, Hindutva sought to provide "a broad basic foundation on bedrock on which a consolidated and mighty Hindu Nation could take a secure stand." In this context, Hinduization was a deliberate act of consolidation. First, Hindutva creatively utilized the binary framework of colonialism, but artfully transposed the unitary Other into the united Self. In other words, the Occidental image of the synthesized character developed by the western orientialists was accepted; however, it was transformed into an active Self from a passive Other. Second, Hindutva constructively projected Hindu India as one composite and tangible nation, which, even if fragmented by colonialism, was in the process of becoming homogenized into one socio-political and religio-cultural entity. Most importantly, it must be noted that in all of this activity religion was utilized as the agent and the object of such homogenization. Precisely at the time in which "most eminent scholars both Indian and English right down to the penny aliner in the daily streets... tried to define the word 'Hindu,'" Indians, under the banner of Hindutva, joined in the enterprise of representing themselves (the East) within the already established representational discourse of the West.

With this in mind, the writings of Savarkar may be cited as representative of an inordinately influential form of nationalist thinking which homogenized the idea of India into one region, religion, and race. The relevance of interrogating Savarkar is twofold. First, he is the most creative proponent of redefining Hinduism in comprehensive terms: religion encompasses the manifold dimensions of geography, society, politics, and culture. Thus, he moves away from merely representing Hinduism as a religious phenomenon confined to rituals, myths, deities, and social norms. Rather, for him, it is much larger and broader, which is why Savarkar coined the term "Hindutva." Second, Savarkar's ideas have gained acceptance with the modern resurgence of Hindu nationalism.

It can thus serve as an ideological base for understanding the main principles of the contemporary political, social and political phenomenon referred to as "Hindutva." In a book entitled Hindutva: *Who is a Hindu,* first published in 1923, Savarkar makes his case that we must move away from the label "Hinduism" and exchange it for the label "Hindutva." Hinduism, for him, is of "alien growth"' thus "we should not allow ourselves to be confused by this newfangled term." Moreover, the term Hinduism is associated only with religious dogma; thus it fails to take seriously the inclusion of other religious offspring of the land of Saptasindhu, i.e. Buddhism, Jainism, and Sikhism.

For Savarkar, the term Hindutva overcomes three of the main problems with the term Hinduism. First, Hindutva speaks of a sacred geography. "The first image that it rouses in the mind is unmistakably of our motherland and by an express appeal to its geographical and physical features it vivifies it into a living being. Hindustan means the land of Hindus; the first essential of Hindutva must necessarily be this geographic one." This sense of motherland is passionately described. Unless one "has come to look upon our land not only as the land of his love but of worship, he cannot be incorporated into the Hindu fold." Second, Hindutva binds all those of the motherland together by a common blood. Again Savarkar puts this emphatically:

The Hindus are not merely the citizens of the Indian state because they are unified not only by the bonds of love they bear to a common motherland but also by the bonds of a common blood. They are not only a Nation but also a race-jati. The word jati, derived from the root Jan to produce, means a brotherhood, a race determined by a common origin - possessing a common blood. All Hindus claim to have in their veins the blood of the mighty race incorporated with and descended from the Vedic fathers, the Sindus. Third, Hindutva asserts that as a result of this biological community, all Hindus (must) share a common culture: "the brave and loving defense of the Hindu culture have been incorporated with and bound to us by the dearest of ties - the ties of common blood." In a longer passage Savarkar expresses this third essential characteristic of Hindutva clearly:

We Hindus are bound together not only by the ties of love we bear to a common fatherland and by the common blood that courses through our veins and keeps our hearts throbbing and our affections warm, but also by the ties of common homage we pay to our great civilization - our Hindu culture, which could not be better rendered than by the word Sanskriti suggestive as it is of that language Sanskrit, which has been the chosen means of expression and preservation of that culture of all that was best and worth-preserving in the history of our race. We are one because we are a nation, a race and own a common Sanskriti (civilization).

Interestingly, though quite predictably, the common culture which binds all Indians together is the one common Hindu culture with deep roots in Brahmanic religion. symbolized by its sacred language (Sanskrit). Accepting and working toward the reclamation of this religio-cultural commonality is crucial to the Hindutva agenda. As Savarkar puts it, "For the first two essentials of Hindutva - nation and jati [race] - are clearly denoted and connoted by the word pitrubhu [Fatherland] while the third element of Sanskriti [civilization] is pre-eminently implied by the word Punyabhu [Holyland] as it is precisely Sanskriti including sanskaras i.e. rites and rituals, ceremonies and sacraments, that make a land a Holyland." .

One geographic region is made to correspond with one race, which in turn is constructed to be religiously and culturally homogenous through the civilization engendered and developed by the Brahmins. The interpretation of Dalit and Adivasi communities in this common nation, common race, and common civilization (religio-cultural heritage) is somewhat mixed. On the one hand, the ideology of Hindutva, as propounded by Savarkar, asserts that all communities, be they Brahmin or Dalit or Adivasi, share in a common blood. This testimony of a common flow of blood "is true not only in the case of those that are the outcome of the intermarriages between the chief four castes, or between the chief four castes and the cross-born but also in the case of those tribes or races who somewhere in the dimness of the hoary past were leading a separate and self-centred life."

This biological connectedness among all communities in India, which affirms the anthropological basis of *Dalit* and Adivasi existence, is a major step in espousing the universalization of human rights for all people. In another passage, primarily referring to specific Adivasi communities and Dalits (Panchamas and Namashudras), Savarkar writes. The race that is born of the fusion... of the Aryan, the Kolarians, Dravidians, whose blood we as a race inherit, is rightly called neither an Aryan, nor Lolarian, nor Dravidian - but the Hindu race; that is, that people who live as children of a common motherland, adorning a common holyland... Therefore the Santals, Kolis, Bhils, Panchama, Namashudras and all other such tribes and classes are Hindus.

On the other hand, there is reason to believe that the hierarchy of the fourfold caste system is maintained in Savarkar's philosophy, even if tacitly. In fact, the relationship of the various caste groups operates on the historical principle of assimilation and absorption by which the "noble stream," the sublime Vedic blood, incorporates the "lost souls," thus saving them from "being lost in bogs and sands." In the following quotation Savarkar illustrates my point in a more nuanced fashion: "All that the caste system has done is to regulate its noble blood on lines believed - and on the whole rightly believed - by our saints and patriotic law-givers and kings to contribute most to fertilize and enrich all that was barren and poor, without famishing and debasing all that was flourishing and nobly endowed." The association of "noble blood" with the twice-born castes and "barren and poor" with Dalits and Adivasis cannot be underplayed. Further, one cannot but think of Manu when Savarkar invokes praise for the "saintly and patriotic law-giver" who brings regulation to the caste system. In the end, in this ideology of nationalistic thought, Dalits and Adivasis can claim common blood with all other Hindus as long as they abandon their religious and cultural differences and give themselves up to the synergy of Hindutva, which promises to harmoniously bring nation, race and civilization together into a homogeneous unity. This harmony, one might add, is rooted in Vedic

Hinduism, which has an amazing propensity to incorporate the lowly and base into the sublimity of the stream of noble blood. Thus Brahminization funds the process of Hinduization into which *Dalit*s and *Adivasi*s are calculatedly absorbed.

The Christian community, which by the first quarter of the twentieth century was identified as consisting primarily of Dalits and Adivasis, is more explicitly vilified in this theory of Hindutva. There is little ambiguity that Christians, along with Muslims, do not find a place in Hindutva, since "they belong, or feel that they belong, to a cultural unit altogether different from the Hindu one. Their heroes and hero-worship, their fairs and their festivals, and their ideals and their outlook on life, have now ceased to be common with our own."

Even though, the Christians belong to the common nation and race (thus fulfilling two criteria of the Hindutva) they do not meet the third criteria because they do not participate in the common civilization. Savarkar expands on this pointedly:

That is why in the case of some of our Mohammedan or Christian countrymen who had originally been forcibly converted to a non-Hindu religion and who consequently have inherited along with Hindus, a common Fatherland and a greater part of the wealth of a common culture - language, law, custom, folklore and history - are not and cannot be recognized as Hindus. For them Hindustan is Fatherland as to any other Hindu yet it is not to them a Holyland too. Their Holyland is far off in Arabia or Palestine.

Their mythology and Godmen, ideas and heroes are not the children of this soil. Consequently their names and their outlook smack of foreign origin. Their love is divided. Nay, if some of them really believe what they profess to do, then there can be no choice - they must, to a man, set their Holyland above their Fatherland in their love and allegiance. Christians are interpreted as not belonging to Hindutva because they do not share in the common civilization. Nonetheless, a careful reading of the aforementioned passage will reveal that in actual fact their loyalty of belonging to the common nation is also questioned.

Christians are portrayed as being more loyal to a foreign land than their own Fatherland. Christians thus cannot really be part of the Indian nation in its Hinduized polity since they are misfits in this civilization and their allegiance to the nation is divided. The fact that Christianity was becoming an attractive option for *Dalits* and *Adivasis* must have been threatening to the forces of Hindu nationalism.

In this coupling, religio-cultural difference was reinforced by ethno-social difference. Variation threatens to become potently dangerous; *Dalits* and *Adivasis* must in no way reassert their difference from Hinduism by embracing Christianity. Thus, those who subscribed to the Hindu homogenization project disseminated the view that embracing Christianity was an antinational and anti-cultural act.

THE WOOING AND WOUNDING OF MINORITIES

Nothing can be more alarming than the resurgence of the Hindutva today? It has gradually evolved from a counterideology that sought to destabilize colonialism into a ruling ideology that seeks to consolidate political power. Thus, the ramifications of its expansive growth are concretely felt every day through the functioning of the Indian nation-state. While Hinduization of the Indian nation has a long history it has become a particularly grave threat to minorities over the last decade with the political ascendancy of the presently ruling Bharatiya Janata Party (BJP). The BJP, in turn, is firmly supported by its Hindu communal network of the Rashtriya Swayamsevak Sangh. The RSS (National Volunteer Corps), founded in 1925, also works through many other related political and sociocultural organizations such as the Vishwa Hindu Parishad (VHP), Bajrang Dal (BD), and the Shiv Sena party (SS). This means that the state has become susceptible to the devices of Hindu nationalism; Hindutva has covertly and overtly gained a foothold in the everyday workings of the nation. The agenda of the Hindutva, sometimes working in collusion with the mechanism of the nation-state, can be seen to operate at two levels. First, there is the persuasive approach, which entices minorities to renounce their cultural and religious differences and embrace the all-encompassing Indian identity in its Hindu visage. Dalits and Adivasis (Christians included) are the targets of a well-orchestrated campaign. There is a systematic effort to educate them at the grassroots level of their religio-cultural space within Hinduism.

The RSS has started village-level educational units that enable teachers well-versed in the ideology of Hindutva to live with and instruct minority communities about their nation, heritage, and civilization. It is estimated that there are at least 2.4 million pupils and 80.000 teachers in these Vidya Bharati schools run by the RSS-VHP coalition. And "much of the text being taught" in such schools "is designed to promote bigotry and religious fanaticism in the name of inculcating knowledge of [Indian/Hindu] culture in the younger generation." Arguing from a study in South Gujarat, Arjun Patel's conclusion is explicit:

The influence of Hinduism on the social and religious life of Adivasis has been considerable, particularly in the last 10-15 years... the BJP and other Hindu organizations such as the Mandir, the Arya Samaj, saints and sadhus, and some Adivasi politicians have succeeded in inculcating the Hindutva RSS, the ABVP, Bajrang Dal, Shiv Shena, the Hindu Milan ideology in the minds of the Adivasi people?

There are ongoing efforts of various Hindu nationalist organizations to "reconvert" Dalits and Adivasis from non-Indian religions (Christianity and Islam) back to their original Hindu fold. For example, on 2 June 2000 as many as 72 Christian Adivasis reconverted to Hinduism in Manaharpur village in Orissa's Keonjhar district? The reconversion is bolstered by a similar presupposition that all those who live in the geographical limits of India are nothing other than Hindus, even if there is a dominant and credible argument made by these communities that they are not only non-Hindu but pre-Hindu in composition.

There is also an attempt to utilize government institutions to hinduize all segments of the nation so as to forge a unitary consciousness at the heart of the nation. This involves the task of restoring the essentialized identity of being Hindu-Indian which was somehow lost through capture (colonialism), conversion, and rebellion (Dalits' and Adivasis' self-assertion). The October 1998 proposal of a commission of educational experts appointed by Dr. Murli Manohar Joshi (BJP, Cabinet Minister, Human Resources Development Ministry) is a stark example of this objective to hinduize all of India. In a comprehensive plan to restructure education, the commission suggests that the government "introduce Sanskrit as a compulsory subject in schools" in order that "the primary to the highest education should be Indianized, nationalised and spiritualised."

It further adds that since "Hindutva is a way of life and not a religion... India's invaluable heritage of the Vedas and the Upanishads should find a place in the curriculum from primary to the higher level courses, including the vocational courses." Second, the coercive left of Hindu nationalism complements the persuasive right. If the latter is meant to entice and cajole, the former is meant to admonish and punish. There can be no doubt that the violence unleashed on minority communities that resist the pan-Hindu identity has increased.

In a methodical and widely-researched monograph published recently, Human Rights Watch documents the increasing violence directed against Dalits: "Between 1994 and 1996, a total of 98,349 cases were registered with the police nationwide as crimes against scheduled castes. Of these, 38,483 were registered under the Atrocities Act. A further 1,660 were for murder, 2,814 for rape, and 13,671 for hurt." It goes on to paint a frightening picture of the rise in recent mass murders in Bihar and Tamil Nadu, which is directly related to the emerging assertion of an authentic and resistant Dalit social, political, and cultural identity. The violence directed against the Adivasis in Northeastern India has also been escalating.

Of course, the rationale of insurgency has been used. There can be little doubt that it demonstrates the hinduizing nation-state's heavy-handed approach as it contains, thwarts, and crushes differences of ethnicity, culture, and worldview.

In recent years Christians have also become the targets of rape, murder, church bombings, Bible burning, and severe beatings. The killing of priests, raping of nuns, and torching of prayer halls and churches are means to terrorize, denigrate and threaten people of different religio-cultural traditions that Christians represent in India.

This violence, incited by the BJP/RSS/VHP/Bajrang Dal/SS, was documented in the cover story of Communalism Combat of July 2000:

> Physical attacks and intimidation of minorities have resurfaced with a vengeance. Incidents in the past three months alone - between April and June 2000 - have crossed the three dozen marks. Christian religious persons running educational institutions or health centres have been singled out for murder or other forms of mistreatment.

In another article, T. K. Oommen purports that "there has been unprecedented violence against [the Christian community in India] in the last one year." He elaborates further: "It is not true that there was no anti-Christian violence in the past. But they [such instances] were few and far between. In the last 50 years there have been only 50 instances of physical violence against Christians. But in the last one year there have been 110 cases of atrocities against them." It must be emphasized that the attack against Christians appears concentrated in Dalit and Adivasi settlements. For example in the Dangs District of Gujarat "the Hindu right was behind a wave of harassment of [Adivasi] Christians in the Dangs, beginning in late 1997."

From November 1997 to January 1999 there were as many as 36 cases of burning and looting of churches, 20 cases of disturbances of some sort between Christians and non-Christians, numerous cases of Christians being beaten and looted, and one killing. Reflecting on the question as to why Christians are the victims of violent attacks in the Adivasi regions, K. N. Panikkar has the following reasons to offer. First, Christians, through their sustained service among the Adivasis, "enjoy considerable appreciation of and support for their work from the local population." This presents an obstacle for the Hindutva organizations to infiltrate the Adivasi areas.

"The advance of the Parivar [Network of Hindutva organizations] in the tribal area is, therefore, possible only if the Christians are discredited and displaced." Second, Christians are targeted because of the secular position they have increasingly taken over the last decade. In the context of Hindu communalism's fascist potential, Christians present a counter model in their "reaching out to secular, liberal and left formations for joint initiative." Christianity, especially among Dalits and Adivasis, must be stopped at any cost from being presented as an alternative option to Hindutva. Panikkar's discussion, I believe, is in line with my claim that Christians are being persecuted because their work among the Dalits and Adivasis is perceived as an effort to thwart the homogenizing aim of Hindutva.

The point being asserted has to do with the tendency in contemporary Hindu nationalism through the various units of the Sangh Parivar (the Bharatiya Janata Party [BJP],the Rashtriya Swayamsevak Sangh [RSS], the Vishwa Hindu Parishad [VHP], Bajrang Dal [BD] and the Shiv Sena party [SS]) to further the process of taming all heterogeneous and plural forms to fit into the unitary construction of a religiously synthesized India, while defining the core of this disciplined pan-Indian identity in Hindu (specifically Brahmanic) terms. On the one hand, the Dalit and Adivasi assertion of distinctiveness and particularity becomes the inner threat to the consolidation of the Hindu nation. On the other hand, Christianity, particularly in its identifications with the Dalits and Adivasis, becomes the external threat that provides an alternate set of religious and cultural meaning systems to the promotion of a unitary nation held together by Hinduness.

INDIAN-CHRISTIAN THEOLOGY

In seeking a solution to this unitary and homogenizing ideology of Hindutva one must be careful to repudiate it as a paradigm. The current efforts should be to reject models that sanction the undercutting of a plurality of religious, cultural, political, and social expressions and to imagine alternate models that legitimate and empower multiple religious, cultural, political, and social self-expressions of the various communities that make up the Indian nation. Minorities, such as Dalit and Adivasi communities who experience and assert their cardinal differences from the Hindutva ideology, are particularly equipped and obliged to project and promote worldviews that are more amiable to plurality and thus less hostile to difference.

The words of Amir Ali are apt here: "The concept of multiculturalism can prove to be an effective counter to the hegemonising project of Hindutva and there exists, on account of this very reason, a strong case for its promotion and encouragement in this country." Such models are extant in the lives of local Dalit and Adivasi communities. They merely need to be recognized and lifted up as worthwhile, serviceable, and satisfactory paradigms for collective human living. Let me share an experience from a Dalit Christian community that exhibits traces of such a pluralistic model. I was the priest of fourteen small Dalit congregations in Karunguli, Chingelput District, Tamil Nadu.

On a July morning I decided to visit one of my congregations at Nagapuram (a pseudonym) to consult with the teachers of our mission school and the elders of the community about a proposed project to reconstruct the school building. I left home at about 9:30 AM on my motorbike. About halfway to the village I met the headmaster of the school coming from the village on his bicycle. He seemed quite surprised and very uncomfortable to meet me. I asked him if it was a school holiday. He said that it was not, but that he had some business at the school administrative office in the city. He informed me that since he was on official work, his assistant teacher was conducting school during the forenoon. He then attempted to persuade me not to visit the school since he wanted to be there to welcome me. Also, his assistant would be too busy to spend time with me.

However, since I was already halfway there I decided to proceed on to the village. I assured the headmaster that I also intended to visit some other parish members to talk with them about the building plan. He was not convinced and started with another line of reasoning as to why I should not go to the village. He insisted that many of the community members were busy with the yearly colony festival to the local goddess, Gangamma. He assured me that it was a real waste of my precious time. Much to the dismay of the headmaster, his reasoning had the opposite effect on me. I really wanted to see some of the village festivity, so set off toward the village, leaving behind a bewildered and unhappy headmaster.

When I reached the village I realized why the headmaster was so upset at my visit to the school. The building was closed and there was no school, not because the headmaster had official duty, but because the whole village community was celebrating the yearly festival of Gangamma, the goddess of their colony. The headmaster, who was also the catechist for the congregation at Nagapuram, was too ashamed to admit to me that all the Christians were also part of this Dalit celebration in the colony. The mission school characterized the ambiguous relationship that Christians in India have toward celebrating Dalit festivals. On the one hand, Christian school officials were not willing to admit that they had anything to do officially with the Dalit goddess. Thus, the school was technically open.

On the other hand, the headmaster was realistic enough to realize that there would be no children in school that day. He had ignored the reason they were not in school and set up some official duty which would allow him to turn a blind eye to the wholehearted participation of his Christian congregation in the yearly festival of Gangamma. When I went around the colony I encountered a similar embarrassment among my congregation members. Upon inquiry I discovered that they were very much a part of the festive celebration. First, they had contributed liberally to the cost of the festival. A month before the festival all the *Dalit*s of the village come together as a community.

On the day designated for the community meeting by the elders the drummers go around an hour before it is time and invite the entire community (both Christians and Hindus). The purpose of this meeting is to set the date for the festival and to decide upon the amount that each family will contribute towards the event. Second, although they did not take leadership roles in the ritual of carrying the goddess, the members of the congregation at Nagapuram did offer their services as drummers and participants in the procession. Third, some shared in the feast at the conclusion of the festival in which the entire community ate the food, which was cooked and offered to the goddess. Although Dalit Christians joined their neighbors in various symbolic ways to indicate their unity in invoking the protection of the colony goddess for their community, they were reluctant to admit to their pastor that they played any significant role in the celebration of their Dalit religious heritage.

On that day, many years ago, I was confronted with a truth that operated practically among rural Christians from a Dalit background: the church's effort to estrange Christians from their Dalit religio-cultural roots and their Dalit Hindu neighbors had not been successful when it came to community practice. The worldview that was functional for them was a pluralistic one: it was fluid and incorporated otherness with some ease. Sabastian Kappen puts this well when he says,

> It is generally believed that the Indian Christians are beings apart, having little in common with Hindus. Such a perception is, in fact, zealously instilled in them by the churches from very early in their lives. But, anthropologically, they are first Indians and only then Christians. They are children of the soil as much as any Hindu. More specifically, as the above-mentioned case illustrates, from the Dalit communities' point of view the economic, social,cultural, and religious distance between Christian and non-Christian Dalits is exaggerated, if not altogether spurious. This is particularly true in rural India where Dalits live together in the same geographical space away from the main village. Because of their deliberate marginalization from the caste Hindu village

and Hindu sociocultural and religious world, Dalits, whether Christian or not, share in a togetherness that is both imposed on them by the dominant caste Hindu worldview and constructed by them in solidarity over against all forces that continuously seek to demean and disrupt their communal life. Through a recent, well-researched ethnography on the culture and religion of the Paraiyars of Tamil Nadu, Robert Deliege confirms the symbiotic relationship between the religion of the Christian and Hindu Dalits. He states:

The religious difference between the Hindus and Christian [Dalit communities] is not as deep as it seems at first sight. For both, religion is pragmatic. The Christians only go to church for a few ceremonies. They have maintained a fair amount of traditional beliefs; in the same fashion, the Hindus have easily come to terms with the cult of Virgin Mary who is the dominant figure in the religious life of Christians.

In a reference that is also inclusive of Dalits and Adivasis, and that lays emphasis on the living practices of common people in India, Achin Vanaik states: "The great redeeming grace of Hinduism lies not so much in its philosophy or in its Brahmanism as in the simple ecumenism of its largely non-Brahminical and popular forms of existence." At least one characteristic of a pluralistic model must be highlighted when we take into consideration the heterogeneous inclination inherent in Dalit communities: conceptions of pluralism stem from the lived reality of Dalit communities. I believe that this can give us directions for a notion of pluralism that will be relevant at a national level.

Rather than being an abstraction from a priori postulates or a theoretical model that arises from philosophically determined first principles, pluralism for Dalits is a way of being in the world. More pointedly, pluralistic living in the community is tactfully maintained in spite of the instruction of exclusivity that Christian teachers and preachers promulgated and that the advancers of Hindutva propagated. Interestingly, one may make the distinction between a model of being in the world that advocates inclusion and one that advances absorption. The Dalits' form of pluralism is not an absorbing of the Other, so that the Other is assimilated into the Self. Rather, there is willingness in this form of pluralism to allow difference to remain even while participating in each other's activities.

Mutual acceptance of difference and mutual participation in such difference without attempts to assimilate it is the main feature of the sort of pluralism that is lived out and offered up by Dalit communities. Such a pluralistic orientation is incorporative, participatory, and cooperative: thus, communitarian. This is interpreted against the backdrop of Vedic-based Brahmanic and Bible-centered Christian unitary, cultural, and religious worldviews, which heralded victory for the exclusive, distancing, and homogenizing ones. Christian reflection on its social and historical context finds itself located in a crucial and strategic position.

Christianity is already outside the walls of the Indian community. Thus, as I have argued earlier, it is positioned alongside the Dalits and Adivasis. In the self-understanding of its role in India, Christianity has sometimes been guided by the philosophical objectives that I have attributed to the Hindutva. Thus, it has tried to eliminate the religious and cultural particularities of its Dalit and Adivasi converts and initiate them into a universal Christian culture. Christian missionaries, in converting Dalits and Adivasis to Christianity, set about instilling a worldview that attempted to surmount all differences and particularities.

Accordingly, there still exists in Indian Christianity the hope that all religions will find their ultimate home in their own one true religion, namely Christianity. Yet there can be another contrasting aspiration for Christian theology in contemporary India. This would involve strengthening and networking the liberating energies that are forging spaces for their own survival - a survival that includes a particular expression of human identity. When this common goal is linked with the desire of Dalits and Adivasis to preserve their respective ways of being in the world, the essence of theology (resistance-liberation) is engendered. The challenge for Christian theology appears in the mirror dimly. Traces of a pluralistic model are manifest in minority communities as they live their lives in quiet defiance against the agenda of Hindu nationalism. In the face of threats to assimilate Christians, Dalits, and Adivasis into a homogeneous Hindu identity, as well as the violent attacks against these minorities, how can Christian theology tap into the energy that fuels the obstinate expression of their religious and ethnocultural difference? What is the role of Christian theology in a context where human beings strive to be free in their expressions of difference within a unity that Hindu nationalism demands today?

In order to answer these questions it may be pertinent to offer a tentative definition of Indian-Christian theology within this particular historical context. Indian-Christian theology involves a critical and constructive reflection on the contextual resistance-liberation movements in India, especially those arising from the dynamics of religious (Christian) and ethnocultural (Dalit and Adivasi) minorities, as they counter the reach of the dominant ideologies of Hindutva and contribute in creative ways to circulate themes of their particularized experience of the Divine One (in Her/His relatedness to human beings and the world), in light of the paradigm of Jesus Christ.

This contextual definition locates theology both within the intercommunity (with Dalits and Adivasis) resistive-liberative momentum of minorities in India and within the intracommunity dynamism of Christian celebration of the source and sustainer of this activity, Jesus Christ. It must also be underscored that theology is not content with merely describing that which is lived out by Christian communities. Rather it aims toward constructing viable possibilities, which of course involves imagining relevant configurations for meaning and action out of and for the specific world of Christians in India.

Let me expand on the two dimensions implied in my definition of theology before I connect them to two traditional sites of theological activity (mission and liturgy). First, the content of theology is intrinsically connected with liberation.

Thus, in the Indian context, it cannot but be related to the resistive-liberative striving of the Dalits, Adivasis, and Christians in the contemporary situation of Hinduization. Liberation is posited as being synonymous with the fabric of Christian theology. As Cone put it in liberation theology's earliest formulation, "liberation is not only consistent with the gospel but is the gospel of Jesus Christ." In placing this pivotal term at the nucleus of Indian-Christian theology there must be contemplation of the historical resistance-liberation striving of religious and ethnocultural minorities in India.

Christian content and resistive-liberative context intersect to supply the locus for and substance of Indian theology. This dynamic undergirds the struggles for the unqualified acceptance of Dalits and Adivasis as equal members of Indian human society and demands their fuller participation in all dimensions (social, economic, political, and cultural) of the processes of building the nation-state. But, of course, one must ask a basic theological question: What is the theological rationale for consciously and concertedly bringing the Dalit and Adivasi dynamic of resistance-liberation with all its religio-cultural and socioeconomic dimensions into the realm of Christian theology? The rationale, as I understand it, stems from our understanding of the everlasting and exhaustive working of God that directs all of creation toward liberation.

The everlasting or perpetual dimension points to the chronological inclusiveness, which joins God's activity from the inception to the telos of creation. While the exhaustive or encompassing dimension emphasizes the geo-spatial comprehensiveness, which extends from the incarnation of Jesus as the Christ to the groaning of every particle of creation. Instead of saying that where the word "God" is named the Divine dynamic is present and active, I am saying the reverse: where resistive-liberative forces work toward gathering creation toward the fullness of life, God is present and active.

In other words, the theater of the working of God encompasses the entire historical and geographical world; and the resistance-liberation striving of Dalits and Adivasis is a significant occasion of this all-embracing working of God. Thus, theology involves a community's decision to take stock of and its offer to join in with the intercommunity dynamic of God, which is understood to be the divine directionality toward life in all its related fullness. Second, because the overwhelming majority of Christians come from Dalit and Adivasi communities, all of their experiences and expressions of God, world and human beings will be interpreted through the paradigm of Jesus Christ.

In a formal sense, Christian theology as advocate for the worldview of the Dalits and the Adivasis is also constricted by its meta-symbol of interpreting the God-human-world configuration. It is estimated that about "72% of the Indian Christians come from tribal and Dalit backgrounds." Thus, these minority communities comprise almost three-fourths of the Christian population. On the one hand, if theology must be relevant in India it must not only incorporate but also define it along Dalit-Adivasi lines. "Without taking into account the experiences and aspirations of the tribals [and Dalits], Indian Christian theology would be incomplete. Their voices will have to be heard." On the other hand, Christian theology cannot but allow its deliberations to be modified in such a manner that they are interrelated with and interpreted through the symbol of Jesus Christ. Dalit and Adivasi communities who have intentionally embraced the Christian system of symbols will not accept anything short of this.

On a positive note we must record that this is already happening. Thus, it can be noticed that the Indian-Christian theologians are attempting to actualize a more conscientious, contextual theology that appropriates much more seriously the Indian people's religion and culture, which is notably Dalit and tribal in character. Michael Amaladoss is referring to Dalit and Adivasi worldviews when he talks of theology basing itself in popular religions: "In the ongoing dialogue between gospel and culture we must devote special attention to popular religion. With other great religions one seeks to dialogue and collaborate. But popular religion is the base with which the gospel as it has developed today has to find integration."

Continuing our earlier discussion concerning the theological rationale for bringing the Dalit and Adivasi dynamic of resistance-liberation into the realm of Christian theology, another related question arises. On what basis does the Christian community judge which of the elements of Dalit and Adivasi resistive-liberative dynamic manifest the presence and activity of God whom they know in Jesus Christ? I suggest that such criteria emerge from within the Christian community through a dialogical discernment of the working of God as it is outlined by the life and teaching of Jesus. Thus, using the key of the life and teachings of Jesus, Christians tend to decide continuously which religio-cultural beliefs and practices represent the God dynamic and which do not.

For example, native beliefs and practices, which exclude persons on the basis of caste, race, color, and gender, are not reflective of the presence and activity of God as revealed by Jesus, whereas symbols, rites, and religious motifs that challenge such exclusions are in continuity with the transformation characteristic of the God dynamic expressed in Jesus. Similarly, Dalit and Adivasi religio-cultural beliefs and practices that celebrate accessible love and solidarity with the marginalized are closer to the God-dynamic as manifested by the life and teachings of Jesus than those that highlight the overpowering, destructive, and violent characteristics of God. Theology thus involves a community's decision to recognize and join in with the intracommunity discernment of the activity of God which is understood to be inline with the life and teachings of Jesus, the embodiment of life in all its related fullness.

A word of clarification is needed on the phrase "life in all its related fullness." First, it is a symbolic theological construct of the goal of liberation that is extrapolated from the activity of God as discerned from the pattern of the life and teaching of Jesus the Christ. It is a contextual interpretation of Jesus' offer of "abundant life." Second, it brings life to the center of theological discourse. In a subtle manner this moves the locus of theological reflection away from the patronizing posture of deliberating only on the issue of survival (existence) when it comes to the Dalits and Adivasis. The marginalized communities also imagine life in the midst of threats to life, of which survival (existence) is an important part.

Third, the life that is daringly and hopefully imagined and worked towards implies a life in all its related fullness. It is life in abundance that does not exclude any from its refreshing wellspring. It is life that mediates fullness in relationship to all creation, particularly for those denied it through systematic and calculated means. The offer of life in all its related fullness thus includes the dimension of abundance and relationality. In fact this notion presents fullness of life as intimately intertwined with the idea of inclusive and cooperative living, which is an alternate worldview to the homogenizing and hegemonizing one promoted by the Hindutva.

MISSION AND LITURGY AS DUAL LOCI

In order for Indian-Christian theology to benefit from the intercommunity (with Dalits and Adivasis) resistive-liberative momentum of minorities in India, as well as the intracommunity discernment of Christians (that aspects of this activity manifest the agency of Jesus Christ), it must reclaim and revitalize its two traditional domains of mission and liturgy. Christian mission involves identifying and participating in the ongoing activity of God in the world.

This is also mirrored in the trajectories of resistive-liberation in its yearning for life in all its related fullness. Liturgy is the Christian community's celebration of this activity of God as interpreted through the pattern of the life and teaching of Jesus, who is affirmed to be the human embodiment of the resistive-liberative dynamic in its journey toward life in all its related fullness. I believe mission and liturgy are the twin fountains that can nourish the enterprise of Indian-Christian theology, and I will now argue this in a more detailed fashion.

Reflections on the Action of Mission

Christian mission involves faithful devotion to participate concretely, reflectively, and joyously in the ongoing working of God in the world in its journey toward life in all its related fullness. One significant activity of God in India, I argue, is revealed in the resistive-liberative efforts of the Dalit, Adivasi, and Christian communities to counter the colonizing propensities of hinduizing forces and to contribute their human resources for life in all its related fullness. The Christian model of radical and full-scale human adherence to this ongoing mission of God for the welfare of God's entire creation is embodied in the life and ministry of Jesus the Christ.

And this advocacy for resisting forces of dehumanization and for strengthening the potential for becoming the free and complete human beings that God created us to be was central to Jesus' life and teaching. That same power of God continues to inspire Christians to endure and follow the path that Jesus revealed, which promises abundant life for every human being and for all creation. Thus, while Christian mission is intimately tied up with the life and teaching of Jesus of Nazareth, it nonetheless invites and equips Christians to live collectively the implications of such a model in their own particular historical context. But this cannot mean that God is wholly dependent on the Christians for advancing this resistive-liberative mission of God in the world. God is continually working in various forms of resistive-liberative activity outside of the contours of the Christian community, which unites a multitude of forces that strive for the fullness of life of all creation.

These are living signs of God's mission, which directs all creation toward fruition. The Indian Church therefore needs to commit herself to being the embodiment of Jesus Christ among God's people today. This is implemented by identifying the stirrings of the resistive-liberative spirit among her fellow Indians in order to join with them in strengthening the forces that cooperate with God in advancing life in all its related fullness in this world. If this activity of participating in the resistive-liberative dynamic of God's mission is the first act then theology becomes a reflection on this action. I would suggest more concretely that Christian mission involves joining Dalits and Adivasis in their resistance to the homogenizing world vision of Hindutva while at the same time enabling them to posit their particular subjectivities into a framework of human community for the nation-state. Christian identity and practice is not isolated from the resistive-liberative activities of other minorities in India. The worldviews held by these minorities are steeped in their religious and cultural life, which in turn reflect their collective identity. Thus, any framework of human community for the nation-state ought to allow for the multiple experiencing and symbolizing of the Universe (usually involving the triadic realities of world, human being, and God) in accordance with the various representations of its people. Indian-Christian theology, by being part of this mission of resisting Hindutva, is also involved in the task of locating, protecting and circulating resources for a more pluralistic model of collective living by valorizing the worldview of religious and ethnocultural minorities.

But the issue is not as simple as it sounds. In order to probe further this aspect of theology, the debate that is taking place in Indian intellectual circles between those who support the secularization option and those who advance an antimodern or critical traditionalist option. The political school of thought that supports the view that secularization is the only way forward argues against the Hindutva proponents who aim to revive and recast the role of religion in contemporary India. Needless to say, the rise of Hindu nationalism has also resulted in the strengthening of Muslim fundamentalism. To counter this resurgence of religious identity politics it submits that the turn to the option of "secularization" is inevitable and judicious.

Building on the western historical foundations of the term "secularization," this option has been interpreted to involve at least three components. First, some religious historians suggest that modernity has ushered in a decline in the social significance of religious institutions, beliefs, and practices. Thus, religion is gradually losing its hold on the evolving modern human being. Second, secularization increasingly carries with it a relative separation between religious space and socioeconomic space, resulting in a disentangling of religion from other public aspects of community life. Finally, secularization's move toward rationality leads to the reevaluation of traditional religious modes of authority in the light of more varied and bureaucratized forms of the same. However, secularization in India, even according to proponents of this view, does not mean a nation-state that is antireligious but rather one that stands equidistant from all religions.

The secular and sacred lines are drawn clearly, so that in multireligious India "this can mean either a fundamental separation of the state from religious activity and affiliation, or impartial state involvement on issues relating to religious interests of different communities. The problem with this school of thought from the point of view of religious (Christian) and ethnocultural (Dalit and Adivasi) minorities is obvious. Minorities safeguard their particularities in the religio-cultural realm, which is under threat through the homogenizing tendency of Hindutva. The resources of religion and culture cannot be separated from the minorities' social, economic, and political activity of resistance-liberation.

Moreover, instead of allowing religion to be disguised in the functioning of the so-called secular nation-state, it is better for minorities that it be out in the open where it can be marked, named, and interrogated. After all, the BJP as a national government has found it convenient to uphold the secularization option while at the same time covertly encouraging its Sangh Combine (RSS, VHP, Bajrang Dal, and SS) to pursue the Hindutva agenda. Arguing that the whole notion of secularization is modernist, western, and tinged with connotations that come from a Christian, antichurch context, some move to oppose the separation of religion from the state and instead push for a national polity that would "use the 'authentic' resources of faith to sustain a socio-political culture with a deeper tolerance for diversity and pluralism than 'Western secularism' can ever generate." One notable and eloquent theorist of such an antimodern alternate theory to secularization is Ashis Nandy. Offering a rereading of Gandhi in terms of an antisecularization proposal, Nandy's "critical traditionality" seeks to get back to a theoretical framework of pluralism that flourished before the colonial and modem epoch.

In order to subvert the pathological processes dictated on India by colonialism there is a need for Indian political scientists to recover and reiterate its prior civilizational paradigms, which are rooted in the premodern religio-cultural worldviews. Such antimodern models of "critical traditionality" come out of the life experience of ordinary people in India and provide working examples of tolerance and pluralism not by ejecting religio-cultural particularities but by utilizing them for the good of all.

Much of my discussion on the constructive role of Indian-Christian theology is related to what Nandy is proposing, particularly with regard to taking seriously the religio-cultural realm of communities as sites of particularized patterns of meaning. And yet there are some differences. On the one hand, I am unable to posit an alternate framework for tolerance and pluralism in the premodern and precolonial heritage of India's civilizational past. In fact, Dalits and Adivasis experienced systematic dehumanization, severe marginalization, and structural oppression through centuries of Indian history. Rather, I am willing to locate such elements of a pluralistic mode of living in the everyday religio-cultural and sociopolitical lives of contemporary minority communities.

These may or may not be related to the grandiose civilizational patterns of the past, but they may exist in the symbolic universe of Dalits and Adivasis and thus provide an alternate model for thinking and living in the world of difference and variety. On the other hand, I see a much more dynamic relationship between the inherited worldviews of these communities and the traditions presently practiced by them. All rituals, symbols, and practices are concrete expressions of that which is inherited interacting with what is contextually experienced. Thus, there is not much scope for the activity of recovery of the pure traditions of the past; instead there is a plethora of hybridized, living religio-cultural symbolic systems.

These are contextual avatars of the wisdom of the past, but they are pragmatic enough to negotiate meaning in the complexities of the present. Christian theology can tap into these and offer them up as resources for the community life of the nation-state as living alternatives to the vision of Hindu nationalism. Dalit and Adivasi religion and culture (and local Christianity, which is predominantly Dalit and Adivasi in constitution) are storehouses of such symbolic expressions of the particularity of minorities in the face of Hindutva's homogenizing and universalizing propensity. Alternate frameworks for collective living in India must be in the business of detecting the elements of distinctiveness (even if through difference) of Dalit and Adivasi culture and religion, which are inscribed into the communicative practices of the community, in order to represent its collective identity to itself as well as to the nation-state.

Thus, through a meticulous study of the Pallars, a Dalit community in Tamil Nadu, Kappadia demonstrates how in their "religious orientation" and "politics of everyday life" they both undercut the valuation of the dominant caste (Brahmanic) values and register their own interpretation of the same. It is the task of theology to reflect on the mission activity of religious and ethnocultural minorities in resisting Hindutva. But theology also involves reflection on the productive task of mission activity that locates and circulates religio-cultural resources of such minorities for developing more pluralistic frames of collective living in the nation-state. The words of Felix Wilfred, who emphasizes both the special need for such a pluralistic paradigm among minorities and the fact that it is among these same communities that one can locate such models, are an apt conclusion to this section:

> The bright light of future falls upon the victims when they begin to see the prospects of their identity and difference being recognized and affirmed. It is understandable, then, why the claims of the oppressed identities are coupled with the assertion of difference.... In other words, the difference is crucial for the construction of their subjecthood as the principal agent for shaping their own future.

Reflections on the Action of Liturgy

Christian worship is the other appropriate site for drawing in and celebrating the Dalit and Adivasi religio-cultural worlds, which in turn can be a source for the theological enterprise.

The liturgical space for Christians can be reimagined as a safe haven for the symbolic representations of minorities that are threatened by the homogenizing co-option of Hindu nationalism. In this sense, worship keeps alive the religious and cultural expressions that reflect the distinctiveness of minorities in India. As mentioned earlier, liturgy is the Christian community's celebration of the God-dynamic, which, as outlined by the life and teaching of Jesus, is affirmed as the pattern and goal of the resistive-liberative dynamic in its journey toward life in all its related fullness.

However, the domain of liturgy in Indian Christianity is hardly a reservoir of people's expressions of their experience of the Divine in its relatedness to human beings and the world. Instead, the dominant paradigm of worship is rooted in the myth of the necessary mediatory role of an ecclesiastical specialist to generate proper homage to God. This mediatory role in fact is continuously transformed into an authoritative and regulatory one. Thus, the liturgy, by which many of the established and traditional churches organize corporate worship, is passed down from the creative workshop of the church specialists. The duty of the priests is to discipline the common worship life of the people so that it conforms as closely as possible to what has been prescribed as "proper" liturgical practice by the church hierarchy.

This older model can be interpreted as arising from the ethos of monarchy, which was prevalent both in the western world and in India during the last few centuries. Accordingly, the figure of God as king must only be approached in prescribed ways and the specialists who belong to the king's court and council are given the duty of making sure that all those who come into contact with the king, especially the commoners, are groomed in the art of the "proper" approach to the king so as not to insult the king's honor and esteem. The conception of liturgy that I am projecting rejects such a notion of God and liturgy. It starts with the premise that there is not a single way in which God is experienced but rather there is a multitude of modes, media, and forms with which this can be expressed among people. Thus, proper worship in the Indian context is not a law that needs to be discerned by the specialist and made binding on the people. Rather, it is a gospel of the free experience of God's engagement in the lives of God's people, which is freely and creatively expressed according to the particularities of various human communities, especially as represented by the Dalits and Adivasis. It is a celebration of the present experience of God by the people (a majority of whom are Dalits and Adivasis) and not so much an obligation to stage the eternal experience of the God of the ecclesiastical fathers.

God, in this emerging model, is symbolized as a faithful and creative companion who sustains and empowers striving people in fruitful ways and fascinating modes in their journey toward life in all its related fullness. God is involved in every aspect of life, particularly preserving those expressions of the subjectivity of human beings that are under attack. Christian liturgy in this context embraces the people's multimodal celebration of their rich God-human experience in all its pluriformity. The drums of the Dalits become the means of invoking, energizing, and encountering the Divine in the Indian Christian liturgy. Christ as drum, thus, may be a Dalit rendition in the arena of music just as Christ as Logos is a reflection of the same in the world of reading and writing. So also can the dance of the Adivasis be an expression of the celebration of God's presence with God's human and nonhuman creation. In the words of an Adivasi theologian, "If the Lord does not dance with the tribal Christians in a victory dance procession, our joy with Him will remain incomplete."

In such inclusion of Dalit and Adivasi culture and religion one must be sensitive to the oral and enacted dimensions of liturgical life. This may move Christian worship beyond the preoccupation with Scriptural texts and literary forms of prayer to a concern with the spontaneous religious life of its daily practitioners. This also calls for a conscious process of de-sanskritization to be set in motion in our collective Christian liturgical journey. While there was an historical period in which Indian Christian theologians attempted to project a false Brahmanic identity by copiously drawing upon classical

Hindu symbols, rites, and philosophical themes, in recent years they have begun to reclaim their Dalit and Adivasi non-Brahminical heritage.

The focus on opening the door of Christian worship to oral-centered and symbolic act-centered religious expression reaffirms our roots in popular and local religions in India. This nontextual character of Dalit and Adivasi traditions influences the direction of contextual liturgical expressions: instead of reaching back to the pristine and original world of the past (mostly inscribed and frozen in sacred texts), they may be intertwined with an orientation towards the future. Harvey Cox's comments regarding the African indigenous churches are applicable in this context:

> The indigenous churches draw on the past to prepare people for the future. They are not burgeoning just because they help people to reclaim ancient spiritual resources that seemed to be lost. They are growing because they help people apply those resources in a new and bewildering context.

When Christian worship is able to embrace the religio-cultural world of Dalit and Adivasi communities it becomes an invaluable source of theology since it taps into the most productive workshop of people's experience of God. We are generally accustomed to idea that theology happens at the level of the academy. Aidan Kavanagh reminds us that such theology, "which we most readily recognize and practice is in fact neither primary nor seminal but secondary and derivative." Instead "primary theology" is that which happens in the liturgical life of the community. "For what emerges most directly from an assembly's liturgical act is not a new species of theology among other. It is *theologia* itself."

This primary theology wills, no doubt, be closer to the unsystematic, bordering on the inchoate, intertwined with the vulgar, and tinged with the nonrational. And yet it merely represents the collective self-expression of the people in their attempt to bring themselves, as framed within their world, before their God. Indian-Christian theology, if conceived of in these terms, becomes a reflection on the action of liturgy: a meditation on the multimodal expressions of experiencing the resistive-liberative activity of God among God's people, particularly among the Dalits and Adivasis.

In doing so, liturgy also becomes an arena in which the multifaceted traces of divine-human encounters in their relatedness to the world are preserved and celebrated. Liturgy is the storehouse for the working out of peoples' multimodal experience of the God. It projects and recaptures Dalit and Adivasi images of God, their views of God's relatedness to God's creation, their visions of the future, their hurts and aspirations, and their ability to hope in spite of the odds against them. And it does this in the particularized forms and media that is part of their own reflexive tradition and practice. I cannot end without returning to readdress the role of Christian theology within the phenomenon of Hindutva explicated in detail at the beginning of this presentation.

The question can be put squarely: based on what I have said about reclaiming mission and liturgy in the service of theology in India, what would be the outlines for a Christian theology of pluralistic nationhood? Though I cannot elaborate on this issue, I wish to begin a discussion by making explicit some of the implications in the treatment thus far.

But I must first reiterate that these are constructive and imaginative projections of what theology can be rather than what it is in the Indian context. In my discussion of Christian mission and liturgy, I suggested that theology be conceptualized in concert with the resistive-liberative working of God that can be discerned through the minority communities' struggle in India. Mission and liturgy occur in intercommunity and intracommunity locales respectively.

On the one hand, mission points to the outward moment of theology: it reflects from its locatedness in the midst of minority communities practicing their particularities and living out their pluralities in the world in a liberated way. On the other hand, liturgy points to the inward moment of theology: it reflects from its position in the midst of the confidence with which minority communities enact their religio-cultural pluralities and perform their distinctive particularities before God and community. In the context of the colonizing forces that aim to homogenize India along the ideology of Hindutva, both these arenas operate to liberate the subjectivity of ethno-religious minorities by conserving and positing their respective particularities for the purposes of constructing a more inclusive framework for the nation-state.

Let me continue this deliberation on the theological import of mission and liturgy in the service of working toward a pluralistic nationhood by indulging in more imaginative theological play. What if we consider pluralistic living among various religious communities in terms of a large, traditional, rural Indian house? Many families from one lineage live in this large ancestral house each with its own appointed area. The house is rectangular with many well-designed apartments to accommodate many nuclear families from the same lineage. In their own portion of the house the members of each nuclear family live in autonomy and security. They evolve their own rites, relational patterns, language, and social practices. This space for primary intrafamily relationships is not closed.

Rather this intimate space for ritualized patterns of rites and practices can also form temporary spaces of hospitality and nurture of others from the extended family. Liturgy can be conceived of as providing such space whereby particular religious and cultural heritages are harbored and celebrated even as they share in the richness of another/other religious tradition/s. In this domain there is thus much freedom for creative and contextual symbolic expression before God and community. However, these expressions must not be in contravention with the negotiated fundamentals of the entire lineage. There are also spaces for secondary interfamily relationships in this house. Two common areas bring all members of the household together. First, there is a large, open foyer, which leads into a corridor that links each of the individual living sections from the front entrance.

This foyer, along with the corridor, is used as a space for social interaction with each other and for entertainment of common visiting friends and relatives Second, there is a rear opening for each unit of the house, which serves as the residence of the respective nuclear family that leads into a common play area. This area is secured from the outer world since the various sections of the house encompass it. This is where intimate interrelationships happen between various members of the lineage. Children are safe to play here and various common facilities are shared to meet the different needs of the larger family. There must be some basic rules that govern relationships.

The mission of the house (which comprises the creator and all the creatures of the household) is to guard the autonomy and security of each individual family unit and enhance the welfare and honor of the lineage as a whole. Christian mission can be conceived along these lines. Resistance to all that threatens autonomy and security of the nuclear families and liberation toward achieving the welfare and honor of the whole household exhibits the dynamic of this mission. Religious and ethno-cultural minorities in India are under a variety of threats in contemporary India.

Dalits and Adivasis, especially in their proximity to Christianity, find themselves in a long and multi-pronged struggle to resist the homogenizing and hegemonizing forces of diverse Hindutva-oriented agencies that are stridently and concertedly overpowering the nation-state. In the first part of this paper I inquire into the historical roots of Hindu nationalism that generated the ideology funding this ominous phenomenon. Through an examination of one influential text (Vinayak Damodar Savarkar's *Hindutva: Who is a Hindu?*) I demonstrated the manner in which the Hindutva ideology valorized the way of life of one vision of Hinduism while undercutting any cultural and religious version that digressed from such a philosophy. I also briefly elaborated on the contemporary manifestations of such a unitary and grand vision, which takes on the guise of modern-day Hindu nationalism.

There can be little doubt that this has taken a violent turn against the Dalit, Adivasi, and Christian communities. I made an effort to document some of this through a process of suggestive interpretation that attributes the continuation of such an operation to the homogenizing logic of the Hindutva. However, the religious and ethno-cultural minorities have not succumbed to the powers that be. Rather, they are involved in their own resistive-liberative struggle. And this becomes the locus for drawing the substance and the agenda for theology.

By being immersed in the resistive struggle of minorities, Indian-Christian theology could also be constructively endeavoring to protect the particularized religio-cultural worldviews of Dalits and Adivasis and to offer these resources towards the building up of a pluralistic framework for common living within the nation-state. I further argue that this will require that we reclaim the two sites of mission and liturgy for doing Indian-Christian theology.

Thus, Indian-Christian theology is invited to live off two fountains. On the broader side it is fueled by the intercommunity dynamic of God's ongoing activity in the world, primarily through the resistive-liberative momentum of minorities striving for life in all its related fullness. This funds theology reflects on the action of mission. On the more confined side it is fueled by the intracommunity discernment of celebrating the experience of God as outlined by the life and teaching of Jesus Christ. This funds theology reflects on the action of liturgy. For many decades Indian-Christian theology has embraced one of these fountains without paying much respect to the other.

Thus, an activist socioeconomic and political agenda for theology concerned itself solely with the activity of God in the world; it ignored the intracommunity celebration of Christian liturgical activity, which nurtured and sustained the Christian community on its journey toward a full celebration of life. Conversely, a contemplative religio-cultural and ecclesiastical agenda for theology was preoccupied exclusively with the specificities of the energy that flows from the God-human encounter; it neglected the fertile activity of God in the other realms of the world. Thus, in a sense, each of these power engines, independent of the other, maintained a truncated version of Christian theology. The future of Indian theology lies in the manner in which these strands creatively interact with each other in the arena of Christian discourse.

The Sangh Parivar has launched a very powerful politico-religious offensive against socio-cultural and socio-political forces and groups, which firmly believe that the Indian civilisation is historically constituted by many cultural streams and the unity of India has been achieved by the intermingling of diverse and multiple cultural belief systems. The forces of Hindutva as represented by the BJP, the Vishwa Hindu Parishad, the Bajrang Dal, the RSS, the ABVP, the Shiv Sainiks believe that India is "one nation based on one culture" and its heritage is linked with Hindu religion.

The real meanings of "one nation and one culture" are that the Hindus have a special privileged position and the various multiple minority groups have to accept the so-called Hindu way of life. The believers in the socalled superiority of Hindu majority culture have launched many socio-cultural and political movements in the whole of twentieth century and in the Nineties they intensified their struggle to capture State power to implement their programme of establishing a Hindu Raj in the country. Since the believers of ``one nation and one culture" have to practise the politics of targetting and confronting other cultural groups, they launched a powerful movement against Babri Mosque at Ayodhya and forcibly demolished it on December 6, 1992. Kalyan Singh himself participated in this activity of the Sangh Parivar and the President dismissed the BJP government in Uttar Pradesh for its acts of omission and commission while dealing with the ongoing agitation of the Sangh Parivar against Babri mosque.

Along with the Uttar Pradesh Government the BJP-led Governments in Madhya Pradesh, Himachal Pradesh and Rajasthan were also dismissed under Article 356 of the Constitution for their involvement in encouraging and patronising the forces of Hindutva. The Supreme Court upheld the dismissal of the four State Governments saying that "secularism was a basic structure" of the Constitution. Not only this. The voters were called upon to give their verdict on the BJP's ideology of exercising political power in the States in defence of the Hindus and against other religions and cultural minorities. In the 1993 State Assembly elections, the voter punished the BJP and Sangh Parivar by defeating them in Uttar Pradesh, Madhya Pradesh, and Himachal Pradesh and in Rajasthan, it succeeded with great difficulty.

The message given by the voters was loud and clear that the BJP definition of Hindu Raj was not acceptable in a multi-cultural plural society. Similarly, the BJP could not electorally cash its ideology of Hindutva in the Lok Sabha elections of 1996 and 1998. In March 1998, the BJP formed a coalition government at the Centre and in November 1998, the "mini-general elections" were held in Rajasthan, Madhya Pradesh, Mizoram and in Delhi. The November 1998 State Assembly elections were contested between the BJP and the other political parties, under the protective umbrella of the BJP-led Central Government. The BJP has been politically humiliated in Delhi and Rajasthan and in Madhya Pradesh; the Congress Party has successfully defended its majority against the challenge of the BJP.

The upshot of the above narration is that militant Hindu mobilisation of the 1990s has not brought great political dividends to the forces of Hindutva. It has been clearly and repeatedly established that the socalled Hindu voter is not enarmoured of the self-appointed guardians of Hindus and this 'mythical' Hindu voter does not hesitate to punish the champions of Hindutva. Any party, in a democracy, examines the adequacy and authenticity of its political agenda if the voters are repeatedly exercising their verdict against its public programme. The Conservative Party in the U.K. under Mrs. Margaret Thatcher and Mr. John Major won successive electoral battles against the Labour Party in the Seventies, Eighties and Nineties. The Labour Party set its house in order and under Mr. Tony Blair's leadership, the party prepared a programme called The New Labour and it abandoned many of its old doctrines regarding public sector. The Labour Party won the elections because it revised its ideology and presented a new programme before the voters. Similarly, after the disintegration of Soviet Union and other East European socialist State systems, the Italian Communist Party along with many other European Communist parties transformed themselves into Social Democracies and they are in reckoning because their newly revised public programme is acceptable to the voters. Are the BJP and the Sangh Parivar rethinking about their ideological position of "one nation and one culture"? The BJP is not getting rewards in politics by patronising the so-called Hindu majority.

If the Hindu voter is not obliging the so-called Hindu Party, the implication is that the political and cultural forces of Hindutva are living in an illusory world of their own self-created Hinduism. But political illusions do not bring electoral successes in democracy. Since the BJP and its other partners of the Sangh Parivar have a clear ideological agenda of establishing a Hindu State, it has not deviated from its ideology of Hindutva. A few will substantiate the statement that the BJP Governments exercise their power to spread the message of Hindutva and create a social situation where Hindus occupy a special position in society.

First, Babri Mosque was demolished on December 6, 1992 when Kalyan Singh was the Chief Minister of Uttar Pradesh. In 1998, Kalyan Singh is again the Chief Minister of Uttar Pradesh, and the U.P. State Police have harassed a respected Muslim Leader Ali Mian. If Ali Mian can be targetted, the ordinary Muslims of U.P. cannot expect any fair play from the BJP State Government. Second, under the direct control of the BJP Government in Gujarat, Christian places of worship and schools are under attack by the Bajrang Dal and the Vishwa Hindu Parishad. The forces of Hindutva have targetted the Christian minority in Gujarat because the protective umbrella is provided by the State Government. Third, the Shiv Sena supremo in Maharashtra has targetted the cricket team from Pakistan and the message to Muslims of Maharashtra is that the Shiv Sena-BJP government does not respect their sentiments. Fourth, the Education and Culture Minister, Dr. Murli Manohar Joshi, created a big controversy at an official meeting of the State Ministers of Education by starting the meeting with a prayer on Saraswati Vandana. Not only did many of the Ministers protest against the place of this Hindu ritual in a public function, K. C. Sundaresan, a Joint General-Secretary of the RSS, stated that "anyone who is opposed to Saraswati Vandana is not an Indian". It was a repeat story of the VHP and Bajrang Dal activists proclaiming during the anti-Babri Mosque agitation that people should "learn to live as Hindus if they wanted to live in India." Hindu cultural symbols are protected and promoted by the governments run by the BJP and the minority cultural ethoses are at the receiving end under the BJP-led governments. A BJP Minister of the Delhi State Government hurt the feelings of the Christian community by making a ridiculous public statement, that "wine was served in churches".

Fifth, believers of the ideology of Hindutva are finding places of pride in public institutions dealing with the writing of history and culture. The BJP-led government at the Centre and in the states has shown their full determination to use political power for the promotion of the ideology and historiography of Hindutva which is directed against all cultural minority groups. Since educational and research institutions are the main intellectual sources of interpretation of history and culture, the BJP governments have nominated and appointed RSS, VHP and Bajrang Dal activists in such organisations. Sixth, Arun Shourie, the BJP Member of Rajya Sabha, has launched a bitter attack against historians who interpret India as a multicultural and multilingual plural society.

The Sangh Parivar on the basis of its present political presence in the central government has launched a three-fold strategy to promote the ideology of Hindutva. First, a project for the re-writing of history and culture has been launched at an intellectual level by using State power. State patronage has been extended to intellectuals to launch an attack against interpretations of Indian history, which do not promote the concept of "one nation and one culture." Second, minorities have been given a political message that the BJP led governments at the Centre or the states will openly pursue discriminatory and anti-minority policies. Third, minorities should not expect protection of life and property from State functionaries under the BJP governments.

Justice Srikrishna's report on the Bombay riots of December 1992 and January 1993 clearly identifies police officials who were practitioners of Hinduism and anti-Muslim. The U.P. Chief Minister is not making public the findings of a judicial enquiry on riots in Meerut. Politics of multi-culturalism has to confront the politics of Hindutva at many levels. It is not absent mindedness of Atal Behari Vajpayee, who appointed three stalwarts of Hindutva as Ministers of Home, Education and Information and Broadcasting. While the Vajpayee coalition government does not have any success story, L. K. Advani, Dr. Murli Manohar Joshi and Sushma Swaraj actively, and aggressively, pursued the Hindu agenda in these ministries. Advani targetted Bangladeshis and wanted an identity card for every Indian as his priority, Joshi and Sushma Swaraj exercised their power to aggressively promote Hindu educational and cultural agenda.

Saraswati Vandana, Vande Mataram, teaching of Sanskrit and recitation of Hindu *mantras* and *bhajans* has suddenly emerged in the Centre stage of public discourse because these ministers attach great importance to the propagation and promotion of Hindu ritualistic symbols. Dr. Murli Manohar Joshi himself wears a tilak on his forehead as a symbol of Brahmanical Hinduism. If on the one hand, the BJP-led government at the Centre has been plagued with serious inter-coalitional conflicts, on the other, the agenda of Hindutva has been on the march and Ms. Uma Bharti wants to organise Hindu youth with State patronage. Whatever may be the election results from 1993 to 1998, the BJP governments pursue their core Hindutva agenda with great determination. The forces of Hindutva are not shy of pursuing their goals with the help of political power irrespective of the fact that the Indian voters keep them punishing in election after election. The cultural agenda of the forces of Hindutva not only has a primacy for all members of the Sangh Parivar, it is also the sole commitment of the BJP government. Social and political forces representing multi-cultural, pluralist and accommodative tradition of Indian civilisation, which is based on composite culture, should understand that the BJP exercises power for its ideology and electoral setbacks do not make any difference to the leadership of the Hindutva forces.

A section of intellectuals believed, though erroneously, that the BJP will become a moderate rightist party in power but the open targetting of Christians in Gujarat under BJP government or Muslims in Maharashtra under Shiv-Sena-BJP government or promotion of Hindu ritualism by the Vajpayee Government should alert wavering intellectuals that without the purist ideology of Hindutva, the BJP will collapse. The BJP has nothing else to offer to the masses of India except the promotion of inter-community hatreds and violence. Without polarising communities of India, the BJP cannot rule over the country and if it comes to power, it accelerates the processes of inter-community polarisation.

This is the reality and essence of the politics of Hindutva. The forces of Hindutva represented by Hindu Mahasabha, Veer Savarkar, RSS, Jan Sangh, and Bhartiya Janata Party have been active throughout the twentieth century in opposition to secular, democratic and pluralist forces in India and ordinary political setbacks do not make them abandon their real Agenda. The results of the elections to the State Assemblies should not make secular forces complacent because there is no evidence in the twentieth century history of India that the behaviour of religion-based politics abandon their path because sometimes masses go against them.

4

Gandhian and Secularist Critique of Hindutva

Gandhism (or Gandhianism) is a collection of inspirations, principles, beliefs and philosophy of Mohandas Karamchand Gandhi (known as Mahatma Gandhi), who was a major political and spiritual leader of India and the Indian Independence Movement. It is a body of ideas and principles that describes the inspiration, vision and the life work of Gandhi. The term also encompasses what Gandhi's ideas, words and actions mean to people around the world, and how they used them for guidance in building their own future. Gandhism also permeates into the realm of the individual human being, non-political and non-social. A Gandhian can mean either an individual who follows, or a specific philosophy which is attributed to, Gandhism.

Eminent scholar, Professor Ramjee Singh has declared Mahatma Gandhi as the Bodhisattva of the twentieth century. *Satya* is the Sanskrit word for "truth," and *graha* (from the Sanskrit root grah cognate with English word "grab") can be rendered as "grasp/obtain/seize(sometimes by force)/take/to obtain/accepting what is given." The term was popularized during the Indian Independence Movement, and is used in many Indian languages including Hindi.

SATYA

Gandhi stated that "I have nothing new to teach the world. Truth and non-violence are as old as the hills." The pivotal and defining element of Gandhism is satya, a Sanskrit word usually translated into English as truth, whose literal meaning is 'what actually is' (deriving from the root verb *as* meaning 'to be'). Truth must pervade all considerations of politics, ego, society and convention. Gandhi did not consider himself to be a pacifist, socialist or on any definable spectrum of politics. He professed to adhere to the pure, existing facts of life to make his decisions.

Gandhi's commitments to non-violence, human freedom, equality and justice arose from his personal examination. Truth is interpreted subjectively. Gandhism does not demand that its adherents agree to Gandhi's own principles to the letter, but in spirit. If one honestly believes that violence is sometimes necessary, it is truthful to believe in it. When Gandhi returned to India in the middle of World War I, he said he would have supported the British in the war. It would have been wrong, according to Gandhi, to demand equal rights for Indians in the Empire, and not contribute to its defence. On the other hand, by the time of the advance of the Japanese in World War II, Gandhi had given up notions of fighting alongside the British and argued for nonviolence instead.

Gandhi developed a way of life by his constant "experimenting with truth" – a phrase that formed the subtitle to his autobiography. He was prepared to learn through trial and error, often admitting to mistakes and changing his behaviour accordingly. This was particularly notable when Gandhi stopped all nationwide civil resistance in 1922 after the Chauri Chaura incident. He would forsake political independence for truth – believing that Indians should not become murderers and commit the very evils they were accusing the British of perpetrating in India. Gandhism is more about the spirit of Gandhi's journey to discover the truth, than what he finally considered to be the truth. It is the foundation of Gandhi's teachings, and the spirit of his whole life to examine and understand for oneself, and not take anybody or any ideology for granted.

Gandhi said: "The Truth is far more powerful than any weapon of mass destruction." Gandhi's philosophy encompassed ontology and its association with truth. For Gandhi, "to be" did not mean to exist within the realm of time, as it has in the past with the Greek philosophers. But rather, "to exist" meant to exist within the realm of truth, or to use the term Gandhi did, satya. Gandhi summarized his beliefs first when he said "God is Truth", which his experimenting later prompted him to change to "Truth is God". The first statement seemed insufficient to Gandhi, as the mistake could be made that Gandhi was using truth as a description of God, as opposed to God as an aspect of satya. Satya (truth) in Gandhi's philosophy is God. It shares all the characteristics of the Hindu concept of God, or Brahman, and is believed by Gandhians to live within each person as their conscience while at the same time guiding the universe.

The concept of nonviolence (ahinsa) and nonresistance has a long history in Indian religious thought and has had many revivals in Hindu, Buddhist, Jain and Christian contexts. Gandhi explains his philosophy and way of life in his autobiography, *The Story of My Experiments with Truth.* He was quoted saying:

"What difference does it make to the dead, the orphans, and the homeless, whether the mad destruction is wrought under the name of totalitarianism or the holy name of liberty and democracy?"

"An eye for an eye makes the whole world blind".

"It has always been easier to destroy than to create".

"There are many causes that I am prepared to die for but no causes that I am prepared to kill for".

At the age of 36, Gandhi adopted the vow of brahmacharya, or celibacy. He committed himself to the control of the senses, thoughts and actions. Celibacy was important to Gandhi for not only purifying himself of any lust and sexual urges, but also to purify his love for his wife as genuine and not an outlet for any turmoil or aggression within his mind. Ahimsa, or non-violence, was another key tenet of Gandhi's beliefs. He held that total non-violence would rid a person of anger, obsession and destructive impulses. While his vegetarianism was inspired by his rearing in the Hindu-Jain culture of Gujarat, it was also an extension of ahimsa.

On July 6, 1940, Gandhi published an article in Harijan which applied these philosophies to the question of British involvement in World War II. Homer Jack notes in his reprint of this article, "To Every Briton" (*The Gandhi Reader*) that, "to Gandhi, all war was wrong, and suddenly it 'came to him like a flash' to appeal to the British to adopt the method of non-violence." In this article, Gandhi stated, I appeal to every Briton, wherever he may be now, to accept the method of non-violence instead of that of war, for the adjustment of relations between nations and other matters. I do not want Briton to be defeated, nor do I want her to be victorious in a trial of brute strength. I venture to present you with a nobler and braver way worthier of the bravest soldier. I want you to fight Nazism without arms, or, if I am to maintain military terminology, with non-violent arms. I would like you to lay down the arms you have as being useless for saving you or humanity.

You will invite Herr Hitler and Signor Mussolini to take what they want of the countries you call your possessions. Let them take possession of your beautiful island, with your many beautiful buildings. You will give all these but neither your souls, nor your minds. If these gentlemen choose to occupy your homes, you will vacate them. If they do not give you free passage out, you will allow yourself, man, woman, and child, to be slaughtered, but you will refuse to owe allegiance to them my non-violence demands universal love, and you are not a small part of it. It is that love which has prompted my appeal to you.

Gandhi espoused an economic theory of self-sufficiency and simplicity. He envisioned a more agrarian India upon independence that would focus on meeting the material needs of its citizenry prior to generating wealth and industrializing. Hindu Universalism denotes the ideology that all religions are true and therefore worthy of toleration and respect. It was articulated by Gandhi:

"After long study and experience, I have come to the conclusion that all religions are true; all religions have some error in them; all religions are almost as dear to me as my own Hinduism, in as much as all human beings should be as dear to one as one's own close relatives. My own veneration for other faiths is the same as that for my own faith; therefore no thought of conversion is possible." Gandhi believed that at the core of every religion was truth (satya), non-violence (ahimsa) and the Golden Rule. He was deeply influenced by the Christian teaching of "turning the other cheek", once stating that if Christianity practised the Sermon on the Mount, he would indeed be a Christian. Gandhi felt that one should be aware of worshipping the symbols and idols of the religion and not its teachings, such as worshipping the crucifix whilst ignoring its significance as a symbol for self-sacrifice.

Although Gandhi was raised as a Hindu he was critical of most religions, including Hinduism. He wrote in his autobiography:

"Thus if I could not accept Christianity either as a perfect, or the greatest religion, neither was I then convinced of Hinduism being such. Hindu defects were pressingly visible to me. If untouchability could be a part of Hinduism, it could but be a rotten part or an excrescence. I could not understand the raison d'etre of a multitude of sects and castes. What was the meaning of saying that the Vedas were the inspired Word of God? If they were inspired, why not also the Bible and the Koran? As Christian friends were endeavouring to convert me, so were Muslim friends. Abdullah Sheth had kept on inducing me to study Islam, and of course he had always something to say regarding its beauty".

He then went on to say:

"As soon as we lose the moral basis, we cease to be religious. There is no such thing as religion over-riding morality. Man, for instance, cannot be untruthful, cruel or incontinent and claim to have God on his side". Gandhi was critical of the hypocrisy in organised religion, rather than the principles on which they were based. He also said the following about Hinduism:

"Hinduism as I know it entirely satisfies my soul fills my whole being. When doubts haunt me, when disappointments stare me in the face, and when I see not one ray of light on the horizon, I turn to the Bhagavad Gita, and find a verse to comfort me; and I immediately begin to smile in the midst of overwhelming sorrow. My life has been full of tragedies and if they have not left any visible and indelible effect on me, I owe it to the teachings of the Bhagavad Gita".

The concept of Islamic jihad can also be taken to mean a nonviolent struggle or Satyagraha, in the way Gandhi practiced it. On Islam he said:

"The sayings of Muhammad are a treasure of wisdom, not only for Muslims but for all of mankind". Later in his life when he was asked whether he was a Hindu, he replied:

"Yes I am. I am also a Christian, a Muslim, a Buddhist and a Jew".

Gandhi's religious views are reflected in the hymns his group often sang:

- Vaishnav jan to call them Vishnava, those who understand the sufferings of others...
- Raghupati Raghava Raja Ram call him Rama or God or Allah...

If one looks at the shifts that have taken place on the political map of India over the past two decades, the single most important change that strikes one is the rise of militant political Hinduism or Hindutva, or broadly, the ensemble of doctrines, social movements and political formations of Hindu-supremacism or Hindu-communalism. Hindutva has mobilised and energised large numbers of people, perhaps comparable to the numbers drawn into struggles for land, work and social justice. It is indisputably India's largest centralised social movement of the past half-century. There is clearly a paradox here. How did a highly plural and assimilative society like India's, which consciously adopted secularism as one of its crucial guiding principles at Independence, come to be, or allow itself to be, dominated by a particularistic and parochial ethno-religious politics within the course of barely four decades or so?

And how did the party-level expression of Hindutva-the Bharatiya Janata Party (BJP) or its earlier avatar, the Bharatiya Jana Singh (BJS)which for long years commanded roughly seven percent of the national vote, and only a modest number of seats (such as 20 to 35) in the 540-odd-strong lower house of the parliament (the Lok Sabha), meteorically rise to pre-eminence with the number of its seats galloping from two (1984) and 85 (1989), to 120 (1991) and now 183 (1999), with its vote-share rising from 7.4 percent of the vote cast at the national level (1984) to 11.4 percent (1989), 20.1 percent (1991) and 26 percent (1998), to fall only marginally to 23 per cent (1999)? The BJP's tenure in power in India's national government for five and a half years also raises a number of other questions.

How strong, committed and enduring are the party's social base and organisational structures? What is the source of its political appeal? What is its relationship with other organisations and movements which are members of that collectivity called the sangh parivar or sangh combine - the 'family' defined around the fulcrum of, and dominated by, the Rashtriya Swayamsevak Sangh (RSS)? What are the strategies that allowed the BJP to break the social and electoral barriers the Bharatiya Jana Sangh faced for over a quarter-century, and thus to come into the 'mainstream' in the late 1980s and the 1990s? What larger social, economic and political processes explain the BJP's growth and the spread of its influence? What is unique about the BJP's policies, its political strategies, and its management of parliamentary processes and elections?

It is equally relevant to inquire into other, related, issues. Has the experience of power at the national level brought about a change in the BJP's ideological orientation, its practical politics and its approaches to international relations, economic policy and to global and regional issues of security? Has it transformed its relationship with the rest of the sangh parivar, in particular, the RSS? If so, what does that spell for the

Hindutva collective? Within the past five years or so, the BJP has lost power (and votes) in a number of states, including important ones like Uttar Pradesh and Maharashtra, mid-sized ones like Madhya Pradesh and Rajasthan, and smaller ones like Himachal Pradesh and the Capital territory of Delhi.

Recent opinion polls show that its national approval ratings are in decline. But has its political influence really plateau decisively and with finality? Can the BJP regenerate and reinvigorate itself, and return to power in New Delhi in a multi-party alliance, like the 24-party coalition which it currently heads? What is the likely future of Hindutva and its impact on South Asia? An attempt to answer some of these questions roughly the first half of those listed above. We start with the premise that the BJP is not just an ordinary political party, but both a political formation and a social movement which is integrally related to and driven by the agenda of establishing a society and state based on the primacy of the Hindus, who form 82 percent of India's population.

The roots of the Hindutva phenomenon go back to the colonial period, in particular the late 19th century, when the encounter between Western modernity and 'traditional' Indian society produced a range of effects and crystallised many social processes, including, especially, what has been called 'disorientation', the reinterpretation of traditional cultures in order to preserve them and at the same time to give them a contemporary sense or new meanings. In India, a substantial section of the Hindu middle class which was exposed to Western education and modernist values adopted a broadly liberal orientation, which aspired to reform tradition and combat hierarchy and superstition (which were integral to that tradition). However, a significant minority of Hindus felt threatened by modernity and by the restructuring of the Indian state under colonialism, and the 'reforms from above' undertaken by the state to abolish certain customs like widow-burning and child marriage.

Some conservative Hindus began to reinterpret their religion and tradition by imitating Western concepts and models in order to preserve the core of that tradition, especially its intensely hierarchical and Brahminical aspects. Some posited the 'Golden Age' of Hinduism, such as the Vedic Age or the 'Aryan period' or some other notion of a 'pure' state of India, identified with dharma (religion), quintessentially Hindu, which preceded the country's 'invasion' by 'aliens' such as Muslims, and later Christians. Thus began the formation of ethnic or ethno-religious nationalism, which received a major impetus in the 1920s, especially in a reaction to the khilafat (Caliphate) movement, the mobilisation of Indian Muslims for an apparently 'global' cause in which the mainstream party of Indian nationalism, the Indian National Congress (founded in 1885) also took part.

Central to this ethno-religious nationalism or communalism was the stigmatisation and simultaneous emulation of the supposed enemy-conquerors - the 'threatening others'. Equally important was the project to reorganise society as a means of producing 'a new kind of people'. This new movement of 'Hindu Sangathan' was to produce organisations like the Arya Samaj, Hindu Mahasabha and the Rashtriya Swayamsevak Sangh. Of these, the RSS (founded in 1925) was the most important and in some ways the most militant: it was a paramilitary organisation right from the outset and stressed physical fitness, exercise, and training in armed and unarmed combat. The uniform of the RSS was derived from the attire of the colonial police and the British Indian army. The RSS was the direct progenitor of the Bharatiya Jana Sangh, and later the BJP.

The principal appeal of these Hindutva groupings lay in their ability to exploit the sense of inferiority that many upper-caste Hindu strata felt, and the attraction of their project of re-creating or reviving a mythological 'Golden Age' of Hinduism based on 'racial purity', dharma and unadulterated devotion to religion in its most puritanical and Brahminical forms. The sense of inferiority was itself rooted in a certain reading of Indian history, largely through colonial eyes, as a succession of periods or epochs based on the religion of the rulers. The 'glorious' Hindu age of Antiquity was followed by the Dark Age a series of alien invasions. In this period, docile, undisciplined, unorganised and unarmed (because unmilitarised) Hindus were conquered and subjugated by aggressive, militant and well-armed invaders and marauders. The conquerors looted, impoverished and ruined prosperous India along with its thriving civilisation and supposedly unparalleled achievements in all fields of science and the arts.

The most stigmatised and vilified of the conquerors, and allegedly the most brutal, were the Muslims. But a more persuasive view is that Muslims came to India's Western shores as traders, not conquerors. Islam took roots in India well before it did in Southeast Asia or parts of Africa. There was flourishing interaction between Indians and Arabs, Persians and Turks long before Mahmud of Ghazni arrived as marauder. There were centuries-long transactions between Hindus, Muslims, and followers of other faiths, reflected in India's composite culture, its languages (many of them influenced by Persian or Arabic), music, dance, cuisines and eating habits, the sciences, and even in the birth of new religions like Sikhism. Distinct communal identities were formed only in the 1860s.

A paranoid, pathological kind of Islamophobia has been integral to all currents of Hindutva. That set their priority: the Muslims were their greatest enemy, the dire 'threat from within'. No wonder the RSS shunned participation in the anti-colonial nationalist movement which had acquired mass dimensions by the 1920s. Its appeal and membership was largely confined to upper-caste Hindus, especially Marathi-speaking Brahmins in Western and Central India, with a sprinkling of shakhas (or branches, the basic unit of the RSS) in areas of the North where Hindu-Muslim riots had occurred, the exception being the Punjab, which had a large number of shakhas. The RSS had no significant presence in the South.

The two most influential theorists of Hindutva before Independence were Vinayak Damodar Savarkar and Madhav Sadashiv Golwalkar, both Maharashtrian Brahmins. Savarkar pioneered the 'Two-Nation Theory', which argued that Hindus and Muslims could not co-exist within the same nation. Golwalkar developed the ethnic-racist and national content of the concept of 'Hinduness' and invested Hindutva with its highly disciplinarian, puritanical, ritualistic and rigid hierarchies which defined it as an all-male secret society led by a small cabal. Golwalkar was notoriously fascinated by Nazism and Italian fascism and directly praised Hitler's view of racial purity: 'To keep up the purity of the race and its culture, Germany shocked the world by her purging the country of the Semitic races the Jews. Race pride at its highest has been manifested here. Germany has also shown how well might impossible it is for races and cultures, having differences going to the root, to be assimilated into one united whole, a good lesson for us in Hindustan to learn and profit by.'

Gowalkar defined the RSS thus: 'The ultimate vision of our work ... is a perfectly organised state of society wherein each individual has been moulded into a model of ideal Hindu manhood and made into a living limb of the corporate personality of society.' For Golwalkar, 'the mission of the RSS was to fashion society, to 'sustain' it, 'improve' it, and finally merge with it when the point had been reached where society and the organisation had become co-extensive.' All the different currents of Hindutva remained fairly marginal in their influence until the 1940s, but then registered a sharp rise, partly as a reaction to the Muslim League's adoption of the Pakistan agenda at Lahore in 1940 and the increasing likelihood, even seeming imminence, of the formation of Pakistan.

The most notable act of Hindutva's adherents in the 1940s was the assassination of Mahatma Gandhi in January 1948. This was committed by a former RSS member who regarded Gandhi as effete and dangerously pro-Muslim, and a disarming and emasculating influence on the Hindus. The RSS was banned following Gandhi's assassination but was later restored on condition that it stop conducting itself as a secret society and become open to public scrutiny, a condition it is yet to fulfil. It is necessary to dwell at length on the origins and ideology of Hindutva in order to understand where some of its appeal lies for the upper-caste, upper or middle class Hindus. But being limited and narrow, that appeal cannot explain how the BJP managed to win vastly greater influence than the RSS some six and a half decades after the sangh was set up.

Nor do the RSS's origins or ideology provide adequate guidance to the practical strategies and tactics which lie at the root of the BJP's phenomenal growth, such as forging identities, gaining influence, recruiting cadres, fighting elections and entering into alliances with other parties. Two other factors are vital to this understanding: The decline of the Congress (which has ruled India for fourth-fifths of its independent existence) and the political vacuum created by *Hindutva*'s adversaries, the decline of the Left, in conjunction with other major changes in India's competitive party politics; the growth of new forms of aggressive ideologies, such as social Darwinism, bellicose nationalism and militarism within Indian society, as well as other changes.

The BJP's original avatar was far less lucky than itself. The Jana Sangh was sponsored in 1951 as a political party by the RSS, which has always sought to pretend as a 'cultural' organisation. The BJS employed a whole range of strategies to gain political influence: ethno-religious mobilisation, (apparent) moderation of hard-Hindutva to gain support from conservative right-wing and feudal classes, such as the former princes; electoral alliances; ideological appeal to anti-socialist ideas (the favoured platform of the Congress in the late 1960s to the mid-1970s); interest-group mobilisation focused on traders, businessmen and white-collar workers etc. Above all, the BJS used communal violence and riots as a means of polarising political sentiment, building cadres and mobilising itself politicallyan exact replica of the tactics of small groups of Muslim fanatics like the Jamaat-e-Islami in certain parts of India.

The BJS consciously projected itself as a Right-wing party in addition to being Hindu- communal: A formation that represents socially conservative values such as respect for the (unequal and hierarchical) caste status quo and one which advocates pro-trade policies, defends privileges inherited from feudal and colonial regimes (like the Privy Purses awarded by the deputing British to former Maharajas and Nawabs) and opposes land reform and good labour standards. The Jana Sangh was strongly supportive of the United States and the Western bloc in the Cold War-contrary to India's long-standing (but now abandoned) policy of Non-Alignment and in sharp distinction to most other political parties. It even went to the extent of supporting America's war on Vietnam, which was deeply unpopular in India.

The Bharatiya Janasangh had by the late 1960s perfected a certain equation and a well-defined relationship with the RSS. The RSS was the Jana Sangh's mentor, ideological guide and political master. It was also its organisational gate-keeper. It would be the arbitrator of all internal conflicts within the BJS. The RSS pracharak (proselytiser-preacher) was crucial to Jana Sangh's vote-gathering strategy. The RSS needed the BJS as its loyal representative in the field of party politics. The two maintained some autonomy from each other. But in a dispute, the RSS would always prevail.

The RSS had the last word in the parivar. None of the various combinations of strategies it tried could help the BJS break its isolation at the political margins for yearsnot even the huge windfall opening produced by the Congress's miserable performance in state after state in the 1967 elections, thanks to the alienation of the middle castes (officially called the Other Backward Classes, OBCs) and the formation of multi-party 'United Fronts' against the Congress, especially in the Hindi heartland.

The BJS's national vote share fluctuated between 3.1 and 9.4 percent in the Lok Sabha elections in the period 1962-77. The average works out to 6.4 percent. The number of Lok Sabha seats held by the BJP varied between 3 and 35 (the highest it ever bagged as the Jana Sangh). By contrast, the Communists alone were at least twice as strong, and their influence and social base was wider and their implantation deeper and more evenly spread. The Left as a whole was at least three times stronger than the Hindutva Right. The BJS was especially badly hit by the 'Left Turn' taken by Indira Gandhi in the late 1960s with the nationalisation of commercial banks and the 1971 slogan of Gharibi Hatao (Abolish Poverty!). However, in June 1975, the declaration of a State of Emergency by Prime Minister Indira Gandhi gave the Jana Sangh a 'dream' opening.

The vilification and the jailing of Jana Sangh leaders by Gandhi's government put them in the same bracket as her centrist and left-wing opponents and bestowed a degree of legitimacy upon them. Most important, RSS and BJS cadres were able to infiltrate the 'J.P. movement', the (somewhat deceptively) credible, respectable and broad-based mobilisation led by the ageing Gandhian leader and former socialist Jayaprakash Narayan, especially in states like Bihar and Gujarat. This gave Hindutva politics the miraculous opening it was looking for an entry into the respectable mainstream from the margins on the Far Right. Thus, when the State of Emergency was lifted and general elections announced in 1977, the Janata Party was formed as a conglomerate or de facto coalition of all the major non-communist parties, both national and regional. The Jana Sangh is became a part of the Janata, piggybacking on Jayaprakash Narayan and on media magnates like The Indian Express's Ram Nath Goenka.

The Janata Party put up straight single-candidate fights against the Congress in a majority of constituencies in the 1977 Lok Sabha elections. The Congress was wiped from the entire Hindi-speaking belt. Of the 294 Janata MPs elected, between 80 and 100 are estimated to have been former Jana Sanghisa number representing the tripling of the BJS's highest seat holdings in the Lok Sabha till then! This was a gain beyond most optimistic projections of the old Jana Sangh. By 1980, however, the Janata experiment ended in disaster thanks to internal contradictions within the uneasy conglomerate. A major contribution to the disintegration of the Janata Party was made by former BJS members, who tried to smuggle in the RSS's sectarian agendaon issues of religion and politics. The Janata's former socialists resisted this and there appeared huge rifts in the party edifice.

In 1980, Indira Gandhi romped back to power, with the Janata reduced to a mere 31 seats in Lok Sabha (of which no more than one-half was estimated to be the former Jana Sangh's share). In April 1980, the former Jana Sanghis got together and launched a new organisation, the Bharatiya Janata Party. The new party promised that its leaders, especially Atal Behari Vajpayee, would be free of the Jana Sangh's jaded ultra-conservative image and some of its ideological constraints. It would put a more liberal facade on Hindutva without compromising with its core agendas. It would in particular emphasise the 'values' of the JP movement and thus widen its base.

Vajpayee emerged larger than life as the BJP's pre-eminent leader, a good orator and campaigner, with a 'soft' style a deceptive appearance. Even sanghi hardliners like Lal Krishna Advani were now advocating a moderate and pragmatic line. For instance, a 1980 issue of RSS journal Panchajanya interviewed Advani, who said: 'In India, a party based on ideology can at the most come to power in a small area. It cannot win the confidence of the entire countryneither the Communist Party nor the Jana Sangh in its original form.' Panchajanya: 'But by ignoring the ideological appeal will you be able to keep together the cadres on the basis of these ideals?' Advani: 'Effort is being made to make them understand. That is why I want the debate to go on.' Panchajanya: 'However, despite its ideological anchorage, the Jana Sangh's appeal was steadily increasing.' Advani: 'The appeal increased to the extent the ideology got diluted. Wherever the ideology was strong, its appeal diminished'.

The tumultuous events of the early 1980s, including the outbreak of a secessionist militancy in Punjab, Indira Gandhi's political disorientation and her turn to soft-Hindutva (she took to visiting Hindu temples by 1982), and her assassination by a Sikh bodyguard following the storming of the Golden Temple by the Indian Army, further polarised Indian politics along religious lines, to the advantage of the Congress which was now courting the Hindu voter. The Congress cynically drove this advantage home by mounting a paranoid and hysterical Lok Sabha election campaign in 1984 about 'the nation being in danger'. This marginalised the Hindutva party once again. The BJP was reduced to a mere two Lok Sabha seats despite having won 7.4 percent of the national vote and having emerged as the second largest party displacing the Communist Party (Marxist). As the RSS organ, *The Organiser* put it: 'It was a Hindu vote, consciously and deliberately solicited by the Congress party as a Hindu party. And this is what steered the party to a grand victory, decimated the "revisionist" BJP and reincarnated Cong (I) as BJP.'

The BJP once again ran the risk of being isolated from support of the RSS and its committed cadres. It vacillated and prevaricated, including on its much tom-tommed yet remarkably ill-defined ideology of 'positive secularism' meaning a politics that purportedly rejects Congress-style minority 'vote-banks' and of 'Gandhian Socialism', a homespun set of ill-digested and mutually incompatible ideas, as far removed from socialism as they conceivably could be, which divided the party's ranks. The vacillation was not to last long. In the early 1980s, the RSS revived the Vishwa Hindu Parishad (VHP), which launched religious propaganda and proselytisation work and focussed on the issue of temples which were allegedly destroyed by 'invading Muslims'. None other than the then Prime Minister Rajiv Gandhi lent a helping hand to the BJP. In adopting an 'even-handed' policy of appeasing both Hindu and Muslim communal hardliners, Gandhi brought in a Bill to override a Supreme Court judgment providing marginal support to an old Muslim widow under the Code of Criminal Procedure-widely seen as a concession to ultra-conservative mullahs who stiffly opposed any reform of personal law or practices.

Simultaneously, he had the locks to the Babri mosque opened, thus allowing Hindus to offer prayers at the images of Lord Rama which were surreptitiously smuggled (with official complicity) right into the heart of the monument in 1949. Both moves helped the VHP mount a strident campaign against 'Muslim appeasement' by the Congress and other 'pseudo-secular' parties, and for the demolition of the Babri mosque and the construction of a 'grand temple' to Rama at its site. In the intervening period, the VHP had gathered additional momentum by launching a 're-conversion' movement to bring back into 'the Hindu fold' Dalits at Meenakshipuram in Tamil Nadu who, oppressed, harassed and humiliated by upper caste Hindus, had decided to embrace Islam in 1980.

Initially, the temple movement only evoked a feeble response, although propaganda about 'appeasement' appealed to many middle class Hindus who are prone to a supercilious and patriarchal view of all religious minorities and deeply cynical about democratic politics in which they only see manipulation of 'vote banks'. But soon, the term 'pseudo-secular' entered the vocabulary of the mainstream media as if it conveyed some profound truth. In reality, by using that term, the BJP was scoring points against whoever rejects Hindu primacy and supremacy. 'Appeasement' is a loaded pejorative term (Correctly, it should only be used in respect of inimical forces). It completely misrepresents the reality of Muslim life in India, which is even grimmer than the life of the average Hindu.

In the mid-1980s, the temple movement too began to pick up momentum when the VHP-RSS leadership, with the BJP's encouragement and participation, launched a series of powerful mobilisations using religious symbols and gestures, for example a campaign to collect bricks for the temple, carrying Ram-Jyotis or lamps in processions, and holding special pujas (worship) in cities and towns, especially near mosques. Some of the most committed early participants in the movement were highly politicised sadhus and upper-caste cadres of the sangh parivar. But it soon began to draw in some low- and middle-caste Hindus, many of them first-generation literates. For them, the temple movement's principal appeal was that it provided a pan-Indian or pan-Hindu and a homogenous, respectable and 'Sanskritised' identity to them, as distinct from the subaltern, marginal and oppressive reality of their (typically rural or semi-urban) existence. As soon as the BJP saw the rising popularity and potential of the Ayodhya mosque/temple movement in 1980s, most of its leaders actively joined it. In 1986, Advani replaced

Vajpayee as BJP president. But even before that, a change of strategic orientation had begun, towards a Hindu 'Sanghatanist' style of organisation and an ethnio-religious strategy of political mobilisation. The BJP by 1987 had clearly formulated the three 'trident' issues, greatly and long agitated by the Jana Sangh, as its principal focus and concerns: A ban on cow slaughter; abrogation of Article 370 of the Constitution, which gives a special status to Jammu and Kashmir, and imposition of a Uniform Civil Code detached from a gender - just, human rights-based, reform of personal lows.

The late 1980s saw many strategy meetings being held among the top-most leaders of the sangh parivar, including the BJP and the RSS and various 'fronts' of the latter such as the Bharatiya Mazdoor Sangh (labour federation), the Akhil Bharatiya Vidyarthi Parishad (students' union), the so-called think tank called Deendayal Research Institute and the newly formed Bajrang Dal. Each of these 'fronts' and parivar members has a special function and a special relationship to the RSS. They are said to number between 150 and 300, spanning such fields as education (the Vidya Bharati network of over 20,000 schools), labour (the BMS claims to be among India's top three union federations), and women (the Bharatiya Mahila Sangh, which loathes modern feminism and women's liberation and believes that the traditional, highly patriarchal, Hindu family provides the best example of the women's rightful place in society).

No less important are organisations like Vanavasi Kalyan Sangh which purports to work for tribal welfare but usually does proselytising work among India's indigenous people, as in Gujarat, and the Swadeshi Jagran Manch, which advocates a fiercely nationalist (but strongly-anti-internationalist and almost autarkic) economic policy, itself opposed to the BJP's naïve and blind dedication to unequal globalisation. The functions of these front organisations are instrumental and well-defined. For instance, the VHP was set up by the RSS in the early 1960s to serve as an explicitly religious-cultural front and to recruit lumpenised sadhus and disaffected sanyasis. The VHP participates in communal and political activities of various sorts and operates worldwide amongst the Hindu diaspora.

The Bajrang Dal functions like the modern-day equivalent of storm-troopers and uses physical violence to intimidate opponents. Bajrang Dal goons and ruffians periodically smash public property and burn churches and mosques, as happened in Orissa, where an Australian missionary and his two young sons were burnt alive in 2001. This is just when Prime Minister Vajpayee was calling for a 'national debate' on religious conversion! The typical relationship between these fronts and the RSS - and most are more loyal to the RSS than to the BJP - is that of the hub-and-spokes variety. They relate to one another not so much directly as through the hub that is the RSS. Some of them are designed and deployed to occupy the space of opposition to BJP policies, and thus to marginalise the true ideological-political opposition.

With the 1989 Lok Sabha elections and the installation of the minority V.P. Singh government in power in New Delhi, the BJP intensified its religious mobilisation campaign. The most eloquent expressions of this intensification were periodic semi-religious mobilisations in Ayodhya, with volunteers pouring in from all over the country, as well as Ram Shila Pujas in different cities. Of particular importance was the Somnath-to-Ayodhya rath yatra launched by Lal Krishna Advani, now deputy prime minister and home minister of India, in a souped-up Toyota van in 1990 made to resemble the cheap commercial-film version of an ancient chariot. This yatra (procession) left a trail of blood in numerous states. There was a close fit between its route, especially between the cities and towns where it evoked the greatest response and ferocious anti-Muslim violence. The most frequently chanted slogan during Advani's rath yatra was: 'There are only two places for Muslims Pakistan or kabristan (graveyard)'.

Advani was finally stopped and arrested in Bihar by Laloo Prasad Yadav's government. But it was clear that the temple campaign and inflaming rank communal passions through hate-speech and open provocation and instigation to violence would become the BJP's principal political strategy. The BJP was only waiting for the right moment to convert the Ayodhya mobilisation into an actual, physical act of destruction meant to 'avenge history's wrongs' and then use that to its electoral advantage. The moment would come with the installation of a weak, compromised and collusive government in New Delhi. This would remove the last barrier between the plans of the Hindutva movement to raze the Babri mosque and its actual demolition. The sangh parivar had for years described the Babri mosque as the most potent symbol of subjugation of the Hindus by Muslims `an 'ocular' insult', as Advani put it.

That moment came at the beginning of the decade of the 1990s when the Indian judicial and administrative systems retreated time and again in the face of the mounting Hindutva assault, and in particular when P.V. Narasimha Rao's Congress government took office after the 1991 elections following Rajiv Gandhi's assassination. This government was in a parliamentary minority for half its term and entered into an informal or unstated half-alliance with the BJP which had by now emerged as the principal opposition party. The Rao government not only failed to hold the BJP-VHP-RSS down to their specific legal commitments not to disturb the status quo in Ayodhya, it allowed them to escalate the tempo of their hysterical mobilisation and close in on their target.

The Babri Mosque had by now become both an emblem of, and a kind of litmus test for, India's commitment to secularism and to defending its multi-religious composite culture against the majoritarian onslaught. Through 1991 and 1992, more and more kar sevaks (volunteers) were mobilised at Ayodhya. At these gatherings, replete with pseudo-religious rituals, they would be treated to highly inflammatory speeches and storm trooper-style propaganda. The chain of events leading to the razing of the Babri mosque on December 6, 1992, and the developments of the day itself, could not have occurred without the collusion of the national and state (Uttar Pradesh) governments. With the mosque's razing, India suffered a terrible trauma, the worst blow since Partition to the very idea of peaceful co-existence between different religious communities. It is impossible to understand the pusillanimity of the Rao government of Congress Party in the face of the Hindutva assault except by reference to far larger social and political processes in particular, the erosion of the 'Nehruvian paradigm' or 'consensus' of democracy, secularism, non-Alignment and socialism (in reality, a modicum of distributive justice). This erosion was reflected in many phenomena: The exhaustion and discarding of the model of import-substituting industrialisation adopted in the early 1950s; the historic decline of Congress party, indeed the 'Congress system' of governance; the shrinking of the Centre-Left space within Indian politics; and the ascendancy of a new illiberal middle class and upper-caste elite detached from the mass of the people, driven by intense consumerism and acquisitive hedonism, and inspired by new, restless, bellicose forms of nationalism.

The BJP moved aggressively into the ideological and political spaces vacated by the Congress. Potentially, the Left could have competed with the BJP in replacing the Congress. But by the 1980s, the Left too had entered a phase of stagnation and decline for a variety of reasons, including the passing away of a generation of pre-Independence leaders; failure to actively develop alternative policies, strategies and perspectives; the contraction of its social base, especially among the urban working class under the impact of policy-driven economic processes leading to the informalisation and casualisation of labour under a neo-liberal model of capitalism; and last but not the least, the disarray in the international communist and socialist movements generated by the fall of the Berlin Wall and, above all, by the collapse of the Soviet Union and the Eastern Bloc.

The rise of the BJP to political prominence and especially to ideological respectability within the middle class cannot be understood without reference to some larger social processes at work in India, as well as the growing weakness of the party's own adversaries. These 'external' factors are probably far more important in explaining the BJP's ascendancy than 'internal' ones such as *Hindutva*'s changed mobilisational and organisational strategies. Among the greatest phenomena of the late 1980s and the early 1990s, especially in the Gangetic plains of Indiaor its Hindi-speaking 'heartland' or 'cow-belt', were the self-assertion of the middle and lower middle castes of the social order the Other Backward Classes (OBC's), or the 'Forward March of the Backwards'.

Secondly, the rise of new tendencies of self-consciousness and self-organisation among the Dalits (the former Untouchables) and the emergence and growth of specifically *Dalit* parties like the Bahujan Samaj Party. Thirdly, the greater regionalisation of politics as state- and region-based (as opposed to national) parties localised caste organisations, etc, playing a more important role than before. The BJP could not relate to the first two processes in any organic or integral way. Indeed, the parties representing the OBC's and untouchables represented the very antithesis of the upper caste-dominated content of the BJP's Hindutva ideology with an emphasis on Sanskritisation and its privileging of Brahminical values and the Greater Tradition (of the literate elite among Hindus, as opposed to the 'popular' or folk-based and plebeian Lesser Traditions). But the BJP became an unintended beneficiary of the backlash produced by the two phenomena, especially the political assertion of lower-middle castes.

Thus, when in 1990, Prime Minister Vishwanath Pratap Singh introduced a policy of limited positive discrimination in favour of the OBCs, there was a violent agitation opposing it, led by upper-caste groups covertly (but increasingly and forcefully) backed by the BJP. That upper-caste backlash immensely helped the party in the Hindi belt in political and electoral terms. As for the third tendency, towards regionalisation of politics, the BJP was its biggest gainer through the accretion of regional parties as its potential and actual allies. Although greatly weakened after the mid-1090s, the Congress was still (and remains) India's most broad-based and widely represented national party. Its state-level opponents became the BJP's convenient allies. This was another major advantage of being a late entrant to a position of national prominence, when the early major incumbent stood discredited and in decline. In the 1996 Lok Sabha elections, the BJP emerged as the single largest party. Buoyed largely by the Ayodhya movement, it had by then formed governments, typically coalition governments, in alliance with other parties, in many states of north-central and western India. But this was the first time when it could ascend to power at the national level-albeit for a mere 13 days. So isolated was the BJP, and so extreme and unacceptable the image of its ideology and politics, that not a single party, (of the 40 to 50 significant ones represented in the Lok Sabha), was willing to join hands with it even to form an opportunist coalition. This isolation ended soon. In March 1998, after barely two years of the rule of the unstable, fissiparous and ideologically divided United Front government of the Centre-Left, the BJP was back in power in New Delhi heading a 24-party National Democratic Alliance (NDA). By this time, strong, even committed, support for Hindutva from the upper-caste, upper and middle class strata crystallised.

This core or committed support base, along with varying degrees of backing from OBC layers (and even from some small *Dalit* groups) explained by local, contingent or transient reasons, was a winning combination. To form the NDA, which included mainly regional parties and some prominent former socialist leaders like Defence Minister George Fernandes, the BJP offered to make a 'sacrifice': Keep in abeyance trademark Hindutva issues like a cow-slaughter ban, Uniform Civil Code, Ayodhya temple and Article 370 from the post-election common programme or National Agenda for Governance. But it insisted that it would not compromise on two issues: Reviewing 'the working of the Constitution' (with a view to promote a more centralised presidential oriented government structure) and reconsidering the country's nuclear policy, in particular exercising the nuclear weapons option. Before exercising it, the government said, there would be a 'strategic defence review'.

A commission to review the working of the Constitution was indeed set up, but the BJP could not find anyone respectable enough to head it. A former chief justice of India finally agreed to chair it on condition that its terms of reference would not include a departure from the Westminster-style parliamentary system centred on the Prime Minister. This review exercise in essence turned out to be a dud. On the second issue, of nuclear policy, the BJP simply proceeded to exercise the nuclear option by detonating a series of five explosions on May 11 and 13, 1998 without the promised 'strategic defence review' and a discussion of the security environment, indeed without as much as a reference to the cabinet or the defence minister.

Also excluded from this decision were the armed services. There is reason to believe the decision to conduct the tests was taken by a small cabal of people, including top RSS leaders and a handful of cabinet ministers belonging solely to the BJP, excluding even Defence Minister George Fernandes. By nuclearising India, the BJP not only fulfilled its own long-standing nuclear obsession and fascination with militarism and weapons of mass destruction; it successfully mopped up, gave a new thrust to and capitalised on a bellicose form of Hindu nationalism growing in the country. The growth of this nationalism is intimately related to the burgeoning of a new consumerist elite under India's neo-liberal capitalism with its intense dualism and grotesque inequalities.

This elite has set its face against the people, indeed sees them as a drag on its own growth and prosperity. It lacks any commitment to liberal values or the spirit of democracy. It is culturally crass and driven by a peculiar kind of hubris and blind faith in India's 'manifest destiny 'Mera Bharat Mahan (literally, my India is great; more accurately, 'right or wrong, My Great Nation!'). This elite nationalism is highly receptive to the Hindutva notion of India's incomparably glorious past: The Vedic Age or the pre-Muslim 'pure Hindu' period, as the source of everything that is great in the ancient world's arts, sciences and cultures. These elite, comprising no more than a tenth of the population, is strongly social Darwinist in orientation. As an ideology, social Darwinism holds that only the fittest survive, and ought to survive, in society as well as nature. There is no place for the weak, the underprivileged and the powerless. This is held to be some immutable law of nature. This idea rationalises the horrendous callousness with which India's globalising middle classes are seceding from, and turning against, the mass of the people, the poor and unwashed, the 'laggards' and losers. These elite is strongly drawn to the culture of authoritarianism and is fascinated by force whether to guard borders, settle disputes, secure the family, or deter rape through capital punishment. This is most starkly manifested in the proliferation of repressive ideas and institutions of the sangh parivar, with its 20,000 Vidya Bharati schools, 30,000 RSS shakhas and its penetration of labour and student unions, as well as institutions of culture and higher education. Of a piece with this is the role of Hindutva as a vehicle for upper-caste domination, with all its anti-liberalism, hatred for the poor, suspicion of modernity, and opposition to the constitutional values of democracy, secularism, pluralism, universal human rights and egalitarianism. Some analysts see Hindutva as an upper-caste and upper class weapon against the weak, which are now asserting themselves and demanding their share in democratic decision-making.

The malign upper-caste orientation of Hindutva, and its utility as an instrument of domination not just of the religious minorities but all underprivileged groups, finds its highest expression in what might be called the Golwalkar Programme, outlined by the RSS's most important ideologue. The Golwalkar Programme consists in systematically assaulting modern-liberal ideas, weakening and undermining all democratic institutions, and using coercion to disenfranchise the minorities politically so as to turn them into second-class citizens without any rights. The Gujarat pogrom of 2002, in which 2,000 Muslims were massacred with state complicity under BJP Chief Minister Narendra Modi, shows the extent to which the Hindutva forces can go in implementing the Golwalkar Programme.

The Vajpayee government has shamelessly colluded with Modi and shielded him in a variety of unseemly ways. This not only proved the secularists' contention that Vajpayee's image as a 'soft' leader or half-liberal is totally deceptive: he is as steeped in *Hindutva*'s toxic ideology and communal politics as anyone else. It also showed that Hindutva remains the most serious and deadly menace to democracy in India.

5

Hindutva and Cultural Nationalism

Accordingly, the National Council meeting (Chennai -- December 27-29, 1999) asked the delegates to endorse this new line of the party in Chennai Declaration. The draft document which maintained that, "The BJP has no agenda other than the common agenda of the NDA", was however amended, due to strong protest of some of the party leaders. The National Council had to replace it with a sentence that "BJP expresses its confidence that every BJP worker understands that our agenda for governance is the national agenda for good governance." The amendment in Chennai declaration did not deter the liberal image builders in the party in their efforts to change the face of the BJP. With the growth in the personal image of Vajpayee both at the national and international level, they successfully stamped the subordination of the party to Vajpayee''s doctrine of governance during its Nagpur National Council session.

Another significant outcome of the Nagpur meet was to create an impression that criticism of the Government policies even inside the party forum would not be acceptable if it were not favourable to the interest of the party in consolidating its ties with allies. Instead of countering the criticism effectively, the new leadership gave an opportunity to its opponents that the BJP in its effort to occupy the position of the Congress has no inhibition to inherit its authoritarian culture, when it is in power. At the same time they cautioned the dissidents with warning that the erring functionaries will be dealt with firmly against indiscipline. Unlike the National Council meet at Chennai, the Nagpur session of the National Council failed to force the new leadership to make any amendments to the Vajpayee''s doctrine of governance.

NEW EXPERIMENT TO WOO THE MUSLIM VOTERS

After diluting the party''s old distinctive agenda on Kashmir and Swadeshi, the National Council made an attempt to expand the party''s base with a new experiment to woo the Muslims. Recalling the Chennai Declaration of the party in which an attempt was made to reinvent the relationship between the BJP and the Indian Muslims, Bangaru Laxman in his written Presidential speech said that "the Muslims have, by and large, neither got rightful share in the nation's development nor been able to join the national mainstream to play their due role in nation-building."

He further said, "the BJP has not yet become the preferred party of governance in the eyes of the people." Quoting from Deendayal Upadhyay's presidential speech at the Calicut session of the Bhartiya Jana Sangh, (the earlier incarnation of the BJP) in 1967 that "Muslims are the flesh of our flesh and blood of our blood" he has now opened a new debate both within and outside the party whether the BJP is serious to change the course of the historical stream of the party or it is simply a ploy to get the votes of the Muslims as suggested by its adversaries.

If the on going debate on the new experiment of the BJP to woo the Muslims is any indication, the possibility of erasing the anti-Muslim image of the party is apparently very remote. Apart from Muslim intellectuals, political opponents of the BJP and a large section of media have refused to be impressed with the "new face" of the party. According to them, this new chorus to entice Muslims with assurance to offer them more seats in future elections is simply an electoral strategy of the party. It has nothing to do with any change in the heart and traditional mind set of the party against the Muslims.

The efforts of Bangaru Laxman to change the course of the historical stream of the BJP are being challenged even by party's sympathisers with many uncomfortable questions. Will the BJP repeat the history of separate electorates to Muslims during the British period by evolving proportional representation to the community in legislatures and Government jobs? Will it give equal status to Urdu along with Hindi? Will it apologise for supporting Ayodhya movement? Will it abandon permanently its agenda of uniform Civil Code, Article 370 and commitment to facilitate the construction of Ram temple at Ayodhya? Until and unless the BJP changes its historical mind set and politics of Hindutva, the Muslim mass may not trust the BJP.

The RSS in a statement on Bangaru Laxman's overtures towards the Muslims did not consider it a case of appeasement. But, it is an irony that hardly within a week of National Council meeting, Kalraj Mishra, UP State President of the party visited Ayodhya, where he was greeted with usual slogans favouring construction of temple there. Similarly, Govindacharya, General Secretary of the BJP has been quoted in media saying that "his party was committed to Hindutva" (Times of India dated September 5). Addressing the State Executive Committee members at Bangalore he said, "In the Indian context, the other name for nationalism is Hinduism, which is a tradition and not a mode of worship. The identity of this nation is Hindutva." Such overtures on the part of senior party leaders vindicate the criticism of party's opponents that the pro-Muslim agenda of the new president is not taken seriously either by the party cadres or by the Muslims.

If the warning signal of the VHP President Vishnu Hari Dalmiya, who was quoted in Media saying that "in forthcoming UP assembly polls VHP cadres may not work for the BJP" and that "We think it was the Ramjanambhoomi movement which brought BJP to power. But having tasted power, they seem to think otherwise. They are not doing anything for the Hindus." (Times of India dated August 25) - are any indication, the new image of the BJP projected during Nagpur Session of the highest policy making body of the party may prove costly.

POWER RETAINING PHILOSOPHY

From the discussion we may conclude that the stagnation in the electoral growth of the party after 1998 and 1999 Lok Sabha polls, the party leadership is apprehensive of erosion in its support base. Bangaru Laxman, the new President therefore, in a realistic approach said, "the BJP has not yet become the preferred party of governance in the eyes of the people." With a view to shed the pro-Hindu image of the party, he tried to down play the Hindutva card in his presidential speech. Similarly, L.K. Advani in his attempt to shed his hard line image cautioned the National Council members to stop behaving like opposition. Advani, who was credited for pushing the party to prominence through Hindutva as its ideological mascot is now also realistic in accepting the coalition pragmatism.

Under the present political scenario ideology hardly has a role to play in retaining the power. Thus, to compromise with the situation as the only agenda of the party, the BJP has now tried to convert its ideological philosophy into the power retaining philosophy. Now the main concern of the party is to ensure its electoral success in future elections. But in the eyes of the new leadership this may not be possible if the party continues to pursue its distinctive old agenda. The ensuing Assembly elections in UP, West Bengal and Tamil Nadu next year will be the test case for the Prime Minister- centric BJP under the leadership of its Dalit President.

To expand the electoral base of the party among the Dalit and minority voters, the National Council down played its aggressive Hindutva card of the past. How far it will help the party to woo the Muslim and Dalit voters particularly in UP Assembly election next year continues to haunt the mind of the BJP cadres, who are now found more and more confused due to prevailing contradictions in the party. The RSS leadership may also prefer to allow the new leadership of the BJP to test its strength on the basis of the new face of the party. The visit of Vajpayee to RSS headquarter as first Prime Minister of the country might have assuaged the Sangh leadership that its "humble swayamsevak" has not abandoned it. But the political observers are yet to assess the mood of the volunteers of Sangh parivar, as it will be very difficult if not impossible for the BJP to win elections without their active support.

On his return from Nagpur, when Bangaru Laxman visited the party headquarters at 11 Ashoka Road, New Delhi, a party MP greeted him along with his supporters with a slogan of *Allah ho Akbar* which vibrated the atmosphere for quite some time. Now many party workers are found greeting each other whether jokingly or otherwise instead of the usual *Jai Sri Ram*. The new leadership might now think to organise a "*Yatra*" to woo the Muslims in pattern of *Ram Rath Yatra*, as the party cadres have already started practising the new slogan. In the history of the world, the Hindu awakening of the late twentieth century will go down as one of the most monumental events in the history of the world.

Never before has such demand for change come from so many people. Never before has Bharat, the ancient word for the motherland of Hindus - India, been confronted with such an impulse for change. This movement, Hindutva, is changing the very foundations of Bharat and Hindu society the world over. Hindu society has an unquestionable and proud history of tolerance for other faiths and respect for diversity of spiritual experiences. This is reflected in the many different philosophies, religious sects, and religious leaders. The very foundation of this lies in the great Hindu heritage that is not based on any one book, teacher, or doctrine.

In fact the pedestal of Hindu society stems from the great Vedic teachings Ekam Sat Viprah Bahudha Vadanti - Truth is One, Sages call it by Many Names, and Vasudhaiva Kutumbakam - The Whole Universe is one Family. It is this philosophy which allowed the people of Hindusthan (land of the Hindus) to shelter the Jews who faced Roman persecution, the Zoroastrians who fled the Islamic sword and who are the proud Parsi community today, and the Tibetan Buddhists who today face the communist secularism: persecution of religion.

During the era of Islamic invasions, what Will Durant called the bloodiest period in the history of mankind, many Hindus gallantly resisted, knowing full well that defeat would mean a choice of economic discrimination via the jaziya tax on non- Muslims, forced conversion, or death. It is no wonder that the residents of Chittor, and countless other people over the length and breadth of Bharat, from present-day Afghanistan to present-day Bangladesh, thought it better to die gloriously rather than face cold-blooded slaughter. Hindus never forgot the repeated destruction of the Somnath Temple, the massacre of Buddhists at Nalanda, or the pogroms of the Mughals.

Thus, the seeds of today's Hindu Jagriti, awakening, was created the very instance that an invader threatened the fabric of Hindu society which was religious tolerance. The vibrancy of Hindu society was noticeable at all times in that despite such barbarism from the Islamic hordes of central Asia and Turkey, Hindus never played with the same rules that Muslims did. The communist and Muslim intelligentsias, led by Nehruvian ideologists who are never short of distorted history, have been unable to show that any Hindu ruler ever matched the cruelty of even a moderate Muslim ruler.

It is these characteristics of Hindu society and the Muslim psyche that remain today. Hindus never lost their tolerance and willingness to change. However Muslims, led by the Islamic clergy and Islamic society's innate unwillingness to change, did not notice the scars that Hindus felt from the Indian past. It is admirable that Hindus never took advantage of the debt Muslims owed Hindus for their tolerance and non-vengefulness. In modern times, Hindu Jagriti gained momentum when Muslims played the greatest abuse of Hindu tolerance: the demand for a separate state and the partition of India, a nation that had had a common history and culture for countless millenia. Thus, the

Muslim minority voted for a separate state and the Hindus were forced to sub-divide their own land.

After partition in Pakistan, Muslim superiority was quickly asserted and the non-Muslim minorities were forced to flee due to the immense discrimination in the political and religious spheres. Again, Hindus did not respond to such an onslaught. Hindu majority India continued the Hindu ideals by remaining secular. India even gave the Muslim minority gifts such as separate personal laws, special status to the only Muslim majority state - Kashmir, and other rights that are even unheard of in the bastion of democracy and freedom, the United States of America. Islamic law was given precedence over the national law in instances that came under Muslim personal law. The Constitution was changed when the courts, in the Shah Bano case, ruled that a secular nation must have one law, not separate religious laws. Islamic religious and educational institutions were given a policy of non-interference. The list goes on.

More painful for the Hindus was forced negation of Hindu history and factors that gave pride to Hindus. Hindu customs and traditions were mocked as remnants of a non-modern society, things that would have to go if India was to modernize like the west. The self proclaimed guardians of India, the politicians of the Congress Party who called themselves secularists, forgot that it was the Hindu psyche that believed in secularism, it was the Hindu thought that had inspired the greatest intellectuals of the world such as Thoreau, Emerson, Tolstoy, Einstein, and others, and that it was Hindus, because there was no other land where Hindus were in a significant number to stand up in defence of Hindu society if and when the need arose, who were the most nationalistic people in India.

When Hindus realized that pseudo-secularism had reduced them to the role of an innocent bystander in the game of politics, they demanded a true secularism where every religious group would be treated the same and a government that would not take Hindu sentiments for granted. Hindutva awakened the Hindus to the new world order where nations represented the aspirations of people united in history, culture, philosophy, and heroes. Hindutva successfully took the Indian idol of Israel and made Hindus realize that their India could be just as great and could do the same for them also. In a new era of global consciousness, Hindus realized that they had something to offer the world. There was something more than tolerance and universal unity. The ancient wisdom of sages through eternity also offered systems of thought, politics, music, language, dance, and education that could benefit the world.

There have been many changes in the thinking of Hindus, spearheaded over the course of a century by innumerable groups and leaders who made their own distinct contribution to Hindu society: Swami Vivekananda, Rabindranath Tagore, Gandhiji, Rashatriya Swayamsevak Sangh, Swami Chinmayananda, Maharishi Mahesh Yogi, and International Society for Krishna Consciousness, Muni Susheel Kumarji, Vishwa Hindu Parishad, Bharatiya Janata Party, and others. Each in their own way increased pride in being a Hindu and simultaneously showed Hindus their greatest strengths and their worst weaknesses. This slowly shook the roots of Hindu society and prompted a rear-guard action by the ingrained interests: the old politicians, the Nehruvian intellectual community, and the appeased Muslim leadership.

The old foundation crumbled in the 1980s and 1990s when Hindus respectfully asked for the return of their most holy religious site, Ayodhya. This demand promptly put the 40-year old apparatus to work, and press releases were chunked out that spew the libelous venom which called those who represented the Hindu aspirations militant and fundamentalist, stigmas which had heretofore found their proper place in the movements to establish Islamic law. Hindus were humble enough to ask for the restoration of an ancient temple built on the birthplace of Rama, and destroyed by Babar, a foreign invader.

The vested interests were presented with the most secular of propositions: the creation of a monument to a national hero, a legend whose fame and respect stretched out of the borders of India into Southeast Asia, and even into Muslim Indonesia.

A hero who existed before there was anyone in India considered himself separate from Hindu society. The 400-year old structure at one of the holiest sites of India had been worshipped as a temple by Hindus even though the Muslim general Mir Baqi had partially built a non-functioning mosque on it. It was very important that no Muslims, except those who were appeased in Indian politics, had heard of anything called Babri Masjid before the pseudo-secularist apparatus started the next to last campaign against the rising Hindu society. It was also important that no Muslim had offered prayers at the site for over 40 years.

Hindus hid their true anger that their most important religious site still bore the marks of a cruel slavery that occurred so very recently in the time span of Hindu history. It was naturally expected in 1947 that freedom from the political and economic chains of Great Britain would mean that the systems and symbols that had enslaved India and caused its deterioration and poverty would be obliterated. Forty years after independence, Hindus realized that their freedom was yet to come. So long as freedom to Jews meant that symbols of the Holocaust in Europe were condemned, so long as freedom to African-Americans meant that the symbols of racial discrimination were wiped out, and so long as freedom from imperialism to all people meant that they would have control of their own destinies, that they would have their own heros, their own stories, and their own culture, then freedom to Hindus meant that they would have to condemn the Holocaust that Muslims reaped on them, the racial discrimination that the white man brought, and the economic imperialism that enriched Britain.

Freedom for Hindus and Indians would have to mean that their heros such as Ram, Krishna, Sivaji, the Cholas, Sankaracharya, and Tulsidas would be respected, that their own stories such as the Ramayana and the Mahabharata would be offered to humanity as examples of the brilliance of Hindu and Indian thinking, and that their own culture which included the Bhagavad Gita, the Vedas, the temples, the gods and goddesses, the art, the music, and the contributions in various fields, would be respected. Freedom meant that as the shackles of imperial dominance were lifted, the newly freed people would not simply absorb foreign ideas, they would share their own as well.

In India, something went wrong. The freedom from Britain was supposed to result in a two-way thinking that meant that non-Indian ideas would be accepted and that Indian ideas would be presented to the world. So long as the part of India giving to the world was suppressed, the freedom was only illusory and the aspirations of the freedom hungry would continue to rise in temperature. The freedom could have been achieved if a temple to Rama was built and the symbol of foreign rule was moved to another site or demolished. The battle was never really for another temple. Another temple could have been built anywhere in India. The humble and fair demand for RamaJanmabhoomi could have resulted in a freedom for India, freedom from the intellectual slavery that so dominated India.

This freedom would have meant that all Indians regardless of religion, language, caste, sex, or color would openly show respect for the person that from ancient times was considered the greatest hero to people of Hindusthan. For the first time, Hindus had demanded something, and it was justifiable that a reasonable demand from an undemanding people would be realized. Imagine if the Muslim leadership had agreed to shift the site and build a temple in Ayodhya. How much Hindu-Muslim unity there would have been in India? India could then have used that goodwill to solve the major religious, caste, and economic issues facing the country. But some of the vested interests in politics and in the Muslim community saw that such a change would mean that their work since 1947 would be overturned and that this new revolution would displace them. Rather than join forces and accept the rising tide, the oligarchy added fuel to the greatest movement in Indian history. One on December 6, 1992 completely shattered the old and weak roots of Indian society and with it, the old political and intellectual structure. The destruction by the Kar

Sevaks of the dilapidated symbol of foreign dominance was the last straw in a heightening of tensions by the government, and the comittant anger of more and more Hindus to rebuffs of their reasonable demands. The ruthless last-ditch effort of the powers-that-be was the banning and suppression of the leaders of the Hindu Jagriti. The effort of the rulers reminds one of the strategies of all ill-fated rulers. Throughout history, when monumental upheavals have taken place, the threatened interests have resorted to drastic measures, which in-turn have hastened their own death.

Hindus are at last free. They control their destiny now and there is no power that can control them except their own tolerant ethos. India in turn is finally free. Having ignored its history, it has now come face to face with a repressed conscience. The destruction of the structure at Ayodhya was the release of the history that Indians had not fully come to terms with. Thousands of years of anger and shame, so diligently bottled up by these same interests, were released when the first piece of the so-called Babri Masjid was torn down. It is a fundamental concept of Hindu Dharma that has won: righteousness. Truth won when Hindus, realizing that Truth could not be won through political or legal means, took the law into their own hands. Hindus have been divided politically and the laws have not acknowledged the quiet Hindu yearning for Hindu unity which has until recently taken a back seat to economic development and Muslim appeasement.

Similarly, the freedom movement represented the supercedence of Indian unity over loyalty to the British Crown. In comparison to the freedom movement though, Hindutva involves many more people and represents the mental freedom that 1947 did not bring. The future of Bharat is set. Hindutva is here to stay. It is up to the Muslims whether they will be included in the new nationalistic spirit of Bharat. It is up to the government and the Muslim leadership whether they wish to increase Hindu furor or work with the Hindu leadership to show that Muslims and the government will consider Hindu sentiments. The era of one-way compromise of Hindus is over, for from now on, secularism must mean that all parties must compromise. Hindutva will not mean any Hindu theocracy or theology. However, it will mean that the guiding principles of Bharat will come from two of the great teachings of the Vedas, the ancient Hindu and Indian scriptures, which so boldly proclaimed.

In holding that not all references to religion in election speeches necessarily amount to corrupt electoral practices; that it is the soliciting of votes on the ground of the religion of the candidate or that of his opponent which is a corrupt electoral practice; that statements made by others do not have the same effect as those made by a candidate himself - in all this, as we saw, the Supreme Court has merely reiterated what the the law itself says and what the Supreme Court has itself held on previous occasions. What then accounted for the fury of the secularists? The first feature which offended them was precisely that the Court had treated candidates at par! On the reasoning of secularists, when a Muslim candidate says, or when a candidate from among the forces of social-change says, Islam is in danger, get together, there is nothing wrong as it is but natural for a minority to feel insecure; but when a Hindu candidate says, Get together, Hinduism is in danger, why that is terrible, he is being communal, he is indulging in a corrupt electoral practice, his election ought to be struck down.

When a Muslim candidate says, Get together and bend this government to concede X,Y,Z, in the reckoning of secularists he is just asking for amelioration; but when a Hindu candidate says, "Get together so that governments do not bend to these communalists and concede X,Y,Z, he is being communal and fomenting religious bigotry. The Supreme Court put the two at par: as asking for something - say, a RS 500 crore bank only for non-Hindus of the kind the Prime Minister announced he was setting up - is not a corrupt electoral practice, opposing it is not a corrupt electoral practice either; as saying that Islam (or Urdu, or Tamil) is in danger is not a corrupt practice, saying Hinduism (or Sanskrit) is in danger is not a corrupt practice. That seems obvious enough. But just as obviously the secularists are not able to stomach it: for a fundamental premise of their verbal assault has been that their has to be an imbalance in favour of non-Hindus, of Muslims in particular.

The second sin of the judgment for them arose from the fact that the Court accepted, indeed adopted in toto the definition of Hindu, of Hindutva which the RSS and the BJP have been maintaining is what they have meant whenever they have used these expressions. There are two different reasons on account of which this caused such offense among secularists. One is of course that the Court had seen fit to endorse the construction which the RSS and BJP have put on the words, that was anathema in itself. But as repugnant if not more so was the fact that in doing so the Court had adopted a description which is complimentary to Hinduism: Hindutva, Hindu, these words signify a culture of tolerance, a universalism, the Court had held. The Court had seen fit to treat the words as a compendium of virtues, complained the Marxist intellectual in Hyderabad.

Now, that is of course unpardonable. For the secularist Hindu, Hindutva etc. signify the dustbin, the compendium of all that is shameful, and much that is positively evil. In this the secularist combines in him two streams - the Macaulay-missionary stream and the Marxist one. And here was the Court affirming the opposite! The very Court whose verdicts the secularists were accusing the RSS-BJP combines of not heeding! Naturally the poor fellows were fuming. And that is precisely why the RSS and BJP proclaimed vindication. Of course they were right in that their description of these words had been accepted by the Supreme Court. But I confess to feeling just about half satisfied. The Court held that the words Hindu, Hindutva, etc. refer to a culture, to a territorial region - the one around and beyond the Sindhu, the Indus that is. It declared that the words are not to be taken to refer to religion in the conventional sense. The words are cultural, geographical, and historical - in a word everything except words that refer to the religion you and I, the vast majority of our countrymen practice. In the Court's view what we practice and have faith in is not a religion at all. It is so diverse. It does not have one book, it does not have one prophet, nor one over- arching Church as a religion has. Therefore it is not a religion. The first point of course is that this is a circular way of proceeding. First religion is defined as that thing which has one book, one prophet, one Church etc., and then, as Hinduism does not have these, it is declared not to be a religion at all. But why should religion is defined in this restrictive way? Why should a system of beliefs and practices which does not have one book, one prophet, one Church, a system which has as one of its central features plurality, a system in which the ultimate referent is not a book or an intermediary like the Church but one's inner, direct experience not be regarded as a species of religion too?

The other point is that this way of defining Hindu etc. is to define the thing out of existence. The Court quotes with approval what an earlier Bench of the Supreme Court had held. In the Commissioner of Wealth Tax, Madras and others Vs Late R. Sridharan, 1976, the Court, starting from the position that it is difficult to define the term 'Hindu' with precision, had declared that Hindu may embrace a non-Hindu religion without ceasing to be a Hindu. That declaration must have provided succor to some tax-payer or claimant to an estate; it may have provided an acceptable defence to some election petitioners in the cases at hand. But I find that sort of a formulation deeply flawed. It calls to mind the sort of thing that missionaries and their allies among Indologists used to say - O' what you people have is not a religion at all; here, let us give you a real religion.

The formulation is also evidence of our state - namely, that the only way in which references to Hinduism in election speeches, say, can be defended is by defining Hinduism out of existence. The RSS, BJP, etc. of course have reason to feel gratified that their description of Hindu, Hindutva, etc. has been accepted. But that way of describing our religion and traditions - even by them - has itself been a reaction. It has been a reaction to the allegations that the religion is narrow-minded, bigoted, iniquitous etc., reactions to the allegations, that is, which were put out by missionaries and their allies in the 19th century and which have been so assiduously regurgitated by secularists over the last few decades. That formulation was also a reaction to the way our electoral laws were being interpreted by the courts. That sort of interpretation in turn was a result of the temper of the times, a temper in which propriety consisted in internalising every calumny about Hinduism. It can be small satisfaction that a formulation which came to be put out as a defensive reaction is now to be the official definition of the faith - a definition of the faith, that is, by which it is not a faith at all. I certainly do not want to belittle the advance. That the highest Court in the land has at last put references in election speeches to Hinduism at par with those to other religions is a major advance. It is also an index of the extent to which the very air is changing.

These two judgements are the seventh and eighth judgements respectively in an entire series. All of them separately and together vindicate the critique of pseudo-secularism which the RSS and others have been advancing. Apart from the facts which were before the Court, apart from the cogency of the arguments which must have been put forward, it is the realisation that if the Hindus continue to be pushed to the wall they will react which has made all the difference. These are in a deep sense post Ayodhya judgements. But the Hindutva judgements also show that there is a good deal of distance to travel as yet. The Court itself did not seem to be fully reconciled to the definition of Hindu, Hindutva, etc. which it endorsed.

Recall what it said in its judgement in the Manohar Joshi case. In urging that the election of Joshi should be set aside as he had used religion to solicit votes, his opponent had cited his statement, Maharashtra shall be the first Hindu state in the country. The Court rejected the submission, and held, In our opinion a mere statement that the first Hindu state shall be established in Maharashtra is by itself not an appeal for votes on the ground of his religion but the expression, at best, of such a hope - that conclusion, is the index of the changed circumstance, for a change the benefit of doubt was being given to the person who expressed that sort of a hope; it also shows how tenuous such things are - for another set of judges could just as well have latched on to this very statement as proof that the candidate was appealing to the voters to help him establish Hindu Rashtra and what not.

But it is what the Court proceeded to say which shows the distance that has to be traveled. However despicable be such a statement, the Court says, it cannot be said to amount to an appeal for votes on the ground of his religion. Assuming that the making of such a statement in the speech of the appelant at that meeting is proved, we cannot hold that it constitutes the corrupt practice either under sub-section or sub-section (3A) of Section 123, even though we would express our disdain at the entertaining of such a thought or such a stance in a political leader of any shade in the country.

As the word Hindu is not to be understood in terms of narrow-minded religion, as Hindutva, Hinduism are just cultural, territorial, historical concepts referring to a broad-minded, tolerant, catholic, inclusive tradition, as Hinduism is merely that compendium of virtues", to recall the words from Hyderabad, how come it became despicable to say that Maharashtra shall be the first Hindu state, by what reasoning did the expression merit the disdain of the Supreme Court? Nor is this just a matter of a little inconsistency. For there is the other side to saying that Hindu, Hinduism etc. refer to compendia of virtues.

In our discourse, even in earlier judgements of the Supreme Court itself only the Hindus are told to abide by these excellent norms. The homilies about being tolerant, broad-minded are addressed only to them - one need go no further for ready examples of this than the pronouncements of the Supreme Court in response to the Presidential Reference on Ayodhya. This way of looking at things equates the arsonist with the structure he is out to set on fire. It is Hinduism as conventionally understood, as the set of beliefs and practices, as the way of life of the vast majority of the people of this land which is under threat. It has been the butt of secularist scorn and scheming, it is threatened by the way the State is being made to bend before the controllers of Muslim votes, by the way it is being rendered impotent before terrorists etc. - the condition of the refugees in Jammu is a vivid illustration of the threat and its consequences. Secularism itself has been converted into an instrument of assault against the way of life which the Court lauds so eloquently. In his excellent little book, *Secularism*, Navratna Rajaram shows how the concept has been stood on its head, and what consequences it now spells for us and our society.

In Europe the Church had asserted and secured the right to lay down the law for all aspects of life. To liberate themselves from these suffocating stranglehold intellectuals and some rulers in Europe constructed the concept of secularism. They argued that while the Church may regulate what was "God's", it ought not to interfere with what was Ceaser's. As Rajaram shows the concept was a device to carve out a sphere of autonomy for the individual in the face of the totalitarian and exclusivist claims of the Church. But in India during the last fifty years the word has become an umbrella to shield totalitarian and exclusivist ideologies; indeed it has become a weapon by which the evangelists of such ideologies have been pushing to the wall the plural tradition of our country, the tradition founded in the basic world-view of Hinduism.

These new judgements of the Supreme Court do recognise that Hinduism has from time immemorial been instilling those principles of plurality and tolerance and compassion. But they do not reverse the standard habit of hurling these principles at the Hindus only. Thereby on the one hand the judgements leave the assaulters free to continue pushing that tradition further to the wall and on the other they thereby leave open the prospect of the reaction among Hindus taking an even stronger form than it already has. But perhaps one should not expect the courts to go all the way all of a sudden. The change in the atmosphere has brought us this far - that instead of the calumnies which have been stuck on to it by secularists, the Court is associating lofty ideals with Hinduism. Further change in the atmosphere will take us the rest of the way.

What the Prime Minister and his colleagues have been doing in the run-up to the elections shows both - the distance we have to travel, and also how difficult it is, in the light of the judgements, to regulate misuse merely by law. The Court held - and necessarily so - that the speeches, documents, videos etc. which may be made the bases for challenging the election of a candidate must be shown to record or depict something the candidate etc. have said during the election campaign - that is, from the date the election was notified to the close of polling. That is as it has to be, no doubt. But there is also no doubt that it leaves the person or his party free to use the appeals of caste, religion, language etc. up to the day elections are notified, and then rely on the associations which he has already formed in the minds of the voters to deliver the votes.

Just see what the Prime Minister and his colleagues have been doing in the last few months. They have been going around genuflecting at every dargah, they have been going about promising salaries to Imams of mosques, and Sitaram Kesari has been promising reservations to Muslims. The Prime Minister has been holding meetings with Ulema and the rest as the representatives of Muslims as a religious group, and he has been giving assurances to them as representatives of a religious community. There can be no doubt that each of these steps has been an attempt to garner votes of Muslims via religion. The first point is the about the nature of public comment on these attempts. How many secularists can you recall who denounced this blatant recourse to religion to garner votes?

The second point is about the law. As technically the elections had not been announced, the Prime Minister and his colleagues were free to deploy the device to the hilt. Moreover, on one thing it does seem that the Court exercised an option which may cost us dear. The matter arose as follows. As is well known, Article 19 (1)(a) guarantees us the fundamental right to free speech. Article 19 (2) specifies the grounds on which reasonable restrictions may be put on this right. Ram Jethmalani argued that from among the grounds which had been enumerated the only one on which the freedom to speak about religion etc during elections could be restricted was public order: and the courts have held time and again that the threat to public order which can be used to restrict fundamental rights is not just the apprehension that there will be some breach of peace; there must be the definite and imminent prospect of a general breakdown of order. The provision in an electoral law which sought to restrict the freedom to an extent greater than this, Jethmalani argued was itself unconstitutional. The Court did not accept this argument. In its judgement it held that in fact restrictions on the use of religion; caste, etc. for soliciting votes can be justified under another ground which is mentioned in Article 19(2), namely decency and morality. There is no reason to restrict decency and morality to sexual morality alone, the Court declared. It quoted with approval what the Supreme Court had held in an earlier case: in Khuller etc. vs Director of Public Prosecutions, 1972, the Court had said, Indecency is not confined to sexual indecency; indeed it is difficult to find any limit short of saying that it includes anything which an ordinary decent man or woman would find to be shocking, disgusting and revolting.

It isn't just that this again is a circular way of defining the ground. It isn't just that given the way things are, while that sort of an approach is not liable to be used to curb vulgarity where it manifestly needs to be curbed - those heavy women being made to shake their thick bodies in our films - and that it might well be used to curb speech where it ought to be untrammeled. The fact is that all reform shocks and offends in the beginning, those who are accustomed to the present ways; those who are the beneficiaries of the present arrangements are revolted by it. The definition of decency and morality which the Court adopted to get over Ram Jethmalani's googly is thus too wide, and in determined hands can be handy for imposing restrictions which the Court itself would not want to ever countenance.

That matter should therefore be reconsidered. And when the occasion to do so arises I would urge two further things. Sub-sections 3 and 3A which were the subject matter of these judgements enumerate caste also among the grounds on which candidates must not solicit votes, on which they must not seek to spread hatred among classes of citizens. I do hope that one of these days the Court will have the opportunity to examine the sort of poison which is being spread on this basis, be it camouflaged in the name of social justice. Second, how come that, while it is an offence under our laws to spread hatred or solicit votes on the basis of religion, caste, language, race, etc., it is perfectly all right to spread hatred and enmity, and to solicit votes on the basis of class? Isn't it high time that the laws were amended to rope in that ground also?

6

Hindutva

The Brahman Conspiracy

TRANSFORMING RELIGION INTO AN ANTI-HUMAN FORCE

It is claimed that all religions preach love, but wars have been waged in the name of every religion, riots and killings have been taken place in the name of religion. The fact that nearly all the charges laid against one religion by followers of another, apply in one way or another to every religion and religious activities is seldom recognised by those who point an accusing finger at practitioners of another religion. When Karl Marx commented that "Religion was the opium of the masses", he never meant it in the sense that religion was a harmful thing in a way similar to narcotic substances. He saw religion as a refuge from the agony of life and as an escapist shelter from painful reality. In his time, opium was not contraband. It had medicinal applications.

Today, unlike in the way Marx meant, religion is being consciously transformed into an evil narcotic substance that would intoxicate and enslave people and make man hate man. We know that throughout history there have been conflicts and wars not only between religions but also between factions within a religion. However, the religious fanaticism that we witness today is far less motivated by the desire to win people over to the 'correct path'.

On the contrary, it is a device to persuade people to apply their religious identity to the elimination of people of other faiths. In Northern Ireland, the catholic who hardly goes to church and the protestant who never attends church destroyed each other in the name of religion. When Yugoslavia was dismembered, the bulk of the population did not have religious faith. Nevertheless, two Christian communities and a Muslim community had much in common, embarked on a genocidal war against each other.

FORCES BEHIND FANATICISM

It is true that there is Islamic fundamentalism. However, it was America that induced, supported and even trained Islamic fanatics in acts of violence and terror. They were used by America, with the support of Saudi Arabia, in its subversive activities against the Soviet Union and China. Today America is reaping what it sowed. Christian fundamentalism has deeper roots, and it has maintained close links with the right wing political establishment of America. Although very little is spoken about it, it is well known that Christian fundamentalists are responsible for a number of acts of violence in America and abroad, ranging from mass suicide to mass killing such as the one that took place only a few years ago in Ohio.

Hinduism is said to be a pacifist religion, but was within the framework of this Hinduism that the practice of untouchability existed. Although there are doubts as to whether Hinduism is a religion, some are actively at work to build a common Hindu identity. But this is not like the progressive identity that men of humane vision like Vivekaananda tried to build in colonial India.

This gang emphasises a new identity that rejects outright the progressive stand of uniting all mankind, accepting and defending gender equality, rejecting the caste system and respecting all religions alike. What is its motive? It is none other than imposing a common identity on the whole of India. How does it seek to address the reality that India comprises a multitude of nations, nationalities, indigenous tribes and religions? There is a system of caste hierarchy in India. How does it propose to deal with it?

THE HINDUTVA VIEW OF THE WORLD

The dominant social class in India enjoys domination over other based on caste as well as wealth. They are not willing to part with their privilege and power, and they need the religious identity of Hinduism to preserve their power. Hinduism holds that the Brahmins are high born and the others low born. Among the others, the Shudras, the caste group comprising manual workers, are placed lowest. Besides that, there is a section of the population comprising nearly a quarter of the Indian population that is too low to be placed within the Hindu hierarchical order. They are referred to as the Panchama, meaning fifth group, who are considered lower than the lowliest Shudra and treated with contempt. Hindutva endorses it and seeks to prolong its existence.

The group of religions referred to as Hinduism has nothing in common by way of a concept of god, prescribed practices, rituals, faith or even a moral code. What has thus far been known as Hindu is an identity referring to a historical region and not one based on philosophy or ideology. But there is concerted effort today to impose the Bhagavad Gita as a common religious text for Hindus. On the one hand, the systems of worship of the depressed communities are denounced as superstition and the people are under pressure to accept the Brahminist system of worship. On the other hand, all manner of superstition among the high castes are encourages as means of exploring the supernatural.

THE POLITICS OF HINDUTVA

Hindutva is not a ploy that that was created by the BJP for mere electoral advantage. Its roots run deep. Hatred towards other religions has been systematically cultivated for over a century. The Hindu Mahaa Sabhaa and the Jan Sangh of the past were organisations that rejected Hindu-

Muslim unity. Their goal was Hindu, in reality Brahmin, domination. Then as much as now, in every organisation that preaches Hindutva, Brahmins are in control. Hindutva was designed to ensure that the Brahmin elite that comprise a few percent of the population could forever lord it over the rest of the society. Religion proved to be a powerful tool in devising Brahminist domination. Hindutva needed the Hindu-Muslim conflict in order to divert the attention of the oppressed people to prevent them from uniting as landless peasants, workers or people deprived of their basic rights.

India needed Hindu-Muslim unity in its campaign for independence from British Colonial rule. That was why the Indian National Congress under the leadership of M.K. Gandhi sought Hindu-Muslim unity. It even went to the point of conceding that caste oppression was a bad thing. However, its loyalty to the elite classes ensured that it did not go much beyond a nominal campaign against untouchability. That was why Ambedhkar and E.V. Raamasaami (Periyaar) rejected Gandhi and deserted the Congress. It was because the roots of Hindutva ran through the Congress establishment that the Congress, especially since the agnostic Nehru, readily yielded to the politics of religion. The need to please the majority in parliamentary politics made such compromises essential.

Once a political party is makes a deal with religious or nationalistic fanaticism, the forces of fanaticism begin to dominate. Each of these forces has wreaked havoc to different degrees in Indian politics in various parts of India. The list of major acts of violence resulting from caste conflicts, disputes based on language and nationality, and communal violence in the name of religion is long and ever growing. Today, however, a form of politics with Hindutva at its centre and portrays Muslims and to a less extent Christians as the enemy is the biggest social evil in India.

THE RISE OF HINDU FASCIST VIOLENCE

This is the tenth year since the demolition of theBabri Masjid in Ayodhya. For over two months, anti-Muslim violence raged unabated in Gujarat. Even today serious incidents of violence are reported from different parts of, mostly urban, Gujarat. Not only did the BJP government of Narendra Modi in that state fail to control the violence, but also encouraged it. The central government has been reluctant to act on this matter, and it got away with its irresponsible approach owing to the lack of will of its 'secular' partners, especially the DMK, MDMK, and Teugu Desam, to challenge the BJP on this matter. The Congress and some of the left parties demonstrated their inherent weakness that arose from their stakes in electoral politics by asking for the removal of Narendra Modi rather than the dismissal of the state government.

Suspicions were expressed by some observers soon after the February incident of arson in Godhraa, where a train carrying Hindu volunteers returning from Ayodhya was set alight, led to the wave of violence against the Muslims in Gujarat, that the arsonists were probably not Muslims. The major political parties did not consider the possibility that it could have been a Hindutva conspiracy to sacrifice a few women and children as moral justification for a well-planned anti-Muslim pogrom. In fact, there are plenty of Nazi and other precedents for staging acts of criminal violence to justify subsequent repression by their forces. Forensic inquiry into the fire has indicated that the fire was started within the train. This leads to two possibilities, namely, that it was an accident or, perhaps more probably, a Hindutva conspiracy.

In either event, the Muslims are innocent, but the acts of violence have gone too far for the truth to be of any good in restoring good communal relations. It is true that the BJP government faces embarrassment internationally because of the violence in Gujarat. It is true that the 'secular' image of India is further tarnished. However, the BJP is hoping to make some capital out of the Hindu-Muslim conflict. It plans to hold fresh elections in Gujarat state with the BJP government in charge of the state. Portrayal of the BJP as the 'true defender' of the Hindus is likely to work in an emotionally charged atmosphere than when people have time to appreciate what really happened. The forces of Hindutva are not wasting time in whipping up anti-Muslim feeling and even the local media is party to the campaign. Their style of work is populist and chauvinistic, and in the style of European fascism three-quarters of a century ago.

If the criminal violence in Gujarat in the name of Hindutva continues, it would lead to communal violence across the whole of India, and that is not for the benefit of any other than a handful of mischief-makers. Therefore, this madness should be halted now. Defeating the BJP or the Shiv Sena at the polls is not the answer. Organisations such as the Bajrang Dhal, Raashtrya Swamsevak Sangh (RSS) and Vishwa Hindu Parishad (VHP) have grown to the point that nothing will be achieved by imposing a ban on any of them. The issue cannot be defined in terms of the dispute over the building the Ram temple at the site of theBabri Masjid or the violence in Gujarat. These are symptoms of a bigger ill, like blisters on the skin caused by a major illness. Treating the symptoms is often needed, but not a substitute for curing the illness, in this instance Hindutva fascism.

The entire society needs to be healed. Immediately, it is necessary to carry the campaign against the ideologies of Hindutva and caste hegemony to the masses through every feasible form of mass struggle. History tells us that a political party steeped in parliamentary politics has approached, on the basis of social justice, the resolution of contradictions among the people. There are plenty of instances in the political history of Sri Lanka to illustrate this point. That is why it is necessary to clearly identify and thoroughly expose the class origin and class interests of those who incite hatred in the name of caste, religion and nationality and to carry out relentless mass struggles against them. In India, only the Marxist-Leninists are ideologically equipped to deal with the issue. Thus, it is urgent and essential that the Marxist-Leninist forces unite and join hands with other progressive forces in the struggle against Hindutva fascism.

The struggle against ant form of fascism cannot be carried out in isolation and without mobilising the masses. Unity of all forces that can be united is essential to any just struggle. It is also important that the struggle against Hindutva fascism should be made an integral component of every just struggle, whether it be a trade union struggle, the struggle of agricultural workers, struggle against caste oppression, environmental protection, women's rights or national liberation. Not only has the potential for this course of action but also the mass support base existed in India. Without the progressive forces acting properly and promptly, screaming about India falling victim to Hindutva fascism will bear no fruit. Thus, the immediate agenda should be the building up under proletarian leadership an anti-fascist united front. This is the biggest challenge facing the Indian proletariat today and the anti-fascist struggle will be the foundry in which the arms that will ensure the victory of the proletariat in India will be forged.

ARYAN INVASION THEORY

Anyone familiar with the uncertainties inherent in historical research will be amazed to notice the immense self-assuredness with which most spokesmen for either side in the Aryan invasion debate are making their case. In reality, a lot in this question of ancient history is undecided: the Harappan script remains undeciphered and the archaeological findings (e.g. Lal 2002) are open to interpretation. Analysis of the historical data in the Rig-Veda fails to find any trace of an Aryan invasion, though along with the Puranas it alludes to episodes of Aryan emigration, but these textual findings cannot be deemed conclusive. Even if they are accepted as solid historical data, scenarios of immigration at an earlier date than hitherto assumed remain compatible with them. So the claim by linguists that the genealogy of the Indo-European language family is best explained by an (as yet not firmly dated) invasion scenario should not be dismissed lightly. We are faced here with an open and undecided question, a fit object for intense but open-minded research.

One of the reasons for the absolutist rhetoric bedevilling the Aryan invasion debate is the enormous investment of various political messages in the competing theories. Their political use in India will be discussed below; but the Western scholar may be expected to know about their political uses in the West, which predate the Hindu nationalist involvement by at least a century. The Out-of-India Theory (OIT) was briefly popular in Europe in the Romantic age as part of the Orientomanic fashion, but the AIT had many more political uses. By relating an ancient instance of white colonization in a dark subcontinent, it confirmed the colonial worldview. The AIT specifically justified the presence of the British among their "Aryan cousins" in India, being merely the second wave of Aryan settlement there. It supported the British view of India as merely a geographical region without historical unity, a legitimate prey for any invader capable of imposing himself. It provided the master illustration to the rising racialist worldview:

1. The dynamic whites entered the land of the indolent dark natives;
2. Being superior, the whites established their dominance and imparted their language to the natives;
3. Being race-conscious, they established the caste system to preserve their racial separateness;
4. But being insufficiently fanatical about their race purity, some miscegenation with the natives took place anyway, making the Indian Aryans darker than their European cousins and correspondingly less intelligent and less dynamic;
5. Hence, for their own benefit they were susceptible to an uplifting intervention by a new wave of purer Aryan colonizers.

The AIT was consequently a must in all Nazi textbooks on race. In this controversy, the AIT camp happens to be Hitler's camp. I would like to caution those who expect to trump the indigenist argument by insinuating political motives: you have no chance of winning that game, for no ugly name, not even "Hindu chauvinism", can trump "Hitler" in branding an opponent with guilt by association and blowing him out of the arena. Contemporary Euro-nationalists uphold the pro-invasionist tradition, e.g. Meerbosch 1992, Van den Haute 1993. Certain rightist circles, vaguely known on the Continent as the *Nouvelle Droite,* devote particular attention to the Indo-European heritage, invariably claiming a European homeland, e.g. Schuon 1979; de Benoist 1997, 2000; Benot 2001:13; or Venner 2002:63.

This trend has enlisted the contributions of eminent scholars, and their political views need not detract from the validity of their argumentation, but the political dimension is undeniably and explicitly present, e.g. AIT supporters Varenne (1967:25) and Haudry are, or were members of the Scientific Committee of the French nationalist party *Front National.* Conversely, the French Left has tried to delegitimize any research into the "tainted" topic of Indo-European ("Aryan"!) culture and origins, leading to the closure of the *Institut d'Etudes Indo-Europennes* in Lyons. Likewise in the US, the *Journal for Indo-European Studies* has been under attack for alleged rightist connections.

Western AIT proponents, right-wing or otherwise, may not realize very well who their allies in India are, and vice versa. The Indian uses of the AIT predate any political use (or even the mere articulation) of the OIT. On this topic, the Western scholars who so unhesitatingly parrot denunciations of the Indian indigenists by Indian invasionists are simply babes in the wood. For their information, a brief overview of the several AIT-exploiting movements is given here:

1. Dravidian Separatism- Sponsored by the British colonial government, a movement of the middle castes in the southern Tamil region started attacking Brahmin and North-Indian interests and symbols, taking the shape of a political party, the Justice Party (later *Dravida Kazhagam*) in 1916. Given the Brahmin leadership in the independence movement, Dravidian self-assertion had obvious uses for the colonial status-quo. To beef up Dravidian pride, a claim was made that the whole of Indian culture, or at least all the good things in it (including, from ca. 1925 onwards, the Harappan cities),

belonged to the aboriginal Dravidians, while the Aryans had mostly brought destruction and reactionary social mores. After independence, the movement opted for a separate Dravidian state, a demand which never caught on outside Tamil Nadu and was abandoned even there after the Chinese invasion of 1962.

In the next years the movement got integrated into the political system and after a split the two successor parties have been alternating with each other in power at the state level ever since, but with an ever-decreasing fervour for Dravidian separateness. The movement's greatest success was when, in 1965, it joined hands with the English-speaking elite in Delhi to thwart the Constitutional provision that from that year onwards, Hindi rather than English be the sole link language of India, - surely a fitting thanksgiving for the British patronage which had groomed the movement into political viability.

2. Dalit neo-Ambedkarism- Dalit, "broken" or "oppressed", is a term applied to the former Untouchable castes, sparingly by the late-19th-century reform movement Arya Samaj, and more officially by mid-20th-century *Dalit* leader Dr. Bhimrao Ambedkar and by his followers ever since. Today, the term has eclipsed the Gandhian euphemism *Harijan*. Ambedkar himself (1917:21) rejected both the AIT and its caste-racialist implication that lower castes sprang from the native race while upper castes were the invaders' progeny. Yet, his followers, along with his 19th-century precursor, the Christian-educated Jyotirao Phule, took the more conformist road of adapting the AIT and staking their political claims in the name of being "aboriginals" deprived of their land, culture and social status by the "Aryan invaders".

Among these neo-Ambedkarites, who claim Ambedkar's mantle but have turned against him on many points (e.g. favouring conversion to Christianity or Islam, which Ambedkar energetically rejected in favour of native religions, esp. Buddhism), strange international alliances abound, e.g. with Islamic militancy, Evangelical fundamentalism and cranky American Afrocentrism. Many of V.T. Rajshekar's brochures are transcripts of lectures at Christian institutions, and one wonders if the latter are aware of the more eccentric parts of his work, e.g. he is the only Indian to merit a mention in an authoritative study (Poliakov 1994) of contemporary anti-Semitism.

His anti-Brahminism is also moulded after the anti-Semitic model, e.g. just like both capitalist plutocracy and Bolshevism have been blamed on the Jews, Rajshekar (1993) treats both religious Brahminism and Brahmin-led Indian Marxism as two hands of a single Brahmin conspiracy. Note that his anti-Brahmin plea opens with a profession of belief in the AIT: "The fair-skinned foreigners, the Aryan barbarians, who strayed into India, came into clash with India's dark-skinned indigenous population - the Untouchables" (1993:1). This kind of company ought to worry those who rely on the principle of "guilt by association" in their argument against the AIT skeptics.

3. Tribal separatism- The first tribal revolts of the colonial age (Santal Hool, Birsa rebellion) had a distinctly anti-British and anti-missionary thrust, administrators and missionaries tried to redirect tribal frustration and aspiration in an anti-Hindu and anti-Indian sense. This caught on quite well among the more peripheral, least "aryanized" tribes, particularly in the Northeast. The claim of being primeval Indians displaced from the fertile plains by the Aryan invaders was a logical rallying-point for their new self-consciousness. To a very large extent, this "pre-Aryan" identity was a total novelty tutored by the Christian missions, who made the tribals their privileged focus of activity and rechristened them as "aboriginals", a pseudo-indigenous term falsely suggesting that non-tribals had all along been seen as foreign intruders. Given the frequency with which journalists and even scholars swallow the invasionist implication of the term, this coinage deserves a gold medal as a brilliantly successful one-word disinformation campaign.

Some of the Northeastern tribes have been converted to Christianity *in toto* and refuse to give "Indian" as their nationality during the census, preferring their tribal identities as "Naga" or "Mizo" instead, thus confirming Hindu nationalist suspicions against Christianity. Ironically, it is these Northeastern tribes who have the least right to be called "aboriginal", as their immigration from the East in the medieval period, much later than any Aryan invasion, is well-documented. Even the older Munda-speaking tribes are widely assumed to originate in Southeast Asia, still the centre of gravity of their Austro-Asiatic language family; while the Dravidians have variously been traced to Central Asia, Elam and even Africa. If the Aryans must perforce pass as invaders, they are not the only ones.

4. Christian mission- The single biggest promoter of the AIT as the bedrock of new political group identities has undeniably been the Christian mission, incidentally also the biggest operator of elite educational institutions in India and a major media owner, hence a powerful moulder of public opinion. Christian missionary authors in the 19th century such as Sir Monier Monier-Williams, Friedrich Max Muller, Bishop Robert Caldwell and Rev. G.U. Pope laid the intellectual groundwork for Dravidian, Tribal and *Dalit* political movements and for a new fragmented self-perception of Hinduism. Quite deliberately, Hindu self-esteem was undermined by breaking the Hindu pantheon into a set of native gods like Shiva and a set of Aryan-invader gods like Indra; by redefining reform movements like Buddhism and Bhakti as "revolts of the natives against Aryan-Brahminical impositions"; and by reinterpreting the *Dharma-Shastras* as nothing but an elaborate apartheid legislation for preserving the race and dominance of the Aryan invader castes.
5. Indian Islam- In recent years, militant Muslims such as *Muslim India* monthly's editor Syed Shahabuddin have tried to integrate the AIT in their anti-Hindu polemics. The thrust of their argument is that if Hindus see Muslims as foreigners, they should be told that they themselves, at least the Aryan elite among them, once were foreign intruders. And that not Muslims but Aryan Hindus were the trail-blazers of destructive invasions pillaging and

destroying native centres of civilization. Further, building on the erroneous but by now widespread belief that most Indian Muslims were low-caste Hindus who sought equality by converting to Islam, it is argued that they are largely part of the native stock, hence more Indian than Hindu nationalists, who are (equally erroneously) identified as upper-caste and hence as Aryan invaders.

6. Indo-Anglian snobbery- English education and more recently the westernization of the workplace, of popular music and other everyday circumstances have generated a class of Indians quite alienated from and ignorant of native culture. More than the English-employed Babus of yore, they delight in mocking and belittling native culture. In their hands, the AIT is simply an instrument to tease Indian "chauvinists" and deconstruct the very notion of a distinct Indian or Hindu civilization. With the decline of ideology and the rise of the commercial outlook in the media, this supercilious and nihilistic attitude is now a rising force in the opinion landscape, but it has always been around in non-Marxist sections of independent India's anglicised elite.
7. Indian Marxism- Among the English-educated elite, a class of Marxist intellectuals has been very active and increasingly influential since the 1930s. Around the time of independence, they emphasized the Leninist theory of national self-determination, favouring the creation of a Muslim state Pakistan and the further partition of India into separate linguistic states. Though not actively militating for separatism later on, they kept on promoting notions like "Bengali nationhood" and refused to accept the Indian state, for "India was never the solution", according to Marxwadi Communist Party politburo member Ashok Mitra (1993). In that discourse, the AIT didn't figure very prominently at first because as Marxists they focused on present social realities rather than the distant "feudal" past.

Well into the 1980s, as long as they thought in terms of socio-economic class, they refused to cultivate casteist and ethnic identities and consequently took only a limited interest in AIT-based identity politics. But with the decline of world Communism, the Indian comrades increasingly compromised with identitarian populism, in some states even with Islamic fundamentalism, in fact with any force deemed hostile to the perceived ruling class, characterized as upper-caste Hindu. In the 1990s, when the AIT was getting challenged, they became its most ardent and most effective defenders, vide e.g. Thapar 1996; Sharma 1995, 1999.

While the other above-mentioned anti-Hindu or anti-Indian groups merely assume and use the AIT, the Indian Marxists have seriously invested in intellectually upholding it. The common denominator in all these uses of the AIT is that it undermines or contradicts India's sense of unity. In Hindu nationalist parlance, the AIT is "anti-national". The reason why the votaries of Hindutva have recently rallied around the position of AIT skepticism is simply to counter these anti-national uses of the AIT.

IDEOLOGICAL POWER EQUATION IN INDIA

To grasp the political dimension of the Aryan invasion debate, it is necessary to clarify the political power equation in the dominant media and academic institutions in India. As former *Times of India* editor Girilal Jain (sacked in 1989 for developing Hindutva sympathies) used to say: "Nothing ever dies in India." Movements long dead in the West are still alive and vigorous in India. That is why the last Communist will not be called Popov or Zhang or Kim, but Chatterji or Bose. Numerically, the Communists' power base in India was always small, but in a few key sectors, including the bottlenecks in the information flow to the West, their presence was overwhelming and remains disproportionate even now.

Around 1970, entryist policies (Communists entering Congress, the ministerial offices and the cultural institutions) and a very gainful *quid pro quo* with a besieged Prime Minister Indira Gandhi made Marxism the dominant ideology in the Indian state and parastatal institutions such as the Indian

History Congress and the National Centre for Educational Research and Training. While ruling parties came and went, the entrenched Marxists defended their position and reserved access for their own kind. The first BJP government at the centre (1998-99) made no dent in the Marxist academic hegemony, and the second one (1999-present) only very partially. Even then, the Marxists didn't take kindly to this first fresh breeze of *glasnost*, hence their campaign against new anti-colonial and allegedly "saffron" accents in the textbooks.

The Marxists don't like to be caught in the searchlight. One of the most respected Marxist scholars, Romila Thapar, chides her critics thus: "Those that question their theories are dismissed as Marxists!" (1996:17) Well, apart from her reliance on a Marxist conceptual framework in her publications, she is also confirmed to be a representative of the Indian Marxist school of historiography in an authoritative Marxist source, the *Dictionary of Marxist Thought* (Bottomore 1988), under its entry "Hinduism", along with R.S. Sharma. For those still in doubt, Irfan Habib, one of the deans of the Marxist school, has put his cards on the table in a book subtitled "Towards a Marxist Perception" (1995).

Among the print media, the one most active in the anti-indigenist crusade is the Chennai-based fortnightly *Frontline*, a consistent defender of the Cuban and North-Korean regimes and of the Chinese occupation of Tibet. After the mock referendum in Iraq in the autumn of 2002, *Frontline* displayed its nostalgia for Soviet mock elections by treating Saddam Hussein's 100% approval rate as a genuine democratic endorsement. Judging from its record, we may take the *Frontline* initiative to prominently feature pro-AIT contributions by Asko Parpola and Michael Witzel, participants in the present JIES debate, to be motivated by something else than a concern for good scholarship.

To be sure, the Marxist motives of the *Frontline* editors and of the old history establishment have no logical implications for the correctness or otherwise of the pro-invasionist argument. Of course not. But then it is not invasion sceptic Prof. Kazanas who tried to twist this debate to his advantage by raising the issue of political motives; that was the doing of some of his critics. If they don't feel troubled by their *de facto* alliance with crackpots like V.T. Rajshekar or with the Marxist school and its record of history distortion, they have no reason to mobilize (false!) rumours of Hindu nationalist connections against Prof. Kazanas.

For all their focusing on the all-purpose bogey of Hindu nationalism (or worse isms), it is remarkable that Indian Marxists and their Western disciples have completely failed to study this ideology. During my Ph.D. research on this very topic (vide Elst 2001/1), I found that practically all secondary publications in the field, including some influential ones (e.g. Pandey 1993, McKean 1996, more recently Hansen 1999), dispensed almost completely with the reading of primary sources. Typically, a few embarrassing quotations, selected by Indian critics of Hindutva from some old pamphlets (mostly Golwalkar 1939), are repeated endlessly and in unabashedly polemical fashion. A shameful example of the total reliance of Western scholars on outright partisan secondary Indian sources while passing judgment on a Hindu nationalist position was the Ayodhya temple/mosque dispute, as I discussed in detail in Elst 2002.

Until the late 1980s, there was a complete consensus among all Hindu, Muslim and Western sources about the fact that the mosque had been built in forcible replacement of a temple, a very common occurrence throughout Muslim-conquered territories. This consensus, nowadays mischaracterized as the Hindu nationalist position, was since confirmed by new findings and remained strictly unchallenged by any counter-findings. Note indeed that all the official and unofficial argumentations against the temple limited themselves to downplaying the impact of some of the evidence for the temple, and never offered even one piece of positive testimony for an alternative scenario. Yet, the dominant Marxist circles decreed that there had never been a temple at the site and lambasted Western scholars who had earlier confirmed the consensus as handmaidens of Hindu fundamentalism, enough to send these scholars into prudent retirement from the Ayodhya debate, vide Van der Veer 1994:161. Lately the Marxists have had to swallow that maximalist position and revert to the more reasonable political position that temple demolitions of the past do not justify mosque demolitions in the present; but for more than a decade, their leaden dogma has stifled the history debate, viz. that the temple demolition was merely a "Hindu chauvinist fabrication". Those who stuck to the old consensus view, the one confirmed by the evidence, have had tons of mud thrown at them not just by Indian Marxists but by their Western dupes as well, e.g. Hansen 1999:262.

Not one of the latter ever took issue with the actual evidence, behaving instead as obedient soldiers carrying out and amplifying the Indian Marxist *ukase*. At the time of this writing, Indian archaeologists are digging up more Hindu religious artefacts from underneath the temple/mosque site, yet the *Financial Times* carries a long article extolling Romila Thapar and Irfan Habib, ridiculing the consensus view on Ayodhya along with the non-invasionist "myth", denouncing Ayodhya consensus representative K.S. Lal (conveniently dead and unable to defend himself), and bluffing about "all the evidence" disproving the Ayodhya temple's existence but not actually mentioning any of it. The same pattern, though less extreme, is in evidence concerning the specific involvement of declared Hindu nationalists in the Aryan invasion debate.

Their positions are systematically ignored or misrepresented, and false motives are attributed to them according to the accuser's convenience. A brazen-faced example is Thapar 1996:8, about the Vedic revivalist movement Arya Samaj, a social-reformist society founded in 1875 whose spokesmen incidentally also rejected the AIT: "The Arya Samaj was described by its followers as 'the society of the Aryan race'. The Aryas were the upper castes and the untouchables were excluded." In reality, the Arya Samaj made its mark in Indian history by working, often at great personal sacrifice, to undo the exclusion of the untouchables; and by redefining "Arya" as "Vedic", away from both its old Indian casteist and its new Western racist interpretation. As for the expression "society of the Aryan race", while I am unaware of its application to the Arya Samaj specifically, it is true that around the turn of the 20th century, the expression "Aryan race" was fairly commonly used by Indian nationalists in the sense of "Indian nation", neither more nor less.

Romila Thapar's use of "Aryan" cited above, by contrast, is a transparent attempt to play on its post-Nazi connotations, as if its meaning hadn't radically changed at some dramatic point between 1875 and 1996. And yet, Romila Thapar remains the most celebrated Indian historian among Western India-watchers, a status recently confirmed by her honorary doctorate at the Sorbonne. In the *laudatio,* the authorities of France's most prestigious university repeated the well-known Indian Marxist rhetoric against "saffronization", with the unusual extra of specifically denouncing the French pro-Indian journalist Franois Gautier, a well-known critic of the AIT (1996). Nobody took the trouble to verify the criticisms rose against the scholarly performance of the honorary doctor.

If we want to know about Hindu nationalist involvement in the Aryan invasion debate, the Indian Marxist School and its Western spokesmen cannot help us. The one extant critical review of the various Hindu nationalist positions regarding the Aryan problem was written by Shrikant Talageri, ironically but significantly a declared Hindu nationalist himself. The following much briefer review is indebted to his input.

ACCEPTANCE OF THE AIT

A number of Hindu nationalists have accepted the AIT. Most prominent among them is Hindu nationalist seed ideologue Vinayak Damodar Savarkar. In his influential booklet Hindutva ("Hinduness"), he wrote of how migrations had "welded Aryans and non-Aryans into a common race" (1923:8) and how "not even the aborigines of the Andamans are without some sprinkling of the so-called Aryan blood in their veins and vice-versa" (1923:56). This way, he rejected the divisive implication of the AIT that India was composed of several distinct nations, arguing instead that they had biologically mingled and culturally fused into a single Hindu nation. Like his leftist opponent Jawaharlal Nehru, he accepted that the nation was a product of historical processes, not an age-old God-given essence. There is no organic link between Savarkar's positions on nationalism and ancient history: as a non-specialist, he merely accepted the dominant paradigm and tried to accommodate it into his political views. But note at any rate, all you who identify OIT with Hindutva, that the founder of the Hindutva ideology was an AIT believer.

Sharply to be distinguished from Hindu nationalists, who are modernists and social reformers for the sake of national unity, there is also a dwindling school of Hindu traditionalist. Among them, you find pandits who are steeped in Sanskritic lore and have never even heard of an Aryan invasion, which is after all unattested in Vedic literature. The one traditionalist who must be mentioned here as accepting the AIT was a Western "honorary Hindu", the French musicologist Alain Danilou (1971, 1975), companion of the traditionalist leader Swami Karpatri. Here again, there is no organic link between his Hindu-traditionalist view of society and his historical beliefs, which were borrowed wholesale from the dominant Western school of thought.

The most well-known Hindu nationalist to actively support the AIT and explore its implications was Bal Gangadhar Tilak, an Indian National Congress leader in the early 20th century. His chronology, worked out in dialogue with Hermann Jacobi (and still upheld by archaeo-astronomers, e.g. Kak 2003), was sharply incompatible with the currently dominant theory: he put the Rig-Veda ca. 4000 BC rather than 1500 BC. If the Vedas were that old, the invasion would have to be pushed back accordingly, as the Vedic geographical setting is obviously South-Asian; but Tilak solved this problem by having the Vedic seers compose their hymns far outside India, in an Indo-European homeland situated in the Arctic region. Except for a handful of European rightist non-scholars, nobody takes this eccentric scenario seriously anymore, not even the Tilak loyalists in Maharashtrian Brahmin circles which happen to be the cradle of both the

Savarkarite and RSS-BJP strands within the Hindu nationalist movement. All the same, Tilak's acceptance of a version of the AIT again disproves the identification of the OIT with Hindu nationalism.

REJECTION OF THE AIT

Few among the Hindu nationalists have really studied the relevant evidence. Some even reject the whole notion of historical evidence as pertinent to this question. From Jaimini's *Mimns-Stra* (BCE) down to Arya Samaj founder Swami Dayananda's *Satyrtha Prakash* (ca. AD 1875), a school of Vedic scholars has believed that the Vedas were not a human creation, but were created by the Gods aeons ago and then revealed in complete form to the Vedic seers. Oddly, for people who held the Vedas in such awe, their theory flies in the face of the Vedic testimony itself: unlike the Quran, the Vedas never take the form of a statement by God addressing man. Instead, they take the form of hymns in which man is addressing the Gods. The names of the seers composing the hymns are also given, and they are put in a historical context, often with their mutual relations, genealogical kinship and faction feuds detailed in the texts themselves.

Moreover, a number of presumably historical events are described or eluded to, most famously the Battle of the Ten Kings. All this points to the historicity of the Vedas: they came about as a creation of human poetry in a specific society at a specific phase in its development. But Vedic enthusiasts like Dayananda and to a lesser extent Sri Aurobindo Ghose chose to disregard this information and reinterpreted all these mundane data as spiritual metaphor. Though they also happened to reject the invasion hypothesis, they excluded the Vedic information as possible source of evidence for their own indigenist position. Aurobindo's correct observation (1971:242-251) that the Vedas contain no mention of an Aryan invasion, thereby loses its force. After Aurobindo's death, his otherwise loyal secretary K.D. Sethna (1982, 1992) abandoned this position and started using Vedic data on material culture to argue the chronological precedence of Rig-Vedic over high

Harappan culture, e.g. that the Harappan cultivation of cotton goes unmentioned in the older Vedic layers so that its early-Harappan introduction must coincide with some mid-Vedic date. More perhaps than the archaeologists' acknowledged inability to discover any remains of an Aryan invasion, Sethna's theses truly were the opening shot in the Hindu nationalist mobilization against the AIT. Within the Aurobindo circle, this work was continued by Danino & Nahar 2000.

Since Sethna's publications, many Hindu authors of divergent levels of qualification have felt emboldened to contribute to the anti-invasionist argument. Some of them lose themselves in projects they are not up to, such as the decipherment of the Indus script, but in matters of textual interpretation and of matching archaeological and genetic data with cultural history, they are often better equipped than their invasionist opponents. Those who care to read this literature will notice how it belies its characterization by hostile commentators as "far-rightist" and the like. It actually taps into the discourse of anti-colonialism, anti-racism and anti-orientalism, which most Westerners would spontaneously describe as leftist. A lone Indian Marxist has also contributed to the anti-invasionist argument, predictably focusing on material and economic data suggesting Harappan-Aryan continuity, and thus upholding the more usual Third World Marxist tradition of anti-colonialism as opposed to the Indian card-carrying Marxists' championing of the colonial view of history.

The political instrumentalization of theories about Indo-European origins has yielded coalitions of strange bedfellows. On the side of the hypothesis of an Aryan invasion of India, we find old colonial apologists and race theorists and their marginalized successors in the contemporary West along with a broad alliance of anti-Hindu forces in India, most articulate among them the Christian missionaries and the Marxists who have dominated India's intellectual sector for the past several decades. This dominant school of thought has also carried along some prominent early votaries of Hindu nationalism. On the side of the non-invasionist or Aryan-indigenist hypothesis, we find long-dead European Romantics and a few contemporary Western India lovers, along with an anti-colonialist school of thought in India, mainly consisting of contemporary Hindu nationalists.

Obviously, among the subscribers to either view we also find scholars without any political axe to grind. And even in the writings of politically motivated authors, we do come across valid argumentations. Consequently, it is best to continue this research without getting sidetracked by the real or alleged or imagined political connotations of certain scholarly lines of argument.

7

Hindu Nationalism
Origins, Ideologies and Modern Myths

Hindu nationalism has been collectively referred to the expressions of social and political thought, based on the native spiritual and cultural traditions of India. Some scholars have argued that the term 'Hindu nationalism' which refers to the concept of 'Hindu Rashtra' is a simplistic translation and is better described by the term 'Hindu polity'- a belief that politics should be organized in accordance with the precepts of the Hindu scriptures and way of life. In its more extreme form, this takes the form of the promotion of a Hindu Rashtra (nation) in the Indian subcontinent. Hindu nationalism emerged in the late nineteenth century, accompanied by the emergence of religious reform organizations such as the Arya Samaj, founded in 1875. The Arya Samaj sought to counter a perceived threat to Hinduism from conversion to Islam, Christianity, and Sikhism.

Hinduism was seen as vulnerable because of its decentralized and non-hierarchical organization; its lack of a core of orthodox beliefs or practices; and because of the operation of the caste system, which imposed social stigma and economic constraints on many Hindus. This was accompanied by a belief that Muslim and British rulers of India had sought to undermine Hinduism, and promote conversion to Islam and Christianity. The Arya Samaj sought to combine the advocacy of a Hinduism based around ancient values alongside programmes of education, social reform, and the ritual of *shuddhi*, a purification ceremony which was used to reconvert people to Hinduism and to remove social stigma from the lower castes.

At first Hindu nationalism ran alongside the Indian Nationalist movement, with leaders such as B. G. Tilak (1856-1920) who was both an organizer of Hindu revivalist festivals and leader of the Congress. However, Congress's need to appeal to Indians of all religions led to tension with Hindu nationalists, particularly under the leadership of Gandhi, who believed that all religions were equally valid. The Hindu Mahasabha, formed in 1915, articulated a much more strident pro-Hindu agenda, aimed at developing centralized organization which would promote a cohesive Hindu doctrine, and countering political concessions given by the British to Muslims. The Hindu Mahasabha could not match the mass appeal of the Congress, and played a peripheral political role in the run-up to Independence.

Another Hindu nationalist organization, the Rashtriya Swayamsevak Sangh (RSS: National Volunteer Corps), founded in 1925, avoided direct involvement with politics, focusing on a programme of physical exercise, military drills, and Hindu teaching. The man who assassinated Gandhi was a member of both the RSS and Hindu Mahasabha, which tainted the reputation of both organizations. After Independence the Hindu nationalist parties struggled to compete with Congress, which often absorbed Hindu nationalist issues—such as the promotion of the Hindi language in the northern States and the prohibition of cow slaughter—into its own programme. With the decline of Congress, however, opportunities arose to develop a mass appeal. The Bharatiya Janata Party (BJP: Indian People's Party: formed 1980) was able to exploit a vernacular religious enthusiasm, partly fostered by the broadcast of two Hindu epics (the Mahabharata and Ramayana) on national TV, with the strong organizational base provided by close links with the RSS, which had by then developed a large membership. This brought electoral success in 1989, and a pivotal position in government formation. The BJP became involved with two often violent agitations in the early 1990s; over the attempt to extend reservations, and in the dispute over the destruction of a Muslim mosque (the Babri Masjid) in the town of Ayodhya. These events consolidated the BJP's support amongst the upper castes and devout Hindus, but alienated many others.

Electoral considerations have forced the BJP to temper its nationalist programme, and through successful coalition building the party's leader, A. B. Vajpayee, became Prime Minister in 1998. In power the party has been constrained in its ability to implement a Hindu nationalist agenda, although it carried out nuclear tests 1998 in a bid to assert Indian power in the region, has pursued an aggressive policy in Kashmir, and has attempted to influence the education system so as to promote the teaching of history in line with the Hindu nationalist agenda. After futher demonstrations in Ayodhya over the right of Hindus to build a temple on the site of the Babri Masjid in 2002, there were widespread riots in Gujarat targetting the Muslim population, which were seen by many to have been encouraged (or even orchestrated) by the incumbent BJP State government.

Outrage following this violence, which some commentators likened to ethnic cleansing against the Muslim population, destabilized the national government. It has further exposed the tension between a populist nationalist programme and the upholding of acceptable limits of tolerance and democratic behaviour. The native thought streams became highly relevant in the Indian history when they helped form a distinctive identity to the Indian polity and provided a basis for questioning colonialism. They inspired the freedom movements against the British rule based on armed struggle, coercive politics and non-violent protests. They also influenced social reform movements and economic thinking in India. The usage of the word 'Hindu' to describe the native polity of India have been found in the historical accounts of medieval India. These usages show that the word Hindu, until the early nineteenth century was emphasized by nativity rather than by religion.

Prominent among the South Indian rulers of the fourteenth century were the Sangama rulers of Vijayanagara empire who were hailed as 'Hinduraya suratrana', the best among the Hindu rulers The Sangama rulers were in constant conflict with the Sultanate of Bijapur, and this usage of the word 'Hindu' in the title, was obviously to distinguish them as native rulers as against the Sultans who were "perceived to be foreign in origin". It has been noted by Historians that "Hindus" did not conceive themselves as a religious unity in any sense except in opposition to foreign rule. For example, the early seventeenth-century Telugu work, 'Rayavachakamu', condemns the Muslim rulers for being foreign and barbarian and only rarely for specifically religious traits.

The other references include the glorification of the Chauhana heroes of Jalor as 'Hindu' by Padmanabha in his epic poem, Kanhadade-prabandha, which he composed in AD 1455. The Rajput ruler, Maha Rana Pratap became renowned with the title of 'hindu-kula-kamala-divakara' for his relentless fight against the Moguls. 'Hindavi Swarajya' (self rule of the natives) was how the rule of Shivaji, the most notable of the rulers of the seventeenth century was described. The usage of 'Hindavi' (translated as 'of Hindus' in Marathi) in 'Hindavi Swarajya' is considered to mean Indian Independence rather than the rule by a religious sect or a community.

HINDU RENAISSANCE IN THE LATE 19TH CENTURY

Many Hindu reform movements originated in the late nineteenth century. These movements led to the fresh interpretations of the ancient scriptures of *Upanishads* and Vedanta and also emphasized on social reform. The marked feature of these movements was that they countered the notion of western superiority and white supremacy propounded by the colonizers as a justification for British colonialism in India. This led to the upsurge of patriotic ideas that formed the cultural and an ideological basis for the freedom struggle in India.

BRAHMO SAMAJ

The Brahmo Samaj was one of the earliest Hindu renaissance movements in India under the British rule. It was started by a Bengali scholar, Ram Mohan Roy in 1828. Ram Mohan endeavored to create from the ancient Upanishadic texts, a vision of rationalist 'modern' India. Religiously he criticized idolatry and believed in a monotheistic religion devoid of any idolatry and religious customs. His major emphasis was social reform. He fought against caste discrimination and advocated equal rights for women. Although the Brahmos found favorable response from the British Government and the Westernized Indians, they were largely isolated from the larger Hindu society due to their intellectual Vedantic and Unitarian views. But their efforts to systematize Hindu spirituality based on rational and logical interpretation of the ancient Indian texts would be carried forward by other movements in Bengal and across India.

ARYA SAMAJ

Arya Samaj is considered one of the overarching Hindu renaissance movements of the late nineteenth century. Swami Dayananda, the founder of Arya Samaj, rejected idolatry, caste restriction and untouchability, child marriage and advocated equal status and opportunities for women. He opposed "Brahmanism" (which he believed had led to the corruption of the knowledge of Vedas) as much as he opposed Christianity and Islam. Although Arya Samaj was a social movement, many revolutionaries and political leaders of the Indian Independence movement like Ramprasad Bismil, Shyamji Krishnavarma, Bhai Paramanand and Lala Lajpat Rai were to be inspired by it.

SWAMI VIVEKANANDA

Another 19th century Hindu reformer was Swami Vivekananda. Vivekananda as a student was educated in contemporary Western thought. He joined Brahmo Samaj briefly before meeting Ramakrishna, who was a priest in the temple of the mother goddess Kali in Calcutta and who was to become his Guru. Vivekananda's major achievement was to ground Hindu spirituality in a systematic interpretation of Vedanta. This project started with Rajaram Mohan Roy of Brahmo Samaj and which had produced rational Hinduism was now combined with disciplines such as yoga and the concept of social service to attain perfection from the ascetic traditions in what Vivekananda called the "practical Vedanta". The practical side essentially included participation in social reform.

He made Hindu spirituality, intellectually available to the Westernized audience. His famous speech at the Parliament of World religions at Chicago in 1883, followed huge reception of his thought in the West and made him a celebrity in the West and subsequently in India too. A major element of Vivekananda's message was nationalist. He saw his effort very much in terms of a revitalization of the Hindu nation, which carried Hindu spirituality and which could counter Western materialism. The notions of White supremacy and Western superiority, strongly believed by the colonizers, were to be questioned based on Hindu spirituality. This kind of spiritual Hinduism was later carried forward by Mahatma Gandhi and Sarvepalli Radhakrishnan. It also became a main inspiration for the current brand of Hindu nationalism today. Historians have observed that this helped the nascent Independence movement with a distinct national identity and kept it from being the simple derivative function of European nationalisms.

SRI AUROBINDO

Sri Aurobindo was a nationalist and one of the first to embrace the idea of complete political independence for India. He was inspired by the writings of Swami Vivekananda and the novels of Bankim Chandra. He "based his claim for freedom for India on the inherent right to freedom, not on any charge of misgovernment or oppression". He believed that the primary requisite for national progress, national reform, is the free habit of free and healthy national thought and action and that it was impossible in a state of servitude. He was part of the revolutionary group Anushilan Samiti and was involved in armed struggle against the British In his brief political career spanning only four years, he led a delegation from Bengal to the Indian National Congress session of 1907 and contributed to the revolutionary newspaper Bande Mataram.

In 1910, he withdrew from political life and spent his remaining life doing spiritual exercises and writing. But his works kept inspiring revolutionaries and struggles for freedom, including the famous Chittagong Uprising. Both Swami Vivekananda and Sri Aurobindo are credited with having found the basis for a vision of freedom and glory for India in the spiritual richness and heritage of Hinduism.

INDEPENDENCE MOVEMENT

The influence of the Hindu renaissance movements was such that by the turn of the century, there was a confluence of ideas of the Hindu cultural nationalism with the ideas of Indian nationalism. Both could be spoken synonymous even by tendencies that were seemingly opposed to sectarian communalism and Hindu majoritism.The Hindu renaissance movements held considerable influence over the revolutionary movements against the British rule and formed the philosophical basis for the struggles and political movements that originated in the first decade of the twentieth century.

REVOLUTIONARY MOVEMENTS

ANUSHILAN SAMITI AND JUGANTAR

Anushilan Samiti was one of the prominent revolutionary movements in India in the early part of twentieth century. It was started as a cultural society in 1902, by Aurobindo and the followers of Bankim Chandra to propagate the teachings of the Bhagavad-Gita. But soon the Samiti had its goal to overthrow the British rule in India. Various branches of the Samiti sprung across India in the guise of suburban fitness clubs but secretly imparted arms training to its members with the implicit aim of using them against the British administration On April 30, 1908 at Muzaffarpur, two revolutionaries,

Khudiram Bose and Prafulla Chaki threw bombs at a British convoy aimed at British officer Kingsford. Both were arrested trying to flee. Aurobindo was also arrested on 2 May, 1908 and sent to Alipore jail. The report sent from Andrew Fraser, the then Lt Governor of Bengal to Lord Minto in England declared that although Sri Aurobindo came to Calcutta in 1906 as a Professor at the National College, "he has ever since been the principal advisor of the revolutionary party. It is of utmost importance to arrest his potential for mischief, for he is the prime mover and can easily set tools, one to replace another." But charges against Aurobindo were never proved and he was acquitted. Many members of the group faced charges and were transported and imprisoned for life. Others went into hiding.

In 1910, when, Aurobindo withdrew from political life and decided to live a life of renounciate, the Anushilan Samiti declined. One of the revolutionaries, Jatindra Das Mukherjee, who managed to escape the trial, started a group which would be called Jugantar. Jugantar continued with its armed struggle with the British, but the arrests of its key members and subsequent trials weakened its influence. Many of its members were imprisoned for life in the notorious Andaman Cellular jail.

INDIA HOUSE

A revolutionary movement was started by Shyamji Krishnavarma, a Sanskritist and an Arya Samajist, in London, under the name of India House in 1905. The brain behind this movement was said to be V D Savarkar. Krishnaverma also published a monthly "Indian Sociologist", where the idea of an armed struggle against the British was openly espoused. The movement had become well known for its activities in the Indian expatriates in London. When Gandhi visited London in 1909, he shared a platform with the revolutionaries where both the parties politely agreed to disagree, on the question of violent struggle against British and whether Ramayana justified such violence.

Gandhi, while admiring the "patriotism" of the young revolutionaries, had dissented vociferously from their violent blueprints for social change. In turn the revolutionaries disliked his adherence to constitutionalism and his close contacts with moderate leaders of Indian National Congress. Moreover they considered his method of "passive resistance" effeminate and humiliating. The India House had soon to face a closure following the assassination of Sir Curzon-Wyllie by the revolutionary Madan lal Dhingra, who was close to India House. Savarkar also faced charges and was transported. Shyamji Krishnaverma fled to Paris. India House gave formative support to ideas that were later formulated by Savarkar in his book named 'Hindutva'. Hindutva was to gain relevance in the run up to the Indian Independence and would also form the core to the political party named Hindu Mahasabha started by Savarkar.

INDIAN NATIONAL CONGRESS

"Lal-Bal-Pal"

"Lal-Bal-Pal" is the phrase that is used to refer to the three nationalist leaders Lala Lajpat Rai, Bal Gangadhar Tilak and Bipin Chandra Pal who held the sway over the Indian Nationalist movement and the freedom struggle in the early parts of twentieth century. Lala Lajpat Rai belonged to the northern province of Punjab. He was influenced greatly by the Arya Samaj and was part of the Hindu reform movement. He joined the Indian National Congress in 1888 and became a prominent figure in the Indian Independence Movement.

He started numerous educational institutions. The National College at Lahore started by him became the centre for revolutionary ideas and was the college where revolutionaries like Bhagat Singh studied. While leading a procession against the Simon Commission, he was fatally injured in the lathi charge by the British police. His death led the revolutionaries like Chandrashekar Azad and Bhagat Singh to kill the British officer J.P. Saunders, who they believed was responsible for the death of Lala Lajpat Rai.

Bal Gangadhar Tilak was a nationalist leader from the Central Indian province of Maharashtra. He has been widely acclaimed the "Father of Indian unrest" who used the press and Hindu occasions like Ganesha festivals and symbols like the Cow to create unrest against the British administration in India. Tilak joined the Indian National Congress in 1890. Under the influence of such leaders, the political discourse of the Congress moved from polite accusation that imperial rule was "un-British" to the forth right claim of Tilak that "Swaraj is my birthright and I will have it".

Bipin Chandra Pal of Bengal was another prominent figure of the Indian nationalist movement, who is considered a modern Hindu reformer, who stood for Hindu cultural nationalism and was opposed to sectarian communalism and Hindu majoritism. He joined the Indian National Congress in 1886 and was also one of the key members of revolutionary India House.

GANDHI AND RAMARAJYA

Though Gandhi never called him a "Hindu nationalist", he believed in and propagated concepts like Dharma and "Rama Rajya" (Rule of Lord Rama) as part of his social and political philosophy. Gandhiji said "By political independence I do not mean an imitation to the British House of commons, or the soviet rule of Russia or the Fascist rule of Italy or the Nazi rule of Germany. They have systems suited to their genius. We must have ours suited to ours. What that can be is more than I can tell. I have described it as Ramarajya i.e., sovereignty of the people based on pure moral authority.

He emphasized that "Rama Rajya" to him meant peace and justice. "Whether Rama of my imagination ever lived or not on this earth, the ancient ideal of Ramarajya is undoubtedly one of true democracy in which the meanest citizen could be sure of swift justice without an elaborate and costly procedure." He also emphasized that it meant respect for all religions "My Hinduism teaches me to respect all religions. In this lies the secret of Ramarajya." Madan Mohan Malviya, an educationist and a politician with the Indian National Congress was also a vociferous proponent of the philosophy of Bhagavad-Gita. He was the president of the Indian National Congress in the year 1909 and 1918. He was seen as a 'moderate' in the Congress and was also considered very close to Gandhi. He popularized the Sanskrit phrase "Satyameva Jayate" (Truth alone wins), which today is the national emblem of the Republic of India. He founded the Benaras Hindu University in 1919 and became its first Vice-Chancellor.

SUBHAS BOSE

Apart from Gandhi, revolutionary leader Netaji Subhas Chandra Bose referred to Vedanta and the *Bhagavad-Gita* as sources of inspiration for the struggle against the British. Swami Vivekananda's teachings on universalism, his nationalist thoughts and his emphasis on social service and reform had all inspired Subhas Chandra Bose from his very young days. The fresh interpretation of the India's ancient scriptures appealed immensely to Subhas. Hindu spirituality formed the essential part of his political and social thought through his adult life, although there was no sense of bigotry or orthodoxy in it.

Subhas who called himself a socialist, believed that socialism in India owed its origins to Swami Vivekananda. As historian Leonard Gordan explains "Inner religious explorations continued to be a part of his adult life. This set him apart from the slowly growing number of atheistic socialists and communists who dotted the Indian landscape." "Hinduism was an essential part of his Indianness". His strategy against the British too included the use of Hindu symbols and festivals. In 1925, while in Mandalay jail, he went on a hunger strike when Durga puja was not supported by prison authorities.

Another leader of prime importance in the ascent of Hindu nationalism was Dr K B Hedgewar of Nagpur. Hegdewar as a medical student in Calcutta had been part of the revolutionary activities of the Anushilan Samiti and Jugantar. He was charged with sedition in 1921 by the British Administration and served a year in prison. He was briefly a member of Indian National Congress. In 1925, he left the Congress to form the Rashtriya Swayamsevak Sangh, which would become the focal point of Hindu movements in Independent India.

After the formation of the RSS too, Hedgewar was to take part in the Indian National Congress led movements against the British rule. He joined the Jungle Satyagraha agitation in 1931 and served a second term in prison. The Rashtriya Swayamsevak Sangh started by him became one of the most prominent Hindu organizations with its influence ranging in the social and political spheres of India.

PARTITION OF INDIA

The Partition of India outraged many majority Hindu nationalist politicians and social groups. Savarkar and members of the Hindu Mahasabha were extremely critical of Gandhi's leadership. They accused him of appeasing the Muslims to preserve a unity that in their opinion did not exist; Savarkar endorsed the concept of the Two-nation theory while disagreeing with it in practice. Some Hindu nationalists also blamed Gandhi for conceding Pakistan to the Muslim League via appeasement. And they were further inflamed when Gandhi conducted a fast-unto-death for the Indian government to give Rs. 55 crores which were due to the Pakistan government, but were being held back due to the Indo-Pakistani War of 1947.

After the assassination of Mahatma Gandhi by Nathuram Godse, the Sangh Parivar was plunged into distress when the RSS was accused of involvement in his murder. Along with the conspirators and the assassin, Vinayak Damodar Savarkar was also arrested. The Court acquitted Savarkar, and the RSS was found be to completely unlinked with the conspirators. The Hindu Mahasabha, of which Godse was a member, lost membership and popularity. The effects of public outrage had a permanent effect on the Hindu Mahasabha, which is now a defunct Hindutva party.

EVOLUTION OF IDEOLOGICAL TERMINOLOGY

The word 'Hindu', throughout the history, had been used as an inclusive description which lacked a definition and was used to refer to the native traditions and people of India. It was only in late eighteenth century that the word 'Hindu' came to be used extensively with religious connotation, while still being used as a synecdoche describing the indigenuous traditions.

HINDUTVA AND HINDU RASHTRA

SAVARKAR

Savarkar was one of the first in the twentieth century to attempt a definitive description of the term 'Hindu' in terms of what he called Hindutva meaning Hinduness. The coinage of the term 'Hindutva' was an attempt by Savarkar who was an atheist and a rationalist, to delink it from any religious connotations that had become attached to it. He defined the word Hindu as "He who considers India as both his Fatherland and Holyland". He thus defined Hindutva ("Hindu-ness") or Hindu as different from Hinduism. This definition kept the Abrahamic religions (Christianity and Islam) outside its ambit and considered only native religious denominations as Hindu.

This distinction was emphasized on the basis of territorial loyalty rather than on the religious practices. In this book that was written in the backdrop of the Khilafat Movement and the subsequent Moplah riots, Savarkar wrote "Their (Muslims' and Christians') holy land is far off in Arabia or Palestine. Their mythology and Godmen, ideas and heroes are not the children of this soil. Consequently their names and their outlook smack of foreign origin. Their love is divided". Savarkar also defined the concept of Hindu Rashtra (translated as "Hindu polity"). The concept of Hindu Polity called for the protection of Hindu people and their culture and emphasized that political and economic systems should be based on native thought rather than on the concepts borrowed from the West.

GOLWALKAR

M S Golwalkar, the second head of the Rashtriya Swayamsevak Sangh, was to further this non-religious, territorial loyalty based definition of 'Hindu' in his book 'Bunch of thoughts'. 'Hindutva' and 'Hindu Rashtra' would form the basis of Golwalkar's ideology and that of the Rashtriya Swayamsevak Sangh. While emphasizing on religious pluralism, Golwalkar believed that Semitic monotheism and exclusivism were incompatible with and against the native Hindu culture. He wrote "Those creeds (Islam and Christianity) have but one prophet, one scripture and one God, other than whom there is no path of salvation for the human soul.

It requires no great intelligence to see the absurdity of such a proposition". He added "As far as the national tradition of this land is concerned, it never considers that with a change in the method of worship, an individual ceases to be the son of the soil and should be treated as an alien. Here, in this land, there can be no objection to God being called by any name whatever. Ingrained in this soil is love and respect for all faiths and religious beliefs. He cannot be a son of this soil at all who is intolerant of other faiths."

He further would echo the views of Savarkar on territorial loyalty, but wifh a degree of inclusiveness, when he wrote "So, all that is expected of our Muslim and Christen co-citizens is the shedding of the notions of their being 'religious minorities' as also their foreign mental complexion and merging themselves in the common national stream of this soil."

CONTEMPORARY DESCRIPTIONS

Later thinkers of the RSS, like H V Sheshadri and K S Rao, were to emphasize on the non theocratic nature of the word "Hindu Rashtra", which they believed was often inadequately translated, ill interpreted and wrongly stereotyped as a theocratic state. In a book by H.V. Sheshadri, the senior leader of the RSS writes "As Hindu Rashtra is not a religious concept; it is also not a political concept. It is generally misinterpreted as a theocratic state or a religious Hindu state. Nation (Rashtra) and State (Rajya) are entirely different and should never be mixed up. State is purely a political concept.... The State changes as the political authority shifts from person to person or party to party. But the people in the Nation remain the same.. They would maintain that the concept of Hindu Rashtra is in complete agreement with the principles of secularism and democracy. The concept of 'Hindutva' is continued to be espoused by the organizations like the Rashtriya Swayamsevak Sangh and political parties like the Bharatiya Janata Party. But the definition, does not have the same rigidity with respect to the concept of 'holy land' laid down by Savarkar, and stresses on inclusivism and patriotism.

BJP leader and the then leader of opposition, Atal Behari Vajpayee, in 1998, articulated the concept of 'holy land' in Hindutva as follows "Mecca can continue to be holy for the Muslims but India should be holier than the holy for them. You can go to a mosque and offer namaz, you can keep the roza. We have no problem. But if you have to choose between Mecca or Islam and India you must choose India. All the Muslims should have this feeling: we will live and die only for this country." In 1995, in a landmark judgment the Supreme Court of India observed that "Ordinarily, Hindutva is understood as a way of life or a state of mind and is not to be equated with or understood as religious Hindu fundamentalism. A Hindu may embrace a non-Hindu religion without ceasing to be a Hindu and since the Hindu is disposed to think synthetically and to regard other forms of worship, strange gods and divergent doctrines as inadequate rather than wrong or objectionable, he tends to believe that the highest divine powers complement each other for the well-being of the world and mankind."

POST-INDEPENDENCE MOVEMENTS

SOMNATH TEMPLE MOVEMENT

The Somnath temple is an ancient temple at Prabhas Patan in the coastal Indian province of Gujarat, which had been destroyed several times by the foreign invaders, starting with Mahmood Ghaznavi in 1025 AD. The last of such destructions took place in 1706 AD when Prince Mohammad Azam carried out the orders of Moghul ruler Aurangzeb to destroy the temple of Somnath beyond possible repair. A small mosque was put in its place. Before Independence, Prabhas Pattan where Somnath is located was part of the Junagarh State, ruled by the Nawab of Junagarh.

On the eve of Independence the Nawab announced the accession of Junagarh, which had over 80% Hindu population, to Pakistan. The people of Junagarh rose in revolt and set up a parallel government under Gandhian leader and freedom fighter, Shri Samaldas Gandhi. The Nawab, unable to resist the popular pressure, bowed out and escaped to Pakistan. The provincial government under Samaldas Gandhi formally asked Government of India to take over. The Deputy Prime Minister of India, Sardar Vallabhai Patel came to Junagadh on November 12, 1947 to direct the occupation of the state by the Indian army and at the same time ordered the reconstruction of the Somanath temple.

When Sardar Patel, K M Munshi and other leaders of the Congress went to Gandhiji with the proposal of reconstructing the Somnath temple, Gandhiji blessed the move, but suggested that the funds for the construction should be collected from the public and the temple should not be funded by the state. He expressed that he was proud to associate himself to the project of renovation of the temple But soon both Gandhiji and Sardar Patel passed away and the task of reconstruction of the temple was now continued under the leadership of K M Munshi, who was the Minister for Food and Civil, supplies in the Nehru Government.

The ruins were pulled down in October 1950 and the mosque was moved to a different location. In May 1951, Rajendra Prasad, the first President of the Republic of India, invited by K M Munshi, performed the installation ceremony for the temple Rajendra Prasad said in his address "It is my view that the reconstruction of the Somnath Temple will be complete on that day when not only a magnificent edifice will arise on this foundation, but the mansion of India's prosperity will be really that prosperity of which the ancient temple of Somnath was a symbol."

He added "The Somnath temple signifies that the power of reconstruction is always greater than the power of destruction"· This episode created a serious rift between the then Prime Minister Jawaharlal Nehru, who saw in movement for reconstruction of the temple an attempt at Hindu revivalism and the President Rajendra Prasad and Union Minister K M Munshi, saw in its reconstruction, the fruits of freedom and the reversal of injustice done to Hindus.

THE EMERGENCE OF THE SANGH PARIVAR

The Rashtriya Swayamsevak Sangh, which was started in 1925, had grown as a huge organisation by the end of British rule in India. But the assasination of Gandhi and a subsequent ban on the organisation plunged it into distress. The ban was revoked when it was absolved of the charges and it led to the resumtion of its activities. The 1960s saw the volunteers of the RSS join the different social and political movements. Movements that saw a large presence of volunteers included the Bhoodan, a land reform movement led by prominent Gandhian Vinodha Bhave and the Sarvoday led by another Gandhian Jayaprakash Narayan. RSS supported trade union, the Bharatiya Mazdoor Sangh and political party Bharatiya Jana Sangh also grew into considerable prominence by the end of the decade. Another prominent development was the formation of the Vishwa Hindu Parishad, an organisation of Hindu religious leaders, supported by the RSS, with the aim of uniting the various Hindu religious denominations and to usher social reform.

The first VHP meet at Mumbai was attended among others by all the Shankaracharyas, Jain leaders, Sikh leader Master Tara Singh, the Dalai Lama and contemporary Hindu leaders like Swami Chinmayananda. From its initial years, the VHP led a concerted attack on the social evil of untouchability and casteism while launching social welfare programmes in the areas of education and health care, especially for the Scheduled Castes, backward classes and the tribals. The organisations started and supported by the RSS volunteers came to be known collectively as the Sangh Parivar. Next few decades saw a steady growth of the influence of the Sangh Parivar in the social and political space of India.

8

The Concept of Hindu Nation

There has been lot of discussion about the nation-state in the 20th century and yet there is no unanimity of views on this controversial subject. The concept of nation-state becomes all the more controversial in a country which lacks religious, cultural and linguistic homogeneity. The classical nation-state came into existence in Europe on the basis of a shared linguistic and cultural heritage and future economic vision. That was not the case in colonised countries in Asia and Africa. The colonial powers did not establish their empires in religiously and linguistically homogeneous areas but wherever they could capture power. These administratively-unified areas became a nation-state when the colonial masters left.

In India, severe conflict took place over the concept of nation-state when the colonial power was about to leave. The Muslim League, which claimed to be the sole representative of the Indian Muslims, rejected the concept of composite nationalism and advanced the theory of religious nationalism. In fact, the idea of religious nationalism was mooted for the first time on the Indian subcontinent. Till then, nationalism was associated with shared history, culture, language and ethnicity. And, the theory of religious nationalism was advanced by the secular elite of the Muslim community and not by its religious leadership.

The two-nation theory was born more out of political considerations than religion. It was result of competition for power between the secular elites of the two communities rather than justified by the theology of Islam or Hinduism. The Muslim religious leaders opposed the theory and justified composite nationalism on religious ground. Territory and not religion forms the basis of nationalism, they argued. The most articulate theorist among those who rejected religious nationalism was Maulana Husain Ahmad Madani of the Deoband School. Among Hindus too it was not the religious leadership which justified the two-nation theory but the 'secular' leadership led by Savarkar and others. Neither the Muslim League nor the Hindu Mahasabha was a religious party.

The leaders of Hindu Mahasabha agreed with Jinnah and his Muslim League that Hindus and Muslims were two different 'nations'. It is a different thing that the Hindu Mahasabha, unlike the Muslim League, did not demand partition. It stood for "Akhand Bharat" under Hindu hegemony. The theory of religious nationalism has been thoroughly discredited. Maulana Husain Ahmad Madani was well aware of the problems and he raised them in his seminal book "Muttahida Qaumiyyat aur Islam" (Composite Nationalism and Islam). There are several Muslim nations today in the post-colonial world. If Islam was to be the basis of nationalism, there should have been only one nation.

It is territorially impossible, one can argue, there being no contiguity. Even if this argument is theoretically accepted, the question arises: why don't countries which have territorial contiguity - Pakistan, Afghanistan, Iran and several of the central Asian nations, and several Arab countries - merge into one nation? No Muslim country will ever take such an idea seriously. An attempt was made during Nasser's time to merge Egypt, Syria and Libya and create a United Arab Republic in the early Seventies. Though all three were overwhelmingly Muslim and Arab countries the union did not last more than a couple of years, though even the language (Arabic) was the same. When the Saudi King objected to Nasser's use of the term 'Arab nationalism', and suggested instead 'Islamic Umma', Nasser asked what was common between an Arab Muslim and an Indonesian Muslim except for religion. How could they come together politically? The question of identity is of primary importance in the formation of a nation. What then is the basis of identity? Identity, most commonly, is based on a shared sense of history, culture and language. Religion may or may not be common. Religion alone cannot provide a viable and cohesive base for common nationalism. In the classical European model too, though Christianity was a common factor Europe was divided into different nations on linguistic and cultural basis. Thus in the formation of a nation a common language, culture and a sense of a shared history play quite an important role. In the case of Malaysia, Malay nationalism, apart from Islam, plays an important role. Malay identity to them is as important as their religious identity. In fact, it is difficult to make a distinction between their Malay and Islamic identities.

This identity is unique to them which they cannot share with other Muslims in Malaysia or elsewhere. There is non-Malay Muslims in Malaysia. They are of Indian origin but they have a very different sense of identity from the Malay Muslims. Malaysia is a pluralist country like India. There are Chinese, non-Malay Muslims, Christians and Hindus. Malay Muslims constitute the largest group at 45 per cent. The Chinese are about 37 per cent. The Malay Muslims, unlike the majority Hindus in India, are socially, educationally and economically a highly deprived group.

It is the Chinese who are educationally and economically dominant. The Malay Muslims organised under the banner of Malay Islam and fought for their rights. They came mostly from rural areas. The revivalist movement represented the aspirations of these rural Malay Muslims. The revivalist movement could easily be co-opted by the state by giving concessions to Malay Muslims. Thus Malaysian Islam has its own unique cultural characteristics and Malay nationalism does not share a sense of common cultural and historical heritage with other Muslims in or outside Malaysia. Indonesian Islam has again its own unique cultural and historical characteristics. Hinduism was a dominant force in Indonesia during the early medieval period and hence there is greater impact of Hinduism on Indonesian Islam, particularly Javanese Islam. Bhasa Indonesia has several words of Sanskrit origin and Hindu names such as Sinta (Sita) and Lakshmi are quite common among the Muslims in Indonesia. Similarly names such as Ram and Vishnu are common among Muslim men. Indoneisa's President, Mr. Abdurrahman Wahid, once told me at a seminar in Jogjakarta that the greatest preacher of Islam in Indonesia was one Maulana Vishnu. These are unique socio-cultural characteristics of Islam in different countries and Muslims and non-Muslims in these countries have a shared sense of culture and history; and it this which imparts them a common sense of national identity.

All these examples clearly bring out the fact that political unity and the sense of a common nationhood need not depend on religious unity but on political, historical and cultural factors. Religious nationalism is not a viable category as the same religion can be, and often is, embraced by different racial, ethnic and cultural groups. Religion, it should be remembered, is a spiritual and moral category whereas nationalism is a political-cum-territorial category. The two should not be confused. A composite culture can be a more viable base for nationalism than religion alone. Religion provides for a common spiritual experience and shared moral and ethical vision whereas nationalism provides for shared political concerns, cultural practices and historical heritage.

South Asia had such a common heritage. Its division was brought about by extraneous factors such as British imperial policies rather than by differences of religion. A South Asian confederation is a must for this region to usher in peace and prosperity. The Sangh Parivar has taken another step towards demarcating the nation as Hindu. So far the attempt has been to stigmatise Muslims as alien and anti-national and thus to exclude them from the nation. Now the net has been extended to include Christians also. Many people are surprised by the sudden attack on this peaceful, small community, with a low profile in politics and hence of no threat to the Parivar. What is really surprising, however, is that it has taken so long in coming. For Guru Golwalkar he had bracketed Christians with

Muslims and Communists as anti-national. His disciples are now implementing his teachings through violent means.

The last one year has witnessed well over a hundred incidents of attack on the person and property of Christians. The attacks are not incidental to communal conflicts to which Christians are a party, but are unprovoked physical attacks and arson and intimidation by the stormtroopers of the Sangh Parivar. They are all criminal acts perpetrated under the political patronage of the Bharatiya Janata Party. Missionaries have been stripped naked and paraded through the streets, even burnt alive, nuns have been gang-raped, churches have been razed to the ground and the Bible and other religious literature have been burnt. The heightened animosity and violence against Christians coincides with the rule of the BJP at the Centre. Prior to the incidence of violence against Christians was relatively low. It is estimated that over a period of 32 years, from 1964 to 1996, there were only 38 instances of violence against Christians. Even in 1997, not more than 15 instances were reported. Apart from the increase in their numbers, the area of incidence of such attacks is also suggestive: most of the attacks have occurred in States ruled by either the BJP or its allies - Gujarat, Maharashtra, Uttar Pradesh and Haryana. That in none of these States governments gave adequate protection to the victims perhaps accounts for the increase in their incidence.

Instead of taking stern action, BJP leaders have either rationalised or justified what the cadres of the Parivar did. In Gujarat, where the attacks against Christians have been intense and continuous, conversions have been invoked as a reason by none other than the Chief Minister himself, suggesting thereby that Christians themselves are to be blamed for inviting the wrath of Hindus. A senior functionary of the BJP justified even rape as a reaction to conversions. The response of Prime Minister A.B. Vajpayee, who is considered a good man and a liberal by many, was the most devious. By calling for a public debate on conversions, he suggests that the blame, in fact, rests with the victims. His move is a veiled threat to individual freedom, guaranteed in the Constitution after extended discussion in the Constituent Assembly. The freedom of conscience and the right to propagate it, be it of religious faith or of atheism, cannot be dissociated from the rights of the citizen in a democracy. The freedom, it is said, is indivisible. Are conversions the real issue? Or is it only a surrogate for advancing the Hindutva agenda?

Christianity in India has a history of about 2,000 years. Beginning almost at the time of its inception, Christian missionaries have spared no effort to "save the souls of the idolatrous, superstitious Hindus". They set up their missions, churches, seminaries and schools whenever and wherever they could gain a foothold. The missionaries learnt Indian languages, set up printing presses and published literature - both secular and religious - to propagate their faith. That in the process they contributed to the enrichment of Indian languages - in several Indian languages, the first codes of grammar were composed by missionaries - is a different matter. The missionaries used the public space to communicate the principles of their "superior" religion and at the same time to "expose the faults and foibles of Hinduism."

Yet there were no Crusades in India - not even what happened in China in the 19th century when missionaries were attacked and driven out from the interior. Hinduism responded in an entirely different manner. Instead of violence and coercion, the claims of the missionaries about their religion and their denigration of Hinduism were challenged through public debates. Theological disputations were integral to the intellectual life of India from very early times. It greatly contributed to the enrichment of its epistemological tradition. Such dialogues took place between members of all denominations - Buddhists, Jains, Christians, Muslims and Hindus. Quite often the rulers provided the platform for such debates.

The Hindu-Christian debates have been theologically quite productive. In the 16th century, continuous disputations took place between Hindu pundits and Portuguese friars. When John Wilson, a missionary of great erudition and scholarship, was pursuing his evangelical work in western

India, a Hindu intellectual, Vishnu Bawa Brahmachari, refuted his arguments against Hinduism at weekly public meetings at Chowpathy in Mumbai, following which a public debate was organised between him and some missionaries. If the pamphleteering of the 19th century is any indication, such exchanges took place between members of other communities also. For instance, in Malabar, Makti Tangal countered the arguments of the missionaries in several of his writings.

Indian rulers have generally adopted an impartial attitude in inter-religious relations. Not that they have not patronised their co-religionists or constructed shrines of their faith: the examples of such pursuits are aplenty from the times of Asoka to the 19th century. But lending support to the persecution of followers of other religions has been rather rare. There are exceptions though, as in the case of the Cholas, the Huns and the Sungas in early history, some Muslim rulers during the medieval period and the Portuguese in more recent times. But the general attitude is exemplified by what Maharaja Ranjit Singh said to one of his Ministers who happened to be a Muslim.

A fakir brought to his court a copy of the Koran, which the Maharaja acquired by offering a large sum. When asked by his Minister as to why he, a Sikh, had done so, the Maharaja, known for his wit and wisdom, reasoned that God had given him only one eye so that he could look upon all religions without discrimination. The colonial rulers, influenced more by expediency than by principles, chose to desist from interfering in religious matters. Until 1813, the East India Company kept Christian missionaries away from its territories. Several British officials, however, believed that Christianisation was both a religious and a political solution, as it was likely to ensure the permanence of the Empire. As a result, whether to Christianise or not was a widely debated issue.

In the aftermath of the Revolt of 1857 - seen by many as a response to British interference in social and religious matters - the colonial rulers reaffirmed the policy of non-interference. The colonial state was not a major player in evangelisation, although a nexus between officials and missionaries did exist in certain areas without receiving official approbation. No mass conversions to Christianity took place under the aegis of the colonial rulers. State patronage was not a decisive factor in conversions. At any rate, conversion is a complex matter. Richard M. Eaton, in an excellent study, *The Rise of Islam and the Bengal Frontier*, pointed out the inadequacies of the existing theories of Islamisation, including those of patronage and social liberation. His contention that the spread of Islam in Bengal was as a religion of the plough is fascinating.

Yet it is true that conversions to both Islam and Christianity have been from the lower caste orders. The increase in the population of the Mappilas (in Malabar) in the 19th century is a telling example. The increase took place from the middle of the century after the abolition of slavery in Malabar, which is now part of northern Kerala. Many of the agrestic slaves freed from their bondage opted for Islam. Mass conversions have often been of a caste as a whole for which the internally oppressive system of Hinduism has been responsible, rather than any external agency. Rather than looking for scapegoats from other communities, Hindu leaders should learn to look inward.

After 2,000 years of Christian presence and almost 200 years of Christian rule, the progress of Christianity in India has not been very substantial. The community is still tiny. The Census of 1991 records the number of its followers at 2.4 per cent of the total population. Nor have they increased in number during the last decade; in fact, their strength has relatively declined from 2.6 per cent in 1981. The missionary efforts at evangelisation obviously have not met with great success. If so, there is hardly any substance in the present hue and cry about conversions being a great threat to Hindus. What is at stake is not religion, but political power. Demarcating Hindus politically and culturally from other denominations is central to the politics of the Parivar. That is the essence of cultural nationalism which provides the ideological basis of Hindu communalism. So far this demarcation was pursued through a hate campaign as well as violence against Muslims. A stage has come when it has become necessary to expand the scope of the enemy, for two reasons. First, the possible political advantage from representing Muslims as alien and anti-national has run out of steam. Secondly, since 1992, Muslims in different parts of the country have shown that they are capable of retaliation. The lessons of the bomb blasts in Mumbai, Chennai, Coimbatore and Kerala are not lost on the Parivar: violence and aggression are nobody's monopoly. Home Minister L.K. Advani, who exudes communal hatred, on the one hand and distributes awards for communal harmony on the other, narrowly escaped being hurt in Coimbatore. Muslim-bashing is not easy any longer. Yet it is necessary to privilege the Hindu, in contrast to the alien other, hence the focus on Christians.

The aggression against Christians is incidental also to the need to expand the electoral base of the BJP. Middle class-upper-caste support is inadequate to gain a majority in Parliament, as was evident from the elections of 1996 and 1998. In the quest to expand its electoral support base, the minorities and, to some extent, the lower castes are out of the reckoning. A group that can be possibly considered is tribal communities, among whom the Parivar has already initiated some work. After the BJP came to power, tribal communities are being wooed with promises of statehood to some areas where they are predominant. But the Parivar has to contend with the influence of Christians in the tribal areas where the missionaries and charity organisations have been active in educational and developmental work.

The tribal communities can be brought to the Parivar's fold only by undermining the Christian influence. The outcry against conversions, as is happening in Dangs, is a result of this. Invoking Christian conversion as an issue is amusing since most of those who belong to tribal communities are not Hindus and their religious practices are not even remotely connected with any form of Hinduism. If Christians are accused of conversions, the Vishwa Hindu Parishad can also be accused of doing exactly the same thing. The latter is no less reprehensible than the former. In fact, in the 19th century, several tribal revolts were reactions to Hindu intrusion into their way of life. Both the missionaries and the VHP are in effect endangering the traditional religious practices of tribal people. Another field in which Christians constitute a hurdle to the Parivar's march is education. The Parivar, conscious of the ideological importance of education, has set up about 20,000 schools under different denominations and is poised to form a parallel system. The Ministry of Human Resource Development, under the control of two Rashtriya Swayamsevak Sangh (RSS) stalwarts, is queering the pitch for it. In a bid to facilitate the expansion of the Parivar school network, Human Resource Development Minister Murli Manohar Joshi recently proposed an amendment to the Constitution so as to extend to all other the privileges so far enjoyed by the minorities.

He also tried to give some legitimacy to the parallel system by inviting the manager of one of the RSS organisations to present a scheme of education, at a meeting of State Education Ministers. Unless Christian educational institutions, which generally enjoy a very good reputation for maintaining teaching standards, are discredited and displaced, the Parivar will find it difficult to advance its network and hence attack on these institutions in the name of abetting conversions. Apart from all these, since the demolition of the Babri Masjid, Christian organisations and institutions have taken some initiatives to promote secularism and to oppose communalism.

They have held workshops, conducted studies and generally promoted activities aimed to sensitise people about secular values. This has understandably enraged the Parivar, particularly the lumpen sections within it, both political and intellectual, which are out to teach Christians a lesson. While the BJP ideologue and eminent journalist Arun Shourie "unmasks" missionaries in his articles and books, the Bajrang Dal strips them naked in the streets and burns them alive.

The anti-Christian tirade is, therefore, not accidental. It is another example of the unfolding of the fascist agenda of the Parivar. That the BJP leadership, including the Prime Minister, has not unequivocally condemned it is reflective of its tacit acquiescence. Christians have been identified as another enemy, a new symbol, to demarcate the nation further as Hindu. The attack on Christians is therefore not a simple law and order issue, as some allies of the BJP seem to believe. It is a profoundly political question which can be overlooked only at great peril to the Indian Republic.

"The concept of Hindu Rashtra is absolutely different from what is known as a theocratic state, like, say, Pakistan or a Vatican... Hindu Rashtra is a geo-cultural concept," says, *The Organiser's* editor, Mr. Seshadri Chari.

The RSS' stand on several issues is articulated by Mr. Seshadri Chari, Editor of the Sangh's mouthpiece, The Organiser, in answering some questions:

Question: What is the main aim and ideology of the RSS?

Seshadri Chari: Founded in 1925 by Dr. Keshav Baliram Hedgewar, a leading figure in the then Congress movement which was spearheading the freedom struggle, the Rashtriya Swayamsevak Sangh (RSS) aims at organising Hindu society as one strong, indivisible entity to achieve all round development of the country. The Sangh believes that dharma and 'sanskriti' (our uninterrupted cultural heritage) form the bedrock of our ancient civilisation which is in the process of continuous evolution. Hindutva has a world vision and the Hindu society has a world mission.

The RSS has always held that the problems encountered by a society can best be solved by the people themselves, who when well organised become a source of strength for the good of society. With a view to finding solutions to various problems, 'swayamsevaks' are encouraged if they start new institutions or join an existing one. Naturally, these organisations are autonomous; they have a constitution of their own, and are not affiliated to the RSS. But the persons working in such organisations do continue to derive inspiration from the RSS and imbibe qualities of dedication, hard work and integrity from the RSS. The BJP is one such organisation in the political field. RSS does not consider politics as the be all and end all of all human endeavours.

Mr. K. S. Sudarshan is 'Sah Sarkaryavah' (joint general secretary) of the RSS. Senior functionaries are generally expected to offer guidance to various organisations and their workers who approach the RSS for assistance. There is, therefore, nothing like somebody being "in-charge of the BJP". Does the RSS see the BJP as the political party of its choice? Is the BJP the preferred instrument for societal change levered from the top? It is the western view that politics is the only medium to bring about change in society. Political parties and their ideologies and institutions have therefore assumed great importance in the West. In the East, particularly in the light of Hindu thought, politics is only one aspect of social life.

The RSS considers the individual to be an effective instrument of change in society and united efforts of a group of such individuals is alone the guarantee for change in society. The BJP is striving to bring about a change in society in its own way. Not all 'swayamsevaks' take the pledge (pratijna). The pledge enables the 'swayamsevak' to remember his pious resolve at all junctures in his later life. Does the RSS agree or disagree with the thesis propounded by Savarkar and re-emphasised by Golwalkar that only those who are born here and consider India to be their 'janmabhoomi' and 'pitrubhoomi' (fatherland) as well as their 'punyabhoomi' (holy land) constitute the Indian nation? Savarkar's thought as explained in his own works like "Hindutva" cannot be said to have been elaborately analysed by the RSS. In the course of his speeches and writings, Shri Guruji (M. S. Golwalkar) is likely to have found it generally in agreement with his own concept of a Hindu nation. The RSS believes in cultural nationalism.

A person who accepts this land as his country and owes unquestioned and primary loyalty to it, owns the basic features of her heritage and culture, imbibes and manifests them in life can be said to be a Hindu national, irrespective of the faith he follows for his spiritual salvation. Many, not born here, have acclaimed this country as their 'punyabhoomi'. And finally, what would be the characteristics of a Hindu Rashtra that the RSS favours, as evident from the writings of the senior leadership of the RSS from the time it was established? The RSS upholds that this is Hindu Rashtra. But certainly there are no elaborate writings on this subject. But the concept of Hindu Rashtra is absolutely different from what is known as a theocratic state, like, say, Pakistan or a Vatican. Hindutva is not a religious dogma. One should understand the distinction between rashtra (nation) and rajya (state). Hindu Rashtra is a geo-cultural concept. Let me begin with some observations that should give any reasonable person pause. In 1998 Hindu fundamentalists proposed that a new Goddess temple be built at Pokharan, 50 km from the site of the atomic bomb tests that were conducted in April of that year. According to their program this would be the 53rd example of Shaktipeeths (seats of strength, literally Goddess power) of Hindu preeminence. Some suggested that radioactive sand from the test site should be distributed as *prasad*, the Hindu sacrament, but cooler heads vetoed that idea.

The Indian military helps to fuel this religious enthusiasm by having named its long range missile after the Vedic god of fire Agni. The followers of Shri Shena, a fundamentalist organization in Mumbai, proudly proclaim that, after the bomb tests, Hindus were no longer eunuchs and now could stand up to the world as real men. At the 1999 Durga festival in Calcutta celebrants found new figures in the traditional tableau of the Goddess Durga and her attendants. They saw life size figures of brave Indian soldiers who won a victory in the mountains of Kashmir because of Durga's divine grace. Hundreds of years ago Hindu kings went into battle only after receiving Durga's blessing by sacrificing dozens of water buffalo to her.

Another chilling experience is to read about the recovery of an original Hindu Empire, extending West into Afghanistan and Central Asia encompassing all Buddhist sites; extending North to recover the Tibet, the original land of the Aryans according to Dayananda Saraswati, extending Northwest to Cambodia to recover the Hindu Khmer kingdoms of Angkor Wat and North Vietnam, where Shiva lingas have been found; and extending Southeast to Java, where a Hindu-Buddhist kingdom once flourished, and Bali where three million Hindus still live. This reminds me of Zionist maps of Greater Israel or plans by some Calvinists for a new Confederate States of America where God-fearing Anglo-Celtic top males will rule their households and their nation of fifteen states.

The origins of Hindu religious nationalism are quite recent considering the long history of advanced cultures in the Indian Sub-Continent. V. D. Savakar's Hindutva (literally A Hinduness) was published in 1923, but the ideas of this book go back to the beginning of the 19th Century. The supreme irony about Hindu fundamentalism is that its first writers were profoundly influenced by European Orientalism and its archeological and linguistic discoveries.

The same Orientalism that gave Europeans the excuse to view Asians as effeminate and impotent, thereby lacking the capacities for self rule, was used by Indian writers to create a view of India as a unified nation that gave birth to not only to the European languages but also to its first civilized peoples and the world's greatest religion. The idea of India as the cradle of civilization and spirituality is, amazingly enough, found in Voltaire, Herder, Kant, Schegel, Shelling, Hegel, and Schopenhauer. Some scholars argue that the Indian philosophy that we now know as neo-Vedanta found in Aurobindo, Vivikeananda, and Gandhi, is just as much German idealism and Indian philosophy.

Hindu fundamentalists were flattered by Aldous Huxley's idea of the Perennial Philosophy and its mystic monism, originally found in the Upanishads and only later, according to their views, spread to other cultures. Thesophists such as Annie Besant turned Orientalism on its European creators, claiming that what they perceived as weaknesses- namely, nondualism, nonviolence, renunciation, meditation, and toleranceBwere precisely what was needed for the salvation of Western societies.

In the 1870s there was a concerted effort on the part of English theosophists to merge with the Indian Arya Samaj (Society of Aryans) as part of Annie Besant's vision of a World

Federation of Aryans. Ironically, in another move of reverse Orientalism, members of Arya Samaj vetoed this idea because they insisted that Indians were the only true Aryans! Interestingly enough, both Indians and Europeans agreed on at least one proposition: Hindu civilization was indeed corrupt and suffering a long decline, but Hindu fundamentalists believed that the solution to that problem was not Christian capitialism; rather, it was the recovery of a glorious Hindu past that Europeans had conveniently rediscovered for them.

Even before Arya Samaj there was the Brahmo Samaj (Society of Brahma, the Hindu Creator God) founded in Calcutta in 1828 by Rammohan Roy, who, although still preserving the idea of Vedic authority, developed a fully modernist, that is rationalist and humanist, approach to Indian identity and nationhood. Debendranath Tagore, father of the more famous Rabindranath Tagore, broke with Roy over the issue of Vedic authority, and another nationalist Keshab Chandra Sen proposed that Hinduism ought to be Christianized. The result of these developments within the Bengal Renaissance was a growing view of Hindu supremacy and exclusivity. One of the most dramatic examples of these views came from Bajnarain Basu, who waxed eloquent as follows:

The noble and puissant Hindu nation rousing herself after sleep and rushing headlong towards progress with divine prowess. I see this rejuvenated nation again illuminating the world by her knowledge, spirituality and culture, and the glory of the Hindu nation agin spreading over the whole world. Rajnarain was insistent that the Hindu Motherland could have no place for Muslims because their religion was alien to India. India's religion should be a cultural Hinduism based on the Upanishads but allowing for the mediation of the one true God by means of the traditional idols. The Brahmo Samaj proposed gradual but sure reform on the elements that had tarnished the image of Hinduism word wide: caste problems, widow remarriage, untouchability, and child marriage.

Arya Samaj was founded by Dayananda Saraswati in 1875 in Bombay, now renamed Mumbai because of Hindutva.

(Madras is now called Chennai and Hindu nationalists want to change all English street names to Hindi and do not want their children to attend English medium schools.) Dayananda's philosophy is sometimes called neo-Hinduism or Semitized Hinduism, what I would call an Abrahamic Hinduism. Dayananda claimed that the Aryans originated in Tibet, an hypothesis that the Nazis tested by sending Ernst Schaefer and Bruno Beger on two expeditions there in the 1930s. (The Nazis were also captivated by an alternative bizarre idea that the Arctic was the home of Aryans, an idea promoted by Hindu nationalist B. G. Tilak.)

While in Tibet the Aryans, according to Dayananda, purged themselves of inferior people (identified as the *dasyus* in the *Rigveda*) and then spread to the rest of the world. In India they established the Hindu Golden Age described in the *Ramayana* and the *Mahabharata*. This great age came to an end with the Bharata War, the beginning of which is dramatically described in the *Bhagavad-Gita* and the result, according to the text, was over a million deaths. Hindu civilization then descended into a long decline that was exacerbated by the pacificism and nihilism of Buddhism and Jainism, which were seen as failed off shoots of Hinduism and not separate religions from Hinduism. During the Second Millennium CE a weakened Hindusim was easy prey for first the Mughal invaders and second British imperialism.

Dayananda saw the Aryans as paragons of virtue and the world's first monotheists. Even though he uses the Hindu epics as proof of the Golden Age, he argued that only the Vedas and the Upanishads have religious authority. (Oddly enough, the members of the Ayra Samaj retained the Vedic fire ritual for their services.) He rejected the authority of the priests to interpret scripture and set himself up, in a way very similar to some preachers in the Abrahamic religion, as the only one that could interpret the Vedas correctly.

He saw the Vedas and Upanishads as the literal Word of God and as the infallible text of the one true Hindu church, a concept alien to the Indian religious tradition, but one again very similar to the Abrahmanic religions and setting the stage for 20th Century Hindutva, Dayananda lauched systematic attacks on traditional Hindus, Buddhists, Jains, Sikhs, Christians, and Buddhists. On the plus side Dayananda believed that the subjugation of women came with the decline of Hinduism and declared that this was a social ill that needed corrected.

He also spoke out against the thousand plus subcastes (*jati*) that divide Indians according to specific vocations and prevent lateral movement in Indian society. With regard to the four main castes Dayananda thought that it was a mistake to think of them as hereditary, a position that was an advance over Gandhi, who, while rejecting the oppression of the Dalits, still maintained the hereditary nature of the four main castes. After Dayananda's death there was a campaign to reconvert Dalits whose families had gone over to Christianity and syncretistic Muslims who, because they so fully participated in Hindu celebrations, and ought according to Arya Samaj, to return to the fold of the true faith. This campaign of reconversion is still at the forefront of Hindu fundamentalist efforts today, especially among the Vishwa Hindu Parishad.

A key figure in the transition from the Brahmo Samaj and the Arya Samaj is Chandranath Basu who is the author that coined the term Hindutva (Hinduness) and he turned Hindu nationalism in a decidedly conservative and reactionary direction. In 1892 he published Hindutva*: An Authentic History of the Hindus* in which he defended traditional views Hindu ritual, caste, restriction of women's education and civil rights, and the maintenance of male authority. Chandranath was firmly committed to demonstrating the superiority of Hinduism over Christianity, especially after the wide spread concern that conversions to Christianity were increasing in the latter half of the century.

In the novels and commentaries of Bankimchandra Chattopadhyaya we see again the profound influence that European philosophy had on the rise of Indian nationalism. Particularly important was the work of Immanuel Kant,

Herbert Spencer, John Stuart Mill, and Auguste Comte. Interestingly enough, Bankim early support for women's equality, presumably under Mill's influence, disappeared in his later works, which also contain stronger claims to Hindu supremacy and more stringent anti-Muslim comments.

He criticized Mill and Comte for their atheism and substituted Krishna's religion of love as the key to human spiritual cultivation and progress. Nineteenth Century Indian nationalists were fully caught up in the idea of evolution and Bankim proposed that Hinduism was the perfect candidate for Comte's idea of Apositive religion, the final stage of human perfection. Huxley's Perennial Philosophy finds a new Indo-European home, but it has a new humanistic twist. Bankim rejects both the abstract monotheism he finds in Abrahamic religions and the impersonal monism of his own Brahmo Samaj in favor of the divine incarnation of Krishna as a human being.

At the turn of the century one of the most important Indian nationalist figure is B. G. Tilak, whose importance and standing in the Congress Party was second only to Gandhi. For purposes of our study of Hindu fundamentalism, Tilak was instrumental in inventing a powerful new form of devotionalism centered on the elephant god Ganesha. Tilak's strategy was calculated and very effective: the new Ganesha festival (first celebrated in 1893) would compete with the Muslim festival of Muharram, which Hindus had always attended.

Hindu nationalists in the state of Maharastra were successful in creating a new division between Muslims and Hindus that would intensify decade by decade into the new century. The Ganesha festival in Bombay is now so huge that it is common to see pictures and stories of it in the international press. Tilak also resurrected King Shivaji, who, by the grace of his patron goddess Bhawani, was by far the most successful Hindu warrior king against the Mughal Empire during the 17th Century. Hindu fundamentalists admire Shivaji's courage and excuse his ruthlessness against the Muslims he defeated.

Tilak also instigated celebrations honoring Shivaji but many of them in the 1890s turned violent, the beginnings of the communal conflict that was to increase in the next century but was an uncommon occurrence in earlier times. Tilak used the *Bhagavad-Gita* to justify Shivaji's campaigns against the Mughals but also the violence that may be necessary to keep the Muslims of his day in line. Shivaji has become a hero and a model for a militant leader who will bring back the glory of all things Hindu.

It is significant, however, in terms of the historical Shivaji that while Muslims repeatedly declared jihad against him, Shivaji principal motivations were Maratha nationalism rather than a broader Hindu nationalism based on the concept of the Indian Sub-Continent as one nation and the idea of Hinduism as a universal religion. Tilak also ignored the fact that Shivaji not only had Muslim allies but employed Muslims in his army and administration, demonstrating that his concept of a Martha nation included non-Hindus as well. Nonetheless, the revival and revision of Shivaji's reign resulted in a number of Shivaji societies that believed that violence against British rule was a religious duty.

Tilak was also involved in researching and writing about the origins of Hinduism and the Hindu nation. I have already mentioned his wacky thesis, defended in a book entitled *The Arctic Home of the Vedas*, that Aryan culture actually goes all the way back to the last Ice Age. Drawing on astronomical allusions in the Vedas, Tilak takes Vedic history back 8,000 years and argues that the Vedic gods were polar deities worshiped by arctic Aryans. From all of his research he drew the same conclusion that many other 19th Century Indian nationalists did, and I will conclude with this illustrative but problematic passage:

During Vedic times, India was a self-contained country. It was united as great nation. That unity has disappeared bringing great degradation and it becomes the duty of the leaders to revive that union. A Hindu of this place [Varanasi] is as much a Hindu as one from Madras or Bombay. The study of the Gita, Ramayana, and Mahabharata produce the same ideas throughout the country. Are not these our common heritage? If we stress on forgetting all the minor differences that exist between the different sects, then by the grace of Providence we shall be able to consolidate all the different sects into a mighty Hindu nation. This ought to be the ambition of every Hindu. The sect of whom Tilak speaks was the Sikhs, the Jains, and the Buddhists. Not at all included, unless they pledge allegiance to Hindutva (conversion itself is not mandatory), are India's 40 million Christians and 120 million Muslims.

The last time the word Hindutva created the confusion was in the case of corrupt electoral practices by Manohar Joshi, who said that if Shiv Sena BJP comes to power they will turn Maharashtra into first Hindu state in the country. He had used the word Hindutva for his politics. The matter went up to the court, and due to the confusions around the word Hindutva, court ruled that Hindutva is a way of life!

This came in handy for RSS combine to wriggle out and to assertively use the word in their political campaigns. Now we hear that Hindutva is an emancipatory concept! What is emancipation? In Indian context emancipation stands for the process which leads to equality of Dalits and women. It also stands for the dignified status of Adivasis and workers. Many of these processes started during the freedom movement as an accompaniment of the struggle against British rule. While we were witnessing these processes steered by the likes of Bhagat Singh, Ambedkar and Gandhi, the country also saw the politics by Muslim League, Hindu Mahasabha and RSS. This latter trio based their concept of politics around religious nationalism.

For Muslim League it was Islamic Sate, Pakistan and for Hindu Mahasabha, RSS it was Hindu nation. Muslim League derived its ideology from the name of Islam and Hindu Mahsabha and RSS developed the term Hindutva, as the guiding ideology for Hindu nation. There is lot of parallel between the pattern of ideology of Muslim League and Hindu Mahsabha, RSS. They all kept aloof from the freedom movement and the associated processes of social transformation of caste and gender.

Freedom movement was not only for freedom from the British rule it also symbolized the values of Liberty, Equality and Fraternity, the values which are emancipatory for those oppressed by feudal rule of Rajas and Nawabs, and the associated clergy (Mullahs, Pastors and Brahmins). Talking of Hindutva in particular, the term was coined by Vinayak Damodar Savarkar in his book 'Who is a Hindu?' in 1923. Hinduism is not a prophet based religion. Originally word Hindu began as a geographical category, for all those living on east of river Indus.

Later all the religious traditions, from caste and gender hierarchy based Brahmanism to egalitarian streams like Nath, Tantra, Siddha and Bhakti all came to be covered under the umbrella of Hinduism. Brahmanism is the dominant tendency within this spectrum, and currently all things Brahminic are identified as Hinduism. Dr. Ambedkar pointed out that Hinduism is Brahminic theology. Savarkar defined Hindu as one who regards this land from Sindhu to Seas as Fatherland and Holy-land.

In this definition all are included barring Muslims and Christians. Savarkar further went on to coin and define the word Hindutva. Hindutva, for him is total Hinduness, a combination of Aryan race, Culture and values. In essence it came to mean a politics based on Brahminic values of birth based inequality of caste and gender. It gives the status of slaves to Dalits and women. RSS picked up the concept of Hindutva from there. Hindu Mahasabha and RSS both stood for status quo in caste and gender relations.

RSS politics did exhibit these values in practical form, over a period of time. Contrary to emancipation, RSS ideology wants not only status quo ante of feudal times, further it wants to push back whatever little process of transformation of Dalits and women has taken place over a period of time. Beginning with gender, RSS is an exclusively male organization. Its women wing is subordinate to it, it is Rashtra Sevika Samiti. Here, Swayamsevak for men, Sevika for women. The word swayam, self, is missing in women's organization. Lets be clear, according to all male dominated patriarchal organizations, Taliban, Fascists, Christian fundamentalists or RSS, women's self is in the pocket of men. Women are subordinate, are property of men. So they are to be dictated, controlled. So one of RSS trained swayamsevak, Pramod Mutalik forms Shriram Sene and beats up women. They dictate that women should be doing or wearing, this that and the other. As far *Dalit*s are concerned Dr. Ambedkar goes on to assert that *Dalit*s need to learn, organize and struggle for their rights, for equality. RSS has come up with Samajik Samrasta Manch, to co-opt the Dalits at subordinate position within the present social structure where Dalits remain subjugated in the social system.

RSS also has the ideology of integral humanism. This essential part of Hindutva politics argues that as the human body has different organs doing their different functions, similarly our society has different groups doing their job. A change in their roles will create disequilibrium, which will be detrimental to the smooth functioning of society. One does concede that the language of RSS is very subtle and clever, but its actions regularly show what it means. RSS is the Father of all other organizations working for Hindu nation.

The politics it has unleashed through BJP, VHP, and Vanvasi Kalyan Ashram etc. does regularly show the real intent of RSS. Few samplers- BJP Vice- president Rajmata Scindia endorsing Sati tradition, VHP-leadership endorsing the killings of Dalits in response to the killings of Dalits in the aftermath of Gohana, on the issue of cow-slaughter. RSS repeatedly emphasizes the 'ancient glory' of the times when Manusmriti was the rule. One is happy to know that the new RSS chief knows the word emancipation. So far so good, as he can't go beyond parroting this word, as the meaning of the word is totally against the agenda of RSS. RSS agenda is opposed to emancipation and stands for suppressing the low caste, and women in perpetual subjugation.

9

The Notion of "Hindu Fascism"

Neo-fascism and religion refers to debates about the relationships between neo-fascism and various religions. Some scholars, using the term *neo-fascism* in its narrow sense, consider certain contemporary religious movements and groups to represent forms of clerical or theocratic neofascism, including Christian Identity in the United States; some militant forms of politicized Islamic fundamentalism; Hindu nationalism in India (Sangh Parivar); and some neopagan alternative religions advocating white supremacism.

The term fascism was first used in Italy during the 1920s, and like Nazism, its meaning came to refer to a type of union of right wing concepts of authoritarian political controls with welfare state economic policies. The term neo-fascism is used to describe fascist movements active after World War II. Modern colloquial usage of the word sometimes extends the definition of the terms fascism and neo-fascism and Neo-Nazism to refer to any totalitarian worldview, regardless of its political ideology. Although the assertion that religious fundamentalists and militants are fascists can often be understood as hyperbole, some scholars have used the term when discussing certain religious movements.

In the late 19th and early 20th centuries, authoritarian ideals saw resurgence in the context of political upheavals across Eurasia, typically anti-aristocratic socio-political revolutions. The ethnic-rooted conflicts of World War I and

World War II arose from the political circumstances brought about by internal societal battles, usually between left-wing revolutionaries and right-wing traditionalists. In addition to the authoritarian political model, most scholars classify fascism as an extreme right ideology, along with ethnic-populist movements that call for increased traditionalism.

In the context of civil conflicts, the demand for increased traditionalism typically promotes ethnocentrism, and in extreme cases this ethnic unity resulted in the persecution of those not within the chosen ethnic group. Religion has often been an aspect of ethnicity, whose moral foundation and message may grow corrupted by the societal acceptance of convergence between political and religious populism. Between the two world wars, there were three forms of fascism: Italian economic corporatism; German racial nationalist Nazism; and clerical fascist movements such as the Romanian Iron Guard and the Croatian Ustashi.

LINKING FASCISM AND RELIGION

Since WWII, neofascists have reinterpreted fascist ideology and strategy in various ways to fit new circumstances." In the context of social conflict in which religious figures and institutions come under partisan influence, religion often becomes a political tool by which principled authority is replaced by authoritarian violence. Early fascism was a mixture of syndicalist notions with Hegelian or idealistic theories of the state. Both early and later fascists viewed the state as an organic entity rather than as an institution to protect collective and individual rights. Fascists often defined themselves in opposition to laissez-faire capitalism, Marxism, and democracy.

During World War II, Karl Popper described fascism as different from Hegelianism, which was bound to a specific "traditional religious form" (Lutheran Christianity in Frederick William's Prussia). Popper suggests that in fascism, religion is usually replaced by a form of evolutionist materialism: "Thus the formula of the fascist brew is in all countries the same: Hegel plus a dash of nineteenth-century materialism (especially Darwinism in the somewhat crude form given to it by Haeckel)." He argues that as a consequence of the popularity of Marxism in the first half of the 20th century, traditional fascism is not endorsing any specific religion. He wrote that while Marxism is seen as atheistic, fascism is not necessarily atheistic:

> ...fascism has not much use for an open appeal to the supernatural. Not that it is necessarily atheistic or lacking in mystical or religious elements. But the spread of agnosticism through Marxism led to a situation in which no political creed aiming at popularity among the working class could bind itself to any of the traditional religious forms.

Later scholarship took several different approaches. Roger Griffin argues that Fascism is best defined as a revolutionary form of nationalism, one that sets out to be a political, social and ethical revolution, welding the 'people' into a dynamic national community under new elites infused with heroic values. The core myth which inspires this project is that only a populist, trans-class movement of purifying, cathartic national rebirth (palingenesis) can stem the tide of decadence. This concept of fascism as palingenesis is complementary with the idea of James Rhodes that fascism is a form of apocalyptic millenarianism – and with the work of Emilio Gentile, who argues that fascism is a form of "political religion" that involves the "sacralization of politics."

Roger Eatwell sees a complex relationship between fascism and religion, noting that "Religions involve some form of belief in a supernatural being(s). However, this misses a point that all modern ideologies exhibit dimensions of religions." Eatwell questions "liberal historiography's demonization of fascism as an un-intellectual creed" According to Eatwell:

> "A more fruitful way of distinguishing between ideology and religion is to adapt Søren Kierkegaard's view that the essence of a religion is not the persuasion of the truth of the doctrine, but a leap of faith to accept a view which is inherently

absurd.... Fascism's essential syncretism meant that it was possible to find forms, which overtly married ideology and religion - for example, in the Iron Guard, or among a limited number of Italian and German clerics (though most failed to see the radicalism at the core of fascism). Moreover, there were aspects of fascism, which were absurd - especially the belief of some Nazis that there was an international Jewish conspiracy against Germany, which encouraged a belief in apocalyptic holy war against the Jew. However, most fascists were not driven by such affective sentiments. Indeed, there is nothing absurd about the core ideology of generic fascism namely the quest to forge a holistic nation and create a radical syncretic Third Way state."

HINDU NATIONALISM

Indian Marxist Prabhat Patnaik has written that the Hindutva movement as it has emerged is "classically fascist in class support, methods and programme" Patnaik bases this argument on the following "ingredients" of classical fascism present in Hindutva: the attempt to create a unified homogeneous majority under the concept of "the Hindus"; a sense of grievance against past injustice; a sense of cultural superiority; an interpretation of history according to this sense of grievance and superiority; a rejection of rational arguments against this interpretation; and an appeal to the majority based on race and masculinity. Some scholars contend that the traditional meaning of the term fascism does not apply to Hindutva groups, and may hinder an analysis of their activities. Academics Chetan Bhatt and Parita Mukta reject the identification of Hindutva with fascism, because of Hindutva's embrace of cultural rather than racial nationalism, because of its "distinctively Indian" character, and because of "the RSS's disavowal of the seizure of state power in preference for long-term cultural labour in civil society". They instead describe Hindutva as a form of "revolutionary conservatism" or "ethnic absolutism".

Before World War II, Sadashiv Golwalkar, head of the RSS from 1940-1973 opined German national pride has now become the topic of the day. To keep up purity of the nation and its culture, Germany shocked the world by her purging the country of the Semitic races, the Jews. National pride at its highest has been manifested here. Germany has also shown how well-nigh impossible it is for races and cultures having differences going to the root, to be assimilated into a united whole, a good lesson for us in Hindustan to learn and profit by." ("We or our nationhood defined" 1938, p.37) However, anti-semitism plays no role in post-1947 Hindutva. Golwalkar in 1966 wrote:

"The Christians committed all sorts of atrocities on the Jews by giving them the label "Killers of Christ". Hitler is not an exception but a culmination of the 2000-year long oppression of the Jews by the Christians."

Contemporary Hindutva groups are overwhelmingly supportive of the Jewish State of Israel. Savarkar himself supported Israel during its formation. Golwalkar too supported Israel in his statement:

"The Jews had maintained their race, religion, culture and language; and all they wanted was their natural territory to complete their Nationality."

A Contention often heard in secularist circles, is that this Hindu revivalism is a form of *Hindu fascism*. Specifically, a BJP in power would soon reveal itself to be a Nazi government- but then it would be too late. I will not bother about quoting all the people who have made such allegations (there are many), and just deal with the substance of this allegation. Actually, there are two radically different allegation of *Hindu fascism*. One merely is an allegation against the current wave of *Hindu communalism*.

The other one says, that Hinduism is intrinsically fascist. The best-known proponent of the latter theory is V.T. Rajshekar, who publishes the fortnightly *Dalit Voice* from Bangalore. He builds his views on Ambedkar's. But at the same time, he strongly subscribes to the theory that the Aryans invaded India, and instituted the cast system to preserve their racial purity, much like the Apartheid system in South Africa.

In fact, all his anti-Hindu views are put forward in ethnic and even racial terminology. The non-caste Hindus and the minorities are for him the oppressed nations of India, oppressed by the Aryan invaders who constitute the upper castes.

Of course, the racial view of caste, a product of the British fascination for race theories, has been debunked scientifically. Even Ambedkar rejected it. By now, the whole notion of Aryan invasions has come under fire. Western scholars start recognizing what many Indian scholars have since long pointed out: that there is not a single piece of proof for the whole theory, and that all the known relevant facts can just as well be explained with alternative and equally coherent theories. But since is lost on Mr. Rajshekar. He has published a book in the West, titled *Dalit - the Black Untouchables of India*. On the cover is a photograph of, I presume, the writer.

And the first thing you notice is: but this man is not black. He is quite a Caucasian, or white man, though slightly more suntanned than Europeans, but not at all a Negroid type. And you start to realize: this man is a crackpot. In order to attract American Black support, or for other propaganda reasons, he makes the caste system into a racial issue. The rich white Aryan Brahmin invaders oppress the poor black non-Aryan Shudra natives.

Now this has a lot to do with Hitler. He too was a crank racist. While the reprehensible racism in South Africa is at least based on a actual racial difference between black and white, Hitler based his anti-Jewish racism on the erroneous notion that the difference between Germans and Jews is racial, which is biological nonsense. Moreover, he too had borrowed the concept of the Aryan race, which the British had developed in India, but which was totally alien to the Hindu tradition. Rajshekar has borrowed the same theory in the same place. He holds the same kind of crank notion that the difference between upper and lower castes is a racial one. So, Hitler-Rajshekar bhai-bhai.

With them, everything gets drawn into racial categories. The only difference is that Hitler is on the side of the Aryan race, while Rajshekar is on the opposite side. Thus, in an article about the Israeli technician Mordechai Vanunu, *Dalit Voice* says that he is a Sephardic Jew (migrated from the Muslim countries), who are oppressed by the Ashkenazi Jews (migrated from Europe, and founders of Israel). When the technician revealed to the world some nuclear secrets of Israel, this was portrayed as an element in the ethnic struggle of oppressed (*Dalit*) Sephardim against Zionist Ashkenazim, who also oppress the Palestinians. So it all fits: *Dalit*s and Muslims should form a front against the Brahmins, therefore *Dalit*s support the Palestinians, and therefore they oppose the Zionists who are Ashkenazi Jews, and link up with the oppressed Sephardic Jews. But here the racist logic breaks down: it so happens that the hard-liners in Israel, like many in the Likud Party, are precisely these Sephardim, who have fled Muslim countries and have no love lost for the Arabs, while the Ashkenazim are generally more liberal. This goes to show once more the nonsense of these racial conspiracy theories on which the Hitler and Rajshekars of this world feed.

So, what remains for the enemies of Hinduism to dub intrinsically fascist about Hinduism and the caste system, of course? Even if it is not racist, it is not equalitarian and institutionalizes inequality on the basis of people's birth (just like in racism). Therefore, the caste system is reprehensible. And therefore Hinduism is reprehensible (through a remote influence of Marxism, everything gets reduced to its social dimension, so Hinduism equals caste system). Firstly, there is a distinction between theory and practice. This may seem an easy way out, often used by soft-Leftists when confronted with criticism of the implementation of socialist theory in the praxis of the Soviet system (*But that is not the real socialism!*). But the distinction is pertinent. On the one hand there were ideologues of the four varnas, the functions in society with their allotted duties and privileges, and they wrote Shastras in which they tried to fit reality into the scheme, complete with a slant in favour of their own caste. On the other there was the existing reality of jatis, roughly endogamous groups, roughly coinciding with occupations, but far more diverse and in motion than the crystalline theoretical framework of Chaturvarnya. Secondly, this social system did not exist in isolation. Thus, centuries of foreign domination must have had an impact on it. We can say a priori that when leading groups in society come to groan under the weight of foreign oppression, they themselves will weigh heavier on the lower groups. That would not be the case if the new rulers would engage in reform of the existing society, but the Muslims never did this (in spite of the new myths about Islam as bringing socialist reforms). A society that is put on the defensive will harden and develop internal friction. Again it may sound like an easy explanation, but it is just quite plausible that a part of the inhuman traits of the caste system as recent generations found it, must be attributed to later outside influences like the impoverishing, brutalizing and demoralizing effect of Muslim rule.

When we study its theoretical conception, we find that the caste system is quite the opposite of Nazism in essential respects. Let us think clearly about this very charged matter. In the caste system, we may distinguish the following components:

1. In society, different groups are recognized.
2. These groups have their own mores and duties.
3. Membership of a group is determined by birth.
4. On the basis of their function, a ritual hierarchy exists between these groups, which do not coincide with either wealth or actual social power.

The first point says merely that difference is recognized. This is not as evident as it sounds. Islam and Communism champion equality, which in practice means uniformity. The second point means that these groups are defined by the role they play in society, and that duties as also privileges are allotted accordingly. This does not mean that the higher ones grab all the privileges. Thus, one who has the duty to guide society by communicating knowledge commits a crime when he is untruthful, or drunk, whereas these things are of no consequence when committed by a manual labourer. This allotting of duties also concerns the different age-groups.

As any anthropologist can tell you, the distribution of duties among age-groups is one of the most evident features of tribal society. That is why the Varna division is considered together with the division of life in stages, the ashramas, so that Hindu social philosophy is known as Varnashramadharma. While this recognition of different roles with their own duties and privileges is by no means a complete answer to every possible social question, it at least provides a framework which is perfectly true to universal human experience. The third point means that one's qualities are largely determined by birth.

The most natural division of mankind, the two sexes, a division which brings with it a definite role, duties and privileges, is determined by birth. One's gunas of qualities, which determine one's vocation in society, are in turn partly determined by heredity. At this point Hindu society has hardened a statistical law, which generally makes people follow in their parents' footsteps, into a rigid steel frame. In reality, an individual's swadharma (own duty, own way) may differ from that of his parents, and that is why the Bhagavad Gita (which is of course only one voice in the plurality of Hindu tradition) simply states that one's varna is determined by one's guna (quality, type), regardless of whether this guna is in turn determined by heredity, by environment and education, or who knows, by the stars at birth.

Of course, this is a point where historically the divergence between theory and practice has become quite substantial. The fourth point is to modern socialists perhaps the most horrible: a hierarchy between the groups. Well, there is an undeniable hierarchy between social functions, even where an equalitarian law system has firmly taken root. Thus, an employee is equal, as a human being and as a citizen, to his employer; the work both do is equally indispensable; yet, the employee's work is by definition determined by the tasks his employer allots him.

So, while there is equality between human beings, there is a logical hierarchy between functions. In that sense, the Vaishya function is superior to the Shudra function. Similarly, a ruler, even while autonomous in his decisions (remember secularism), is dependent on knowledge and a social philosophy, but the thinkers who devise this intellectual and ideological framework, should be independent in their thinking, free from the rulers' interference. In that sense, the Brahmin function is logically superior to the Kshatriya function, even while rulers are more powerful and wealthy than thinkers. In my opinion, it is this logical hierarchy of social functions which the early ideologues of Varnashramadharma had in mind.

It is but human that people with a higher function were also honoured accordingly. But in how far that was translated into a cruel anti-human inequality in actual village and city life, is another matter. It is too vast to go into it here. Suffice it to say that I have become a bit skeptical of the abysmally grim picture of the caste system which all of us have been fed, after actually living among Hindus of both high and low castes, and after studying the research done by modern-educated Indian scholars. As Meenakshi Jain has indicated, it is not because certain Brahmins were particular about not eating with other people etc., that other castes felt inferior or oppressed by this uptight and unprofitable kind of behaviour (much less inclined to imitate the difficult Brahmin lifestyle, as the Sanskritization theory would have it).

In Catholic circles, like in religion class, we used to get some testimonies from the missions, now and then. When asked for examples of how horrible the caste system is, missionaries would always mention the distance Brahmins keep from the inferior non-Brahmins. But so what? For orthodox Brahmins, as I have known some in Varanasi, I myself am an avarna, and they will not have dinner with me. But I don't feel offended by that. If they think I am impure (and I am: I have eaten many a beef steak in my life), then that is their choice. I don't really care, and I think most Shudras in India's long history didn't care. But they did *not care* in the intolerant way of the iconoclastic modernists, who like to trample on somebody else's rules and taboos: while they themselves did not observe the near-obsessive purity rules of Brahmins, they would not think of forcing Brahmins out of their purist seclusion. The effort to rewrite history and to see integration instead of separation and enmity as the norm of interaction between the different communities, should not be directed to the history of Hindu-Muslim relations (where it is gross distortion), but at the history of caste relations (where it is a correction of the extremely divisive picture created by the missionaries and colonialists). There was plenty of co-operation, amity and human concern across caste lines. On the other hand, as in other societies, there has existed oppression in Hindu society too. And this has been aggravated in the last few centuries by the decreasing prosperity, which in turn was due to Muslim oppression and plundering, to the disruption of India's economy by its forcible integration into Britain's colonial trade system, and to the victory of modern industry over the indigenous industries (which also affected non-colonies like China and Iran). Increasing poverty invariably increases social friction and oppression.

While rejecting the immensely black picture which the missionaries have painted of Hindu society, and which has been very much interiorized in the Indian collective consciousness and is still being reproduced by the self-proclaimed Ambedkarites today, we need not deny that oppression and misery existed. And it must have taken the shape of the social structure in force, which happened to be the caste system. No-one in his right mind is inclined to denigrate the efforts at *"bringing the backward castes into the mainstream of Indian society"* (to use the politicians' expression).

On the stand taken by the Hindutva people on the caste system. Now, in essential respects the caste system is the opposite of Nazism. This counts not only for the idealized theory but even for the raw practice. First of all, this system is not at all centralized. The traditional Hindu society knows many layers of social organization: family, *kula, upajati, jati, varna*. Now, this layeredness of society, this devolution of many organizational functions to intermediary levels, is the strongest possible buffer against dictatorship and totalitarianism. When analyzing why the French Revolution quickly degenerated into a reign of terror and a dictatorship, Hegel state that it was the destruction of the intermediary levels of social organization which led to this polarization between the naked individual and the all-powerful state authority.

The first task of totalitarian-minded people is to break down those organizational units which they cannot control. In Orwell's Nineteen Eighty-Four, the protagonist of the narrative regains a measure of mental independence from Big Brother's total control, when he falls in love with some girl. Suddenly there is an emotional relationship, i.e. another form of human interaction than Big Brother's state, a bond which escapes Big Brother's control. These simple natural forms of human togetherness, like the family, the clan, the tribe, no matter what their drawbacks, are the strongest possible protection against totalitarianism.

Traditional societies all had clans and tribes. With the building of empires, these lost some of their importance. But the atomization of society into isolated individuals, who find nothing above them but the all-powerful state, is largely a modern phenomenon, and fascism is one extreme outgrowth of it. It is not only factually incorrect to attribute the characteristics of fascism to a traditional society like the Hindu society, it also gives proof of a total incomprehension of larger historical categories, like modern vs. traditional, hierarchy vs. totalitarianism. The unique thing about Hindu society is that it kept this tribe-wise and clan-wise organization even after setting up very large integrated state structures.

By contrast, Mohammed in his bid to form a state (after the admired models of the Persian and Byzantine empires) wanted to destroy these intermediary levels. Thus, he is not at all clan- and family-minded. While Confucianism, Judaism or Hinduism are very family-centered, Islam does not ordain family stability, but gives a man all the freedom to break up the family he started, by simply declaring to his wife: Talaq Talaq Talaq. Moreover, Mohammed explicitly wanted his followers to put the loyalty to Islam above the loyalty to the clan. One may consider this an element of universalim, rising above narrow loyalties. That is certainly how Muslim apologetics puts it. But the other side is that the primitive loyalty to the natural family unit merely gets replaced by another, more demanding narrow loyalty: to the Prophet, to Big Brother.

All dictators like uniformity. The Spanish dictator Franco worked hard to destroy the linguistic diversity in Spain by suppressing the use of Catalan and Basque. Similarly, Stalin wanted to abolish all ethnicity and language diversity. These subnational identities were anathema to a centralistic dictatorial mind. It so happens that Islam too insists on uniformity, even in very small things. In world history, it is perhaps only the Mao outfit of the Chinese communists that matches the uniformity of appearance among Muslims. Women should wear burqa, and men should trim their beards after the Prophet's example. This outer uniformity is expressive of an imposed uniformity of behaviour and belief. I do not find this uniformist loyalty to the Prophet any more open-minded or Universalist than the "narrow loyalty" to a tribe.

There is reason for suspicion against people who need to trample upon natural loyalties before they can establish their *brotherhood*. It is like a scorpion, which lifts his prey up from the ground and then stings. These natural social units are the ground under people's feet, and if you want to enlist them in your own power trip, you have to take them out of these natural units, and make them vulnerable to your claims on them, by isolating them. It is quite possible to teach people universal values and awareness of the larger whole, without breaking opens the existing divisions in society. Actually, calling clans and tribes a division conceals the fact that they are just as much *units*, levels of integration.

Few buildings these days are built from one massive rock; the normal thing to do is to integrate smaller units into bigger and yet bigger ones. The global civilization which we are building today will not be made up of scattered individuals. Organizationally, it will be a hierarchy of intermediary levels of integration, a two- way combination of unity and diversity. The current revival of ethnicity throughout the world is just one example of man's natural resistance against atomization.

The essence of varnashramadharma, the social philosophy that allots different duties to differently minded groups of people, as well as to the different age-groups, and that allows communities to develop at intermediary levels between individual and state, is quite the opposite of the uniformization so typical of totalitarian systems.

HINDUTVA AND THE "EVILS OF HINDU SOCIETY"

In the secularists' tirades, the Hindutva people are systematically portrayed as upholders of inequality and of all the evils of Hindu society.

Remark: the very expression evils of Hindu society, which Nehru routinely used, is totally out of bounds when Hindu is replaced with Muslim or another community. The expression "the crimes of the Muslim conquerors", or "the evils of Muslim society" (like anti-modern backwardness, persecution of non-Muslims, slavery, the inferiority of women), are sure to provoke shouts of communal! There is also no one to describe the social problems in the West as "the evils of Christian society", as if all worldly problems can be reduced to the impact of the prevalent religion.

In fact, the unity of Hindu society, and the promotion of the backward castes in the mainstream of society, has always been a major plank of Hindu organizations like the RSS. In its literature, the RSS boasts of having received compliments from such non-communalist people like Mahatma Gandhi and Jayaprakash Narayan, for its entirely caste-free structure and working. Nonetheless, for decades after it was set up, it was mostly an organization of Brahmins and, increasingly, Vaishyas.

It seems that recently, the caste-wise composition of the RSS is changing. According to a recent report, "much to the despair of the Marxists and secularists alike, it is not the upper caste that dominates the Sangh's shakhas. It is ironically the middle castes and rising Dalits." An RSS member is quoted saying:"All our best attended shakhas are in the poor areas, not in the alienated middle class or rich upper caste suburbs or cities or towns. In simple words, the new Sangh Swayamsevak is mostly a backward caste or Dalit."

So, the following analysis by Sunil Adam is just another Leftist lie: "The Muslims only serve as a negative target of Hindu consciousness so as to marginalize the contradictions of the Hindu social order and at the same time maintain the social and political status quo, which is the actual object of Hindutva." While totally denying the historical fact of the unprovoked all-out Muslim attack on Hindu society during centuries on end, and while reducing the thrust of the Hindutva movement to an anti-Muslim thrust, it repeats the classic Marxist fallacy of reducing everything to a matter of class (c.q. caste) contradictions. Moreover, it ascribes to the Hindutva movement an intention of maintaining the social and political status quo: this goes contrary to all statements of intention by the Hindutva leaders.

Of course, we may be dealing here with the rhetorical trick of ascribing intentions to people: "You say that this is what you want, but it is not what you want. I will tell you what you really want." This is a venomous act of psychological imperialism: not even letting people decide for themselves what they intend. Unless of course you can prove from their actual behaviour that it is something else they want. But the burden of proof is on the accuser. So, the Hindutva movement is innocent of casteist conservatism until the contrary is proven. For establishing such proof, Mr. Adam will have to explain away all the anti-caste statements of Hindutva leaders (all eyewash?) and all the testimonies that the RSS and affiliated organizations are indeed caste-free.

But no, Mr. Adam gives no proof of anything. Assured that no-one in the arena will contradict him, he continues:"The economic and political mobility of lower castes is one of the factors that stirred the upper castes to resurrect the question of Hindu identity during the early eighties. In other words, for Hindutva to succeed it has to accomplish the twin and contradictory tasks of uniting the country's majority under the Hindu banner and also ensure that a majority among them accept their place in the social and political hierarchy prescribed by the pristine Brahminical religion..."

Now, this is where Mr. V.P. Singh's decision to implement the Mandal Commission Report recommendations comes in. This Commission recommended that, after the Scheduled Castes and Tribes, who have been getting 22.5% reservations in recruitment and promotions in government service as well as in education (though these quota have not been filled up in many cases), the principle of reservation be extended to the Other Backward Castes (*Classes*, says the Report, but then it enumerates castes). V.P. Singh's decision was clearly meant to attract the Backward Caste vote (46% of the Indian population, according to an old census). It could at the same time split the Hindu vote, pitting high against low castes.

Opponents feared that this split would not be limited to Election Day, and that Mandal would tear the whole social fabric apart. Enemies of Hindu society also looked at it that way said Prof. Rajni Kothari:"*The Mandal Report has the potential to finish off the supremacy of Vedic Hinduism.*" The effect of the caste-based reservations would be, to strengthen caste identity (with opposing caste interest). But while in traditional society the caste system was a harmony model (this nice-sounding term is a curse to Marxist ears), this newly strengthened caste consciousness would foment caste enmity. It would also frustrate the drive to unify Hindu society.

As Mr. Adam says:"It is this [Hindu-unifying] scheme of things that the Mandal Report is capable of upsetting. Whether the Hindu identity will submerge caste identity or vice versa will depend on which is a better agent of politicization, caste or religion? In other words, India today has the paradoxical choice of choosing between caste, which has a secularizing impact, and Hindutva which can lead the nation to an unknown destiny."

Paradoxical indeed. While anti-Hindu pamphletry and rhetoric largely focuses on the horrors of the caste system, which is depicted as intrinsic to this horrible Hinduism, we now get to read that caste will break Hinduism. Caste is the evil of Hindu society, it is a hierarchy prescribed by the pristine Brahminical religion, but now we get to read that it has a secularizing impact. It is not only a logical paradox, or rather contradiction. There is also a moral contradiction in Mr. Adam's reasoning, which I would re-word as follows:"Hinduism is reprehensible because of caste; because we want to kill caste, we want to kill Hinduism; now, in order to kill Hinduism, we are going to strengthen caste."

These secularists have been saying that they think they can use it as a weapon against Hinduism; they have no scruples in promoting it as progressive and *secularizing*. So, the Janata Dal people who have been decrying the Janmabhoomi movement as a threat to national unity, as well as the communists (from whom one had expected many ugly things, but not the promotion of a non-Marxist category like casteism), as well as most non- Congress secularists, have applauded the divisive Mandal plan. Anyway, while the secularists use every occasion to demonstrate how unprincipled they are except for their commitment to the destruction of Hinduism, Hindus need not unduly worry over the issue of caste-based reservations.

Its impact would not be all that deep. In some southern states, large reservation schemes have already been implemented during the eighties. While it is said that these have harmed the efficiency of the administration, they have not spectacularly affected caste relations. And while it may be unfair against upper-caste people, it may have the beneficial effect of encouraging them to enter and develop the private sector, instead of settling for a life in the bureaucracy. If I may make a few blunt generalizations about caste, I would venture to say that the rise of the Backward Castes may well be a very beneficial development for Hindu society.

When I look at the caste titles of the Communist leaders and of the most rabid secularists, I notice they are mostly high-caste people. The upper castes have intensely collaborated with the Muslim and then the British ruler; they are largely an alienated lot with little sympathy for their own culture and society. Some of them, in fairness, have fought until their back was broken. Others have simply prostituted themselves with the rulers for generations. By contrast, the lower castes have fought the Muslim invaders tooth and nail. Contrary to the modern myths of Islam bringing relief to the oppressed low-castes, they suffered badly under the Islamic onslaught: e.g. the lands the Muslim rulers took to set up their zamindari were mostly taken from these agricultural and cattle-rearing castes.

Moreover, thanks to their limited schooling, these low-castes have not yet massively imbibed all this pro-Muslim and anti-Hindu propaganda that passes as history in the school curricula. So today, the Backward Castes are not only the numerical centre of gravity in a democratic Hindu society, they are also less contaminated with anti-Hindu bias. With that, I have said more than enough in terms of caste considerations. The real work for revitalizing Hindu society has to be done by individuals, and these are found in any caste and community. Incidentally, the upheaval over Mandal has brought out a fact which should be rather embarrassing for the missionary propaganda.

The Dalit Christians are low- caste people who have been lured into conversion with the promise of (1) eternal Salvation by Jesus Christ the Saviour, our Lord, and (2) freedom from the low-caste status as well as from poverty. These *Dalit* Christians held a demonstration in Delhi to demand reservations, on the plea that they are still as poor and low-caste as before conversion. The Ram Janmabhoomi movement has demonstrated, more than anything else, the fact that Backward Castes and Scheduled Castes and Tribes, in spite of all the ploys to wean them away from Hinduism, still very much identify themselves with Hindu demands, such as a symbolic restoration of the damage Islam has done. In the tribal belt in southern Bihar, Mr. Advani's rathyatra got a rousing welcome.

The communal riots too show how the efforts by Muslim parties and by the anti-Hindu Bahujan Samaj Party to forge an alliance of low-castes and Muslims against the high-castes, are not having much of the desired result. In the Hyderabad riots, Muslims attacked a Harijan quarter, primarily because they expected these Harijans to be unorganized and weak. A local Harijan leader has confirmed this to me. Even more telling was the violence in Bijnor, U.P. on October 30. There, the District Magistrate confirmed to journalists that the violence had been instigated by a local Muslim politician, and he added that the city was a stronghold of the BSP, but that the communal riots had just as much pitted the Muslims against the Harijans. The Ghaziabad riot on 26 January 1991, with nine casualties, was nothing but an attack of a Muslim pro-Saddam demonstration on Valmikis (a Scheduled Caste) who were celebrating Republic Day.

These incidents conform to a larger pattern in Indian history. Contrary to the fables of the low-castes being sympathetic towards Islam, it is they who have always opposed it tooth and nail. Today in Pakistan, the large majority of the remaining Hindus are very poor Backward Caste people. If Islam is so good for them, and Hinduism so harsh, why have they continued to stick to Hinduism and suffered so much trouble and oppression by Islamic society for it? It is time we realize that the caste system has in fact protected Hindu society against total islamization, and that even low-caste people took pride in their caste so that they preferred their place in Hindu society to absorption in the atomized Muslim community.

So, the stand of the Hindutva people is not: Hinduism has sinned terribly by having this caste system; therefore it has to imitate Islam and abolish caste. It is rather:the caste system had its use sometime in the past, over the centuries it has come to carry a lot of unhealthy social equations and attitudes, and now it has become socially irrelevant and a factor of divisiveness, therefore it is time for us to abandon it.

ARYA AND SWASTIKA

A very crude kind of anti-Hindu propaganda, sometimes used by American Protestant sects in warning the youth against the dangers of Hare Krishna etc., points out that

Hinduism and Nazism have a central symbol in common: the swastika. I have also heard the comparison from Ambedkarites who, taking V.T. Rajshekar's lead, systematically refer to Hindus as "Hindu Nazis". For the latter category, it may be of interest to know that the swastika is just as much a central symbol in Buddhism, Ambedkar's chosen religion. In China, the swastika is known as a Buddhist symbol. Moreover, in the Aryan mythology of the post-Ambedkar Ambedkarites (if a teacher gets killed, it is by his pupils), the Hindus were invaders who destroyed the Hindus civilization, of which the *Dalits* are the legitimate descendants.

Now, this pre-Hindu Indus civilization already used the swastika. The swastika is quite a sanatana symbol, not bound up with any nation or ideology. It is also found among peoples outside the Hindu sphere of influence. It is because of his fallacious doctrine of the Aryan race that conquered both Europe and South Asia, and because of a mistaken belief that the swastika was typical of the Aryan peoples, that Hitler adopted this symbol as a symbol of his Aryan state. But of course, the legitimate Aryans, i.e. the Sanatana Dharmins of whatever ethnicity or race, and of whatever sect including Buddhism, cannot be blamed for Hitler's misconceptions nor for Hitler's crimes that gave a bad connotation to this symbol.

People, who believe in magic, and in the independent power of symbols, infer from this primary belief that Hitler's spectacular rise to power may have been due to the power inherent in the swastika. In a moralistic variant on this superstitious theme, some people believe that the evil which Hitler committed under the swastika flag must somehow be inherent in the swastika symbol. And from there, as they keep on inferring, they start suspecting that some mysterious evil is inherent in Hindu culture. This reversal of the swastika's meaning, from a sign of luck (always depicted on the hand of opulent Ganesh) to a sign of evil, is somewhat like the story of the Christian image of the devil: he is depicted with buck's horns, a clear reference to the horned god of Paganism (like the Pashupati on one of the Indus seals).

The positive imagery of Paganism got integrated into Christian imagery, but then as the symbol of evil. Now that we are no longer bound by the compulsions of the missionary project, we may clear the horned god, as well as the swastika, of the evil aura with which outsiders have covered them. For Hindus who have migrated to the West, especially the U.S., there is a practical problem: if they display the swastika on the gates of mandirs, or other places, outsiders think that this is some Nazi outfit. Worse, people who have personally suffered under the Nazi regime may feel painfully reminded. I think it is a matter of sensitivity to display those swastikas only in very modest ways, for as long as people who have lived through the horrors of the Nazi regime are with us.

Meanwhile, the Hindus abroad should educate the public about the real meaning and hoary tradition of this symbol, so that some time in the next century the Swastika may regain its rightful place as a profound and timeless symbol, untainted by the accidental and misconceived association with Nazism. With all this talk about the misuse of the swastika, it may be useful to briefly restate its basic meaning. The word comes from su-asti, it be good, as in the Sanskrit greeting Pratah swasti, good morning. So, swastika means auspicious-maker or sing of auspiciousness. What the swastika visually depicts is the solar cycle, be it during the day or during the year. It shows the circular movement at the four cardinal points: sunrise, noon, sunset, midnight; or spring equinox, summer solstice, autumn equinox, winter solstice.

As such, it is shorthand for the Zodiac as well as for all macrocosmic and microcosmic cycles. It signifies the completeness as well as the dynamics of the Whole. Being primarily a solar symbol, it is normally (except in black-and-white print) painted in solar colours like red, saffron or gold; while the Nazi swastika was black. Like the swastika, the term Arya, which is rather central in Hindu tradition and more so in Nazism, is in need of rehabilitation. Of course, the term does not indicate a race, but a quality of character. When Buddha gives a short formulation of his teachings, he calls it the Arya

Satyani, the four Noble Truths. If the secularists have been inhibited about the use of the word Arya as proving the Fascist character of Hinduism, it is partly because of this terminology used by Buddha, the hero of their mythical anti-Brahmin revolution.

The term Aryan was used by the Nazis in opposition to the term Semitic. It so happens that both have

1. A primary linguistic meaning (the Indo-European and the Semitic language families),
2. A fallacious racial meaning (with Semitic standing for Jewish), and
3. Aderivative theological meaning, derived from the language groups in which the main texts of two religion families have been written the Hindu tradition in the largest sense, and the Jewish-Christian-Islamic tradition. The Nazis used the terms in the second meaning, vaguely basing it scientifically on the first meaning. For the third meaning, they didn't have the brains not the philosophical inclination to go into it.

Aryan and Semitic are shorthand for two radically differing approaches to religion. With "Semitic" are meant the religions claiming revelation from the one and only God. In primitive Shamanistic cults, there may be spirits speaking through the Shaman, but that is never a unique and definitive revelation from a unique Creator- god. Similarly, there were oracles where a god was supposed to speak through a human medium; the point is that there were many of them. But the revealed monotheistic religions carry with them a typical fundamental doctrine that sets them apart from all other religions.

On the one hand, their God speaks to people at a specific moment in history, at a specific place, so that the beneficiaries or immediate witnesses are limited in number, certainly less than all of humanity. On the other hand, their God is the only one, so that all the other people on earth either have to get other revelations from this one God, or they are not getting revelations at all, except false ones from false gods. While the first option was theoretically possible, the Semitic religions have effectively chosen the second. This implies that humanity gets divided into two: those whom God has personally addressed, and those whom he has ignored. So, we get Jews and Gentiles, Christians and Pagans, Muslims and Kafirs.

Of course, every tribe used to divide the world into the tribe and the rest. The tribe was home, the rest was unsafe and foreign. And every group identity, tribal or other, can give rise to hostility against other groups. As an application of this general rule, even religious group identity could be the basis of polarization and conflict. However, the polarization between the One God's Chosen Community and the rest of humanity was of a radically different nature than these ordinary group antagonisms. The tribal division was a division between people on an equal footing. The others had their own identity and interests, with which our own might sometimes be incompatible, but there was nothing intrinsically evil or wrong about them.

We had gods, and so had they. Both of us worshipped the sun god, or the goddess of fleeting time who devours us all, or the Unknown god, with local accents and variations, but not radically different. For instance, in Homer's epic about the Trojan War, you see some of the god's side with the Greeks and other god's side with the Trojans. They shared the divine sphere between them. This basic equality is broken in the Semitic religions. There, one part of humanity has God on its side. That implies that whoever stands against it, stands against God, with no divine friends on his own side. There is now a fortunate part of humanity, and another part which is doomed and cursed.

Religion in its public aspect used to be a unifying thing, a celebration of a cosmic oneness transcending the biological social and other differences between the realms of nature and the members of a society. Now it became a divisive thing, pitting the Chosen against the doomed. In this psychology, it is quite normal that all the non- human layers of the cosmos, who, just like the doomed part of humanity, were ignorant of God's unique revelation, were all deprived of their sacredness. The golden calf and other idols of the Gentiles were smashed.

The sacred trees of the Pagans were felled. The holy cows of the Kafirs were slaughtered. And this entire cosmos was given to Adam and Eve for their pleasure. Henceforth, a tree was nothing but timber.

Thus, the Semitic religions constitute a radical break with natural religiosity, which had always made nature share in the manifestation of the divine, and which had never thought of limiting the awareness of the divine to one community. In books written in a monotheistic cultural milieu, this revealed monotheism is always portrayed as a great step forwards in the march of humanity. However, in real terms I cannot see one genuine advantage that has accrued to humanity thanks to the revelation-based monotheism. It is said that this monotheism meant the end of superstition, of people praying to godlings for favours. But people have prayed to this new. One God for the same favours. Worse, is there a bigger superstition than the belief that you are specially favoured over the other part of humanity, and that God is on your side?

By contrast, the Aryan religious tradition has not pretended to be the special recipient of a unique divine revelation. The divine is manifest everywhere, be it in different ways and to different degrees. It is not excluded that some elements/times/places/animals/people are more sacred than others, but the difference is only gradual. There is a divine oneness of all entities in the cosmos. If at all you want to give this outlook a philosophical name, you could say that roughly, it is monism. That means, the assumption or perception that somehow everything is of one essence. This Aryan tradition has found its classic formulation in the Sanskrit writings of entire lineages of human beings, referred to as Rishis. However, it is also present in Pagan traditions outside the area where Sanskrit was the language of culture.

There are outward differences but a fundamental akinness with Pagan traditions the world over. If you analyze Pagan practices of ritual, sacrifice, incantation, you find the same presupposed attitude towards the cosmos: a basic awareness that it is one. This basic awareness will be present in the religious feeling of many a member of the Semitic religions. But there, it is overlaid with the doctrinal assumption of a fundamental and irreducible two-ness of the cosmos: on the one hand God and His chose ones, on the other hand the godless remainder. The degree, to which individuals feel bound by their formal allegiance to this doctrine, may differ widely.

And we will not judge the individuals. But we may give an opinion on the doctrine of the One God who reveals Himself to/through a specific individual, has brought an absolute division of mankind in the minds of its adherents, and this mental division has in turn caused untold suffering in persecutions and holy wars.

They may not denote races, as Hitler thought, but they do denote language groups, and people identify to quite an extent with their language. Moreover, these two types of religious outlook do not historically coincide with the said language groups. The Bible was written in Hebrew and the Quran in Arabic, while Jesus spoke in Aramaic (though his words were preserved in Greek translation), all three Semitic languages. Nevertheless, there was a lot of Paganism in this language area before revelation-based monotheism took over. It is often forgotten that the Arabs whom Mohammed tried to convert, were just as much polytheists as the Hindus, and that they fought equally hard to preserve their Kaaba as the Hindus fought to repeat that the Jewish tradition lost the aggressive edge, which form the most reprehensible effect of the Semitic outlook, long ago.

Conversely, in Aryan Iran, under the Sassanian dynasty, we see the Aryan religion of Zoroaster take on an equally exclusivistic attitude as is typical for the Semitic religions, complete with temple-destruction, idol-breaking and persecution of Manichaeans and Buddhists. Later, many Aryan-speaking people have been converted tot he Semitic creed of Islam. In Europe, most followers of the Semitic religion of Christ are speakers of Aryan languages. In Africa and other places, the division in Aryan and Semitic has no linguistic (much less a racial) relevance. So, I propose to renounce the habit of using Semitic as shorthand for "revelation-based monotheistic" religions. The use of the word Arya as shorthand for Sanatana Dharma can continue, but one should be careful not to give secularist slanderers a chance of falsely associating it with the Aryan race nonsense.

But before renouncing the Semitic habit myself, I will use the term Semitic one last time, in order to show how Nazism itself, for all its anti-Semitic rhetoric, very much fitted into the Semitic tradition. As Girilal Jain has convincingly argued, Nazism was an extreme realization of the 19th century secular nationalism in Europe. This secular nationalism was in its general attitude towards mankind a direct heir to the Semitic legacy carried into Europe by Christianity. There is a straight lineage from Moses' Chosen People to Hitler's Herrenvolk (superior people). The radical division of mankind into the chosen insiders and the lost outsiders is very much present in this secular nationalism.

A not-so-secular slogan of the impeccably secular Nazi state, written on the belt of the German soldiers, was: Gott mit unsp (God with us). This notion can be traced straight to Moses, from whom it had made a second lineage to Mohammed's jihad. Because of Hitler's dislike for Christianity, and because of some Nazi intellectuals' rhetoric involving the pre- Christian German mythology, many people, especially Christians, have considered Nazism as a return to Paganism. That is a case of being fooled by a superficial semblance. In the Nazi ideology, the Germanic mythology had no place whatsoever.

There was a certain flirting with themes from Germanic mythology since the mind-19th century at the latest, the best-known being Richard Wagner's operas (as there had been an exploration of Greek mythology since the Renaissance). So, by the time of Nazism, there were some artsy upper class people and some weird intellectuals playing with this ancient Germanic imagery, but there is no trace of any ideological influence from those fairytales on the actual political thought of the Nazis. Incidentally, today there is a new revival of Pagan religion in Europe. In Britain we have had the New

Druids, both formal groups who claim to revive the ancient Celtic traditions and individuals who explore whatever lore has survived, combining it with astrology, Oriental mysticism, and more such ingredients.

This movement started in the romantic 19th century, in the same climate in which Wagner wrote his Ring der Nibelungen and Lohengrin, and it has continued with ups and downs till today. In Germany too, there is now a rediscovery of pre-Christian Germanic religion. Apart from the fact that these new heathens have to reconstruct this lost tradition from stray fragments and outsiders' testimonies, they also face the problem of this association of ancient Germanic lore with Nazism. But they manage to convince themselves and others of the utter superficiality in the Nazis' appropriation of this ancient imagery, and of the inherent tolerant and open-minded attitude of the Pagan civilization. In today's Germany, an estimated 20,000 people regularly participate in gatherings where the ancient or neo-ancient rites are conducted, most of them intellectuals with decent jobs.

If we look at the basic points in the Nazi programme, we do not find anything there that can be traced to Germanic Paganism. Anti-Semitism (i.e. anti-Judaism) has nothing whatsoever to do with Germanic Paganism; it is a strong Christian tradition. Especially the Russian Orthodox Church and the Roman Catholic Church in Hitler's Austria gave it implicit or explicit ideological support. Authoritarian political thought has nothing whatsoever to do with the Germanic tribal organization, which was largely democratic, with an elected king and a regular all-tribe assembly meeting. It had more to do with the secular organization of the Roman Empire (which model had loomed large over the European polity all through the Christian period), which has also influenced the Church organization. The same Roman influence we find in outward forms like the uniformist discipline, the Roman salute and the fondness of grand parades.

Secular nationalism, glorification of the state, genocide, racial purity and uniformity, all these essential ideological elements of Nazism has nothing whatsoever to do with the Pagan religion and neither the Germanic Paganism, nor the Hindu Paganism with its swastika. It is important to stress this profound foreignness of Nazism to pre-modern Paganism, because once Hindus set out to rediscover the social philosophy and other elements of their own traditions, there will of course be some secularist ignoramus who will say that "*this is just what Hitler did*". The Nazi kind of nationalism was also of the Semitic kind. Rather than seeing the nation as one step on the ladder in the organizational hierarchy, below civilization and humanity, and above regional, tribal and family units, it denied this gradedness.

Instead, it divided the world in outsiders and insiders, thus in principle opposing itself to the rest of the world, and imposed uniformity on the nation, discouraging all subnational groupings. Again, this exclusivistic and uniformist nationalism is opposed to the Pagan outlook. The dominance of monotheism has strongly promoted that single most essential trait of the monotheistic mind: simplistic crudeness. For a well-known example, monotheists are idol-breakers: they are for God's unity, therefore they are against diversity. Their mental culture is too crude to see that multiplicity does not exclude unity, even while polytheists know fully well that there is one divine essence in all their gods (who anyway are all projections of the one but multi-faceted human consciousness).

Most modernizers these days are appallingly limited to black-and white categories in their thinking. For instance, in the present discussion of multi-level integration, they are of course for slogans like unity and integration, and therefore they are against any narrow and chauvinistic championing of region, sect, language group etc. Their only concept of unity is to raze everything flat, then there will be no more difference and disunity, so that will be the realization of unity, equality etc. This is Hitler's and Stalin's approach to national integration. Yet, real modern scientific thinking is gradual. It handles in-between categories (such as probability between certainty and uncertainty). This is formally a rediscovery of the old Pagan world-view. There is not just the absolute one God and the absolutely profane plural world, as in monotheism. There is a lot of life between the two. There is both sacredness and profaneness within the world, as there is both oneness and plurality within the divine. Similarly, there are in-between levels between the individual and the state, with units who entertain certain specificity rather than submitting to uniformity. A typically simplistic fallacy of the monotheistic mind is the one heard so often in the anti-Mandir rhetoric:"But Ram is everywhere! Ram would be ashamed if he saw how attached you people are to something as profane as a spatial location and a structure of bricks!" Of course God is everywhere.

And yet, there is a sanatana, ineluctable tendency in man to make the sacred present within the world, by consecrating certain parts of space and time, and demarcating them from the profane parts. We like to create difference, and make some places and some times special. Even the monotheists have had to yield to this natural tendency. Even though Allah is not in any place and time in particular, the Muslims have places of pilgrimage, festival days, a special day for prayer (Friday), a special month for fasting (Ramzan). The uniformizing monotheists can't help recognizing certain more sacred parts in space and time. So it is quite alright for Hindus to say: no, not any place will do, we want the one site that we have considered sacred since centuries. Sacred means: not just any.

This Semitic simplistic crudeness, the same which prevents secularists from properly understanding the Ayodhya issue, is present in many modern unhealthy forms of nationalism, among them Nazism. They see their nation in isolation, as an absolutely independent unit, which on the other hand excludes all subdivisions within the nation. In a healthy international set-up, there are grades of independence, which are proportional to the grades of separate identity between ethnic and linguistic units. A case in point is "Khalistan". The Sikh community is distinct by its dress, and by its specific choice of Hindu scriptures and parampara. It is not distinct by language, for Panjabi (if at all it can be considered a language rather than a Hindi dialect) is also spoken by Hindus and

Muslims; and its scriptures are in Hindi, the language of crores of non-Sikh Hindus. It is not distinct geographically, for it has always lived mixed with other communities. It does not have a separate political history, for Ranjit Singh's empire was a state ruled by a Sikh, but by no means a Sikh state in which Sikhdom was shared by all or even the majority of the citizens. So, by the United Nations criteria for recognition as a separate nation, the Sikhs don't qualify at all. To the extent of the distinctness of their identity, they are entitled to, well, cultivating the things that make up their identity, but not to a separate state. There has been a gradual increase of Semitic influence on the Sikh community during this century, or rather, on the Akalis who have set themselves up as the leaders. They have exchange the Hindu concept of God's oneness, through many forms, for the Semitic concept of God's unicity, inimical to all personified depictions or goods.

They have reshaped their gurus into prophets, intercessory mouthpieces of God, with Guru Govind Singh as the "last and final prophet". These prophets have revealed the words that make up Sikh Scripture, and made the Sikhs into a "people of the Book". The chief influence is of course that of Islam, but the general depreciation for polytheism and idolatry which the British brought, has also played a role. It is no wonder that with this artificial Semitic identity, some Sikhs have developed a *Semitic* concept of nationalism, not admitting of any gradations. They began applying the crass simplistic reasoning of absolutizing their small measure of distinctness into a separate nationhood, and denying their internal differences and sub-identities for the sake of uniformity. They have a separate dress, therefore they have a separate identity, and therefore they are entitled to an independent state.

On the other hand, within their own community, they accept no differences and impose the Khalsa Sikh identity on the otherwise pluriform Nanakpanthi community: any Sikh who is not a Khalsa Sikh is not a real Sikh. Absolute cleavage with other communities and uniformity within the community, these are the essential ingredients of modern nationalism, generated in the Semitic cultural context of late- Christian

Europe. For the sake of national integration in India, it is imperative to set the record straight, to reverse this process of absolutizing any minor difference in identity into a separatist claim to a nation-state.

In the specific case of the Sikhs, the obvious fact should be made clear, that Sikh identity is integrated in a hierarchy of differentiation within Hinduism: it is a Bhakti sect within the broad Vaishnava tradition within Sanatana Dharma. In general, a theory of graded integration of distinct communities via a hierarchy of political levels that does justice to this distinctness should be evolved. That is the Aryan answer to a world-wide problem of plural-identity states, which has been aggravated by the Semitic absolutist approach.

"They killed the Mahatma" "It is extremely symbolic that Advani is the heir of Nathuram Godse who, in pursuit of what he was convinced was his duty to India, shot dead the man who had chanted the name of Ram all his life till his last breath", writes M.J. Akbar. Many others make the same allegation, mostly more sharply.

Before going into the facts of the matter, let us make the observation that today the name and especially the murder of the Mahatma are being exploited to the fullest by people who are crusading against that which was Mahatma Gandhi's first concern and loyalty: Hindu society. As is clear from the Mahatma's polemic against the Christian missionaries, he was first and foremost a Hindu, who opposed all designs to destroy Hindu culture. And it was because he loved and served Hindu society, that he could take the freedom to criticize it.

Those who criticize Hindu society and its defenders today, not as its well-wishers but as its enemies, and who do not hesitate to invoke the Mahatma's authority to prop up their Hindu-baiting designs before a population with an increasingly hazy memory of the Mahatma's real commitment, are traitors to the Mahatma's message. These people, from the shameless Jawaharlal Nehru down to his sycophants like M.J. Akbar, are in no position to lecture Advani about Gandhi the Ram bhakt.

In 1948, Nathuram Godse was an active member of the Hindu Mahasabha. Many workers and leaders of this organization were also members of the Congress, the party which Akbar in his article seeks to portray as the absolute antipode of the communal forces. Since 1925 there existed another Hindu organization, the Rashtriya Swayamsevak Sangh, which did not intend to be political. Godse, who was a Maharashtra Brahmin just like the founders of the RSS, had left this organization some time before he killed Gandhi, because he didn't find it radical enough.

In 1947, the Mahatma's decades-long attempts to forge Hindu-Muslim unity ended in utter failure, when the Muslim League, supported by an overwhelming majority of the Muslim electorate, forced Partition on India. It should be a lesson for those who talk lightly of national integration and Hindu-Muslim unity, that even the Mahatma couldn't influence the Muslim community leadership. In the perception of millions of Hindus, especially those who had too flee their homes in what had suddenly become Pakistan; this Partition was very much the Mahatma's personal failure and responsibility: he had carried on a policy of concessions to the Muslims in order to appease their ever-increasing demands, and they had only become more arrogant in the process.

As if to confirm their views, he went on a fast to death in order to force the Hindus and the Indian government into a number of concessions. Among them: the Hindu refugees who were staying in mosques in Delhi had to vacate them and find a place elsewhere, and the Indian government had to pay Pakistan's share of the treasury which the British had left, to Pakistan, a country with which it was actually at war in Kashmir. All his demands were meeting, and he stopped his fast. This one-sided string of demands on the Hindus, and this masochistic habit of instilling guilt into his own community and swallowing all the Muslim crimes without protest, immensely angered many Hindus, among them Nathuram Godse. He couldn't take it any longer, for him the very name of the Mahatma made my blood boil. So, with the complicity of a few friends, he murdered the Mahatma.

The Indian people were so angry with the Mahatma the day before, now re-installed him as the living saint they used to venerate, and as he was now dead, they made a myth out of him. A myth that contained the beliefs the day before had been seen by everyone to lie shattered by reality. Conversely, there was a lot of violence against the Hindu Mahasabha. There was also large-scale violence against the Maharashtra Brahmin community to which Godse belonged, much like the anti-Sikh violence after Indira's murder (in both cases M.J. Akbar's Congress is generally believed to have actively fomented this violence). The great beneficiary of the Mahatma's murder was undoubtedly Jawaharlal Nehru.

It marginalized the Hindu Mahasabha, and whatever other Hindu activist party existed, completely. Without the murder, Nehru and his Congress would have had to answer for his betrayal of the election promise that India would remain united, and for the immense suffering to which they were a party by accepting Partition.Now, he had an occasion to ban and possibly destroy what he hated most of all: the organizations which championed Hindutva. In this case, the fact that Nehru benefited immensely by the Mahatma's murder, will not lead us to the conclusion that he must have been behind it. For, the principle that he who benefits must have committed the crime, only applies if people act rationally.

Now, Nathuram Godse's act was anything but rational. Not only did he do the biggest possible damage to his own political cause. He also did not even punish the source of the Partition disaster that had angered him so much. If he had killed Jinnah, it would still have been murder, but it would somehow have been logical. But killing the Mahatma was like being beaten up by street toughs and then coming home and killing your father in revenge. It was quite irrational. It is therefore quite improbable that the Hindu Mahasabha as such had a hand in the murder. In fact, Godse had been angry with party leader Savarkara for being too co- operative with the new Indian government. At any rate, the party leadership was not involved in the murder: that was the judge's opinion, when he fully acquitted Savarkar, whom the prosecutor for the state, at the express instigation of Nehru, had also accused of complicity in the murder. The party leader's non- involvement was so clear, that the prosecutor did not appeal against the acquittal. As is well known, Godse and his accomplice Narayan Apte were hanged, and several others were sentenced to life imprisonment, of which they actually did some fifteen years.

Now, what does L.K. Advani have to do with all this? He has been a member of the RSS since decades. His party, the BJP, or at least its earlier incarnation, the Jan Sangh, was formed by RSS members who wanted to give a political dimension to the movement, in 1951. So, his party did not exist at the time of the Mahatma's murder, but the mother organization RSS was very much around (in fact, RSS chief Guru Golwalkar was one of the first to condemn the murder as a heinous crime, but that condemnation was of course so common that it couldn't prove much. So the question becomes: is the RSS anyhow *"the heir of Nathuram Godse"*, as M. J. Akbar wants us to believe?

After the murder, Nehru, who saw his chance, banned not only the Hindu Mahasabha but also the RSS, and jailed many RSS workers. However, the prosecutor could not find any trace of complicity, and did not prosecute any RSS man. So, in a juridical sense, the RSS had nothing at all to do with the murder. And M.J. Akbar and similar propagandists have to exploit people's ignorance in order to pass off their association of L.K. Advani with Nathuram Godse. Now, one could say that the RSS was co-responsible for the murder in the vaguer sense that they crated the atmosphere for it (the same way secularists today allot guilt for the riots). And it is undoubtedly true that the RSS was against Partition and therefore against the Partition managers, including the Mahatma. He had done so many fasts unto death to force Hindus, why had he not done one to stop the Muslims from partitioning the country?

This question lived in the minds of many Indians, and probably the RSS was vocal in expressing this anger against the Mahatma's passivity in the face of Partition. There is no doubt that they did their part in strengthening the anti-Gandhi mood in the country. But they did not create the atmosphere for Godse's act: Godse knew them since years and he was through with them. Godse didn't need the RSS (on which he looked down as being merely a culture organisation) to make up his mind about Gandhi and about how to punish him.

There is quite a difference between demolishing the Mahatma's myth (a myth which M.J. Akbar's Congress Party continues to exploit even today) or criticizing his policies, and killing the man. The anti-Mahatma things which the RSS people said and wrote were to my knowledge not more vicious than the anti-Advani propaganda which the secularists spread today (being a bigot, vicious, rabid, fascist, another Barbar, Jinnah, Hitler, etc.) And if tomorrow a lunatic kills Advani, we will not accuse the secularists of committing or even inspiring the murder. They may be proven liars, but that does not make them murderers.

HINDU NATIONALISM

"The Hindu communalists' claim to being patriotic is wholly suspect. The RSS and the Hindu Mahasabha have a shameful history of collaboration with the British, especially in 1942. Their support to the colonial state, unlike the communists', did not even have that redeeming feature or fig leaf: the choice of a lesser evil against fascism. It came from utterly despicable, base and crass motives." Thus spoke Praful Bidwai.

Praful Bidwai repeats here a classic from the communist gallery of lies: that the communists collaborated with the British as a matter of choosing the lesser evil and first fighting fascism. It is simply not true that the communists joined hands with the British because they wanted to fight fascism. When England formally, declared war on Nazi Germany in 1939, the communists didn't move. Stalin had a pact with Hitler, and so the communists did not fight Hitler. It was only when Hitler attacked the Soviet Union, that the communists joined the anti-fascist struggle. The communists' loyalty was not to India, not to Britain, not to the cause of anti-fascism, but solely to the Soviet Union. The only redeeming feature in the communists' collaboration with the British was that it was part of their collaboration with the Soviet Union.

Praful Bidwai writes articles against communalism and accuses communalists of *"utterly despicable, crass and base motives"* for their collaboration with the British. So that must be his judgment about the Muslim League, which always consistently collaborated with the British, and which was wholly unconcerned with fig-leaves like the anti-fascist struggle. We may add that Bidwai's communist friends supported the Muslim League's Pakistan demand and that they spied for the British and got many freedom fighters jailed. The Hindu Mahasabha had always been in the anti-colonial struggle. Its leader Savarkar had spent many years in a penal camp on the Andamans for complicity in anti-colonial murder.

We may disagree with what he said, but as titles go, he had deserved his title Swatantryaveer (hero of independence). When he wanted Hindus to join the British army during the war (*"Hinduize all politics, militarize Hindudom"*), this was not a betrayal of the freedom struggle, but rather a potentially very effective strategy for obtaining quick independence. Savarkar's calculation was that after the war, the British would find before them a Hindu army, well-trained in the war against the Japanese, well-armed and well-organized, against which they would not even want to wage another colonial war.

Why does Bidwai mention 1942, and not, say, 1944? Because in 1944 all parties including Congress collaborated with the British, while 1942 was the year of the Quit India movement. This movement was no doubt patriotic, but it was a great failure. It did nothing for independence, and it did not even achieve its real objective: bringing Congress back in the centre-stage of Indian politics. But at the same time, Subhash Chandra Bose was joining the Axis powers and organizing the Indian National Army to invade and liberate British India. Now, let's see who collaborated with the British against his own people. Jawaharlal Nehru declared that when Subhash Chandra Bose would set foot on Indian soil, he would fight him. That is, Nehru would collaborate with the British against the Japanese-backed Indian National Army. Taking our cue from Praful Bidwai, we must ascribe to Nehru "utterly despicable, crass and base motives".

Anyway, what a strange exercise: dealing with the allegation that the Hindu activist parties are not India nationalists. I had thought that at least would be granted to them. It just goes to show how rabid (to use one of their favourite terms) the secularists' hatred for the Hindu communalists has become: they just kick around whichever way they can, now reverting to the more familiar allegation of national revanchism, irredentism (reclaiming territory on historical grounds) and narrow chauvinism.

Let us consider these more familiar allegations, which would be an element in common with the aggressive nationalism of Germany, Japan and Italy in the thirties (and with that of China in 1950-62). Take irredentism: designs to annex territory based on historical claims. In some RSS publications, you see maps of Akhand Bharat, which are roughly British India: including Myanmar (Burma), but not including Afghanistan. So, it might seem they somewhere have a design to annex Myanmar one day. In fact, Myanmar was never a part of India; it was only the British who lumped the two together for a while.

On the other hand, Afghanistan was a full part of the Hindu cradle up till the year 1000, and in political unity with India until Nadir Shah separated it in the 18th century. The mountain range in Eastern Afghanistan where the native Hindus were slaughtered, is still called the Hindu Kush (Persian: Hindu slaughter.) It is significant that one of the very few place-names on earth that reminds us not of the victory of the winners but rather of the slaughter of the losers, concerns genocide of Hindus by the Muslims. It seems that many people, who champion the Hindu cause, do not have a good knowledge of Hindu history.

But others do at least know of Afghanistan's having been a part of Hindu culture, for I have heard once, as an illustration of the expansionist ambitions of the Hindu communalists, that they want the shuddhi of Afghanistan. It was quoted by a secularist, with the suggestion: isn't that irredentist, and therefore fascist? Well, no. As long as shuddhi means the Hindu variety of conversion, there is nothing wrong with organizations like the Arya Samaj going to Afghanistan and performing shuddhi of the Afghans, that is, ritually leading them back into the Hindu fold. Of course, one doesn't see it happen just like that. But then, one doesn't see it happen after military conquest either.

No cases are known to me of forced shuddhi, even in the heady twenties when Shuddhi and Tabligh movements competed for converts. Shudhi can only come after a conscious and free decision of the human being involved. On that condition, there is nothing wrong with the Shuddhi of Afghanistan. There are also, no doubt, some cranks who think that all countries with some Indian influence have to be brought together in a Greater India: Iran, Tibet, Sri Lanka, Malaysia, Thailand, Cambodia, and Indonesia. But since some of the same cranks also believe that everything comes from India (my native tongue, Dutch, is said to have been brought by the Daityas), this Greater India would really comprise the whole world.

The thing is that such people, while politically totally unimportant, are somehow visible enough within the Hindutva movement, to give the whole movement a bad name. The one questionable and even objectionable element in the nationalism of Hindutva prophets like Savarkar and Golwalkar, as well as of Jawaharlal Nehru for that matter is this 19th century European concept of a territorial nationalism. Savarkar defined a Hindu as someone for whom India is both his fatherland and holyland. The two words are important in the definition: a Chinese Buddhist may consider India his holyland, but since he is not an Indian native, he is not a Hindu; and an Indian Muslim, conversely, is not a Hindu because his holyland lies in Arabia.

Now, why tie the definition of Hindu to this piece of land? The Hindus in Bali, Guyana, etc. are just as much Hindus as those in Bharat. One can migrate and yet retain Hindu culture. Of course, the name Hindu is really a geographical term (Hind is Persian for Sindh), but then the task for Hindu thinkers should be to free Hinduism from this territorial definition, rather than to confirm it. It is said that Shintoism is Japan's national religion (as opposed to so-called universal or imperialist religion). Alright, but Shinto does not mean Japan, it means the way of the gods. So, if you define a religion, you should say something about its contents, not just about its geographical location.

"The way of the gods" may be still very rudimentary as a definition, but it says at least that it is a method or practice (a way) involving the divine in a kind of personalized way (the gods, as opposed to an atheist or nirguna system). That is more than Hindu, which means just of India. Savarkar put things upside down. He was a nationalist, pledging allegiance to this piece of earth now called India. But what is special about this country, so special that Savarkar builds a religion on it? There is nothing special about this country, except that historically it happens to be the cradle of Hindu society, and that society in turn derives its worth from its practicing and embodying a certain culture, Sanatana Dharma.

It is because of Sanatana Dharma that this society is worth serving and preserving, and in turn it is because of Hindu society that Hindusthan is worth loving and defending but this culture can be transplanted or re-created elsewhere, and then that other country is as much fatherland and holyland. This territorial nationalism centered on Bharat Mata only confuses the issues before Hindu society. For instance, it occasions all this silly talk about Muslim Indians cheering for Pakistan in cricket games, and having extra-territorial loyalties to the area from which their religion was imported. But so what?

The problem with Islam is not at all that it is foreign. The problem with Islam lies not in its geographical but in its ideological origins. The problem is not one of nationalism vs. extra-national loyalties; it is one of culture and ideology: an exclusivist anti-humanist creed vs. a pluralist and integrally humanist culture. The Islamic problem is not one of loyalty to Pakistan or Mecca, but one of self- righteousness and intolerance. As long as the Hindu nationalists continue to define the Muslim problem as a problem of nationality, of "joining the national mainstream" and of "being Indian first and Muslim next", they are trapped in 19th century state nationalism, with its entire puffed-up patriotic emotionalism.

They are evading the confrontation between two incompatible ideologies/cultures, which no patriotism or loyalty to the state can unit. For instance, asking the Muslims to identify themselves as Mohammedi Hindus is not only very unrealistic, it constitutes a refusal to recognize the true (exclusivist and therefore averse to assimilation) character of Islam, in the name of a superficial Hindu nationhood. There is no good reason why Muslims or anyone else should direct his first loyalty to the Indian state. That state is nothing but an instrument to regular society and facilitates the citizens' fulfillment of their own life aims.

If Muslims want to direct their loyalty towards an international religious community, they are free to do so, as long as they abide by the law of the land. The way forwards for the Hindu movement, is to redefine the problem in terms of ideology and civilization, and to address the challenge of Islam not at the level of ineffective emotional categories like loyalty and identifying with the nation, but at the ideological level. And when it comes to loyalty, this should not be directed towards such accidental matters as a territory or a nation in which we happen to be born, but towards the eternal values embodied in Hindu civilization.

Hindutva ideologue V.D.Savarkar was a territorial Hindu, but culturally he was quite alienated. The well-known example: he advocated meat-eating and even meet-eating. Savarkar reasoned: if beef is more nutritious, then drop all the taboos, and kill cows for their meat. If seems many of his (formal and informal) followers still think that the Hindus can only defeat the meat-eating Muslims if they give up vegetarianism. What nonsense this is: what are you fighting for if you believe that "in order to better defend Hindu culture, I have to give up Hindu culture"? If you think you have to forsake your culture identity, you only have this territorial identity left. And then, paradoxically, you arrive at the same point where the Nehruvian secularists are. They too advocate a culturally neutral, territorial patriotism. Both in the Hindu movements and in the anti-Hindu secularist movements, people are saying that you should be Indian first. What is this, being India? What is that, Bharatiyatva?

Human beings are not different by the land they inhabit. They develop certain distinctiveness by the value-system they practice, by the social ways that mould them, by the mental outlook that is instilled in them. So you can have a commitment to certain values. But a commitment to a certain piece of earth can only be superficial. And if this basically superficial attachment to this territory gets mystified, as happened with the secular nationalisms in some European countries, then the consequences are evil. Of course, when there is a football game, I want the team from my town to win. If it's an international game, I want my country's team to win.

It would be a bit ridiculous to support the other town, the foreign country. So, that much territorial patriotism is alright. But one's basic commitment should be to more substantial things than that. A country can only acquire a value, and be an object of commitment, if it becomes historically linked with a substantial value. As long as India is conceived as culturally neutral, it is just a piece of land, not really worth any commitment. Forget about Bharatiyatva. The day when the world has one global culture, and that day is not too far off, these concept of territorial patriotism, of Indian-ness or American-ness etc. will only apply in football stadiums.

However, today the Indian state has an important function as the abode and defense of a culture which could hardly thrive otherwise. Since Hindu society is surrounded by Islamic and Communist enemies out to destroy Hindu culture, this state acquires a more than territorial importance. India is not culturally neutral, because objectively it is the only defense of

Hindu culture against its enemies. So, as abode and defense of Hindu culture, this land and this state can count on the Hindus' allegiance and attachment.

At this secondary level, nationalism becomes meaningful. That Savarkar, one of the foremost Hindutva leaders, could be so careless about Hindu culture even while defending it, is significant for the advanced state of self-forgetfulness that threatens to submerge Hindu society and in this nationalistic and directed to Bharat Mata, than cultural and directed to Sanatana Dharma.

If at all the nationalism in the Hindutva movement would develop fascist overtones (and I do not see that at present), it would be due to its not being Hindu enough, and being too secular-nationalist. Compare with the relative unimportance of national borders in medieval Europe when it was all Catholic and unconcerned with nation-states. It was the larger religious and cultural idea (the Brahmin level) that could keep in its place the political idea of the state (the Kshatriya level). Similarly, a deeper knowledge and understanding of Sanatana Dharma would soon dedramatize and ultimately dissolve the problems of religionalism and sectarianism.

For instance, Sikh separatism is based on externalities like beards and turbans, and on a defective and distorted understanding of Hindu and Sikh doctrine. If today Hindu politicians have to advocate a tough line in Punjab, and sending in the army, it is because they themselves (as well as all the traveling sadhus and other consciousness-raisers of Hindu society) failed to check the spread of ignorance and misconceptions about the Sikh tradition. Saying that India only makes sense as the eggshell in which Hindu society lives, and that India takes its identity from Hinduism, may not be the position taken by Savarkar, who put this the other way around, but at any rate it is the position considered Hindu communalist par excellence by the secularists. Yet, the position is wholly correct.

But for Hinduism, there would not have been an Indian Union. Suppose that, as some foresaw a century ago, all Hindus would have been converted to Islam or Christianity. What would happen then, can be seen from such happy Muslim-Christian bhai-bhai countries like Lebanon, Cyprus, Sudan, Kosovo (Yugoslavia), Nagorny-Karabakh. The country would have been split at the very least into a Muslim North and a Christian South. In the sense that Hinduism is the cultural reason for India's very existence, India cannot exist but as a Hindu Rashtra. Let us see what the secular alternative is. In a secular India, there is room for different religions, right? This pluralism is either a negative pluralism: we don't care, be whatever you want to be.

In that case, you have a neutral state. That is the official position today, and it is not generating much enthusiasm. The minorities don't want it, because they feel threatened by majority rule. They fear that a neutral state regulated by majority vote, would uniformize at the expense of the weaker elements in the plural set-up. They allege that, against its own professing, the preserving of the minorities' identity is made an issue, and when the majority of the weak, an anti-democratic policy of championing the minorities against the majority is enforced. And so, everyone is unhappy. The alternative to this neutral pluralism is a positive pluralism. Underlying it, there is philosophy that positively gives a full-blooded foundation and justification to plurality.

That philosophy exist: it is called Sanatana Dharma, and a state founded on it could well be called a Hindu Rashtra. In this state, the different components of the plural set-up are recognized as such. This state would be different from a uniform democracy, in that it would recognize plural subsystems. This recognition of plurality is, once more, the very opposite of fascism. Integrating different units of identity into a large identity is one of the foremost socio-political problems of today. And it is an issue on which the Hindu tradition has interesting approaches to offer.

MAJORITYISM

The BJP has been saying that the government and some political parties indulge in minorityism. This means that they have promised or given special privileges to the minorities, chiefly the Muslims, in exchange for their political support. Two other reasons for this pampering the minorities may be " the approval of the Muslim countries, with whom Nehru and his successors established a special relationship (party made necessary by the Nehru-created Kashmir problem, on which a united Muslim front had to be prevented), and the satisfaction of a mental desire to be secular. In my opinion, the last factor, the mental cluster of secularism, the need to prove oneself non-Hindu and pro-minorities, is the most important one.

The examples of systematic institutional minorityism cited most often are the separate personal law based on the Shariat, the special status of the Muslim-majority state Jammu and Kashmir, the immunity of minority schools and places of worship from government interference or take-over. Examples of occasional political minorityism are the numerous unequal treaties before independence between Congress and the Muslim league, the creation of a Muslim-majority district in Kerala by redrawing of district borders, the overruling of the Shah Bano verdict with legislation, the creation of a minorities commission (under the Janata government of which some BJP leaders were Cabinet ministers). These do not add up to a full oppression of Hindu society by the Muslim minority, but they do constitute real discriminations.

Opposing this minorityism, the BJP has put forward the slogan: Justice for all, appeasement of none. This means that there should be no discrimination between individuals, between states, or between any intermediary levels of organization, on the basic of religions. Thus, instead of a Minorities Commission, there should be a Human Rights Commission, because members of the majority can have grievances too. Instead of immunity for minority schools, there should be immunity for schools run by any community. In fact, many members of the Constituent Assembly who voted this Articles 30 giving guarantees to the minority educational institutions, acted on the assumption that majority institutions would wrong, the Article should be reconsidered. A common civil code should be enacted. Articles 370 should be scrapped and Kashmir should be fully integrated.

So, what the BJP demands here, is that the rules of democracy be applied without any exemptions or exceptions on communal grounds? To any democratic-minded person, this would seem quite unobjectionable. Not so to the Indian secularists. Of late, they have coined a new term, which should brand this democratic equality as really a component of fascism: majoritarianism. The right term to oppose minorityism would have been majorityism, i.e. espousal of the majority cause, but they chose the uglier majoritarianism. This is too bad for them, because the term can be analyzed as "espousal of the majoritarian cause", so not championing a (majority) community, hence communalism, but championing the majoritarian principle.

And there is nothing objectionable in the majoritarian principle: it is the very working principle of our democracy. In fact, the secularists are quite correct in not describing the opposition to minorityism as majorityism. Opposing the favouring of minorities need not indicate a favouring of the majority, it may just as well stem for a concern of the working principle of the current from of democracy, viz. decision by the majority. "The true test of a democracy is the justice that the minority gets in the system. The majority will always get its share whatever the system", writes M.J. Akbar.

With that, white minority rule in South Africa certainly passes the true test of democracy. M.J. Akbar implies that all struggles against minority regimes oppressing majorities were futile, since majorities cannot possibly be oppressed. But Hindus point out that they are really discriminated against in the laws of the land, and that minorities do get privileges which are unthinkable in most genuinely secular states. If we apply Bipan Chandra's definition of communalism, viz. attributing common secular interests to people on the ground of a common religion. Then we must consider M.J. Akbar's statement as an application of communalist thought categories. There is absolutely no questioning of the religious rights of the minorities in India, so if Mr. Akbar raises issues involving the minorities, it must be non-religious issues, in which the category of religious community (minority) does not properly apply. From the moment the religious rights of the minorities are guaranteed, any other talk of minorities is fundamentally communalist. Every single article of law not dealing with the exercise of religious community as a legally relevant unit of organization, is an element of communalism in the legal framework of the state, and should be repudiated in a truly secular-set-up.

A religious community is only a lawful category in strictly religious matters. In these, there is already discrimination against the Hindus. The states governments can (and do, as recently in Kerala) take over the management of Hindu temples, not of minority places of worship. They can (and do, as in West Bengal) take over school started by Hindu organizations. Apart from the secular aspects of education, there is religious discrimination against the Hindus in that the imparting of Hindus tradition is hampered, as well as the creation of a Hindu atmosphere in a school (e.g. through the selective recruitment of teachers, to which the minority schools are fully entitled).

Both in the letter and spirit of the Constitution and in actual practice, Hindus as a religious community are discriminated against in matters of temples management and education. These discriminations are at least partly encroachments on the exercise n the exercise of the Hindus' constitutionally guaranteed religious freedom. Just imagine what rhetoric and agitation would be lunched if such discriminations had applied to the minorities. Then there is the matter of the separate civil code for the minorities. Marriage and inheritance laws are, perhaps on top of some sacramental dimension, quite secular matters. Recognizing and institutionalizing inequality between the citizens of India in these secular matters on the basis of their religion is definitely a case of constitutional communalism.

Or rather, let us not be too harsh on the Constitution itself, for it does call on the law-maker to eventually abolish the religion-based law systems. It is political communalism on the part of the parties that refuse to implement the constitutional provision for the eventual enactment of a common civil code. It has been said, by commentators ranging from Girilal Jain to Mani Shankar Aiyar, that this common civil code should not be forced on the Muslims that they should agree to it voluntarily, without any pressure being put on them to do so.

As a matter of practical policy in the given situation, that makes good sense. However, as a matter of principle, the position that a common law decided on by a democratic majority, should not be imposed on an unwilling minority, opens the door for all kinds of minority veto rights that make a mockery of the democratic principle that decision are taken by majority vote. One can justify this position by saying that a minority's personal law is not the whole country's business, so that the relevant majority whose choice should determine the democratic decision, is not the majority of the entire nation, but merely the emerging in the democratic process within the community.

This reasoning would from part of a philosophy of multi community integration, in which as many powers as possible are devolved to the lowest possible level, in this case the religious community (since personal law is associated with religious commandments). This philosophy is currently gaining in relevance in a world which, with its increasing global integration, is discovering the socio-political value of decentralization: while matters of global concern are to be decided at the global level, national decisions should be retained at the national level, which in turn should not usurp decisions that can be taken at the regional level, and this in turn should devolve to the local level decisions that can be taken at that level.

This decentralization trend (which is visible, for instance, in the increasing recognition of the substate regions as political units in the European Community) is linked with the modern small is beautiful philosophy, applied to political decision-making. Of course, this decentralization of power to the proper and lowest possible level is akin to the decentralized structure of Hindu society, which always was commonwealth of (occupational as well as religious) communities. It is quite in the spirit of Hindu tradition, tough not in the spirit of the Constitution, to leave the Muslim community its personal law.

The separate status for the state of Kashmir (Article 370) is again discrimination in secular matters on the basis of religion, viz. its being a state with a Muslim majority. Nehru sycophants have tried to explain this irresponsible and communalist Article as follows: "The special problems of Jammu and Kashmir do not arise only out of the fact of its being a Muslim-majority state. It is also a state coveted by a foreign power which has thrice gone to war with India to capture the state, whose territory is partly under hostile foreign occupation, which is geopolitically located in the cockpit of international intrigue."

In fact, each of these problems can be reduced to this one fact that it is a Muslim-majority state and is therefore claimed by Pakistan under the terms of the Partition of British India. With a Hindu majority this would be radically different, and it would not even want the separate status granted by Article 370. Moreover, none of the said problems justifies a separate status. On the contrary, in most countries they would lead to an extra strong integration into the Union, if not permanent central rule. But our Nehruvian knows it all better: "It is with a view to addressing ourselves to these very special problems that the constitutional device of Article 370 was evolved." If that is true, then we must recognize in all sincerity that this device has been ineffective.

It has not stopped the Chinese from annexing parts of Karakoram and Ladakh, it has not stopped Pakistan from invading it twice more, it has not prevented the ongoing skirmishes over the Siachen glacier, it has not prevented the general spread of secessionism, it has not prevented the Kashmiri Muslims from practicing majorityism at the expense of the Hindu and Buddhist areas of Jammu and Ladakh and from hounding out the Hindu minority of the Kashmir valley, and it has not given private investors the confidence to go in and bring some genuine economical development. Short, in every geopolitical, communal and even economical respect, it has been an outrageous failure. But our Nehruvian spokesman remains, like his mentor, adamantly blind to the feedback from reality:"In the circumstances, the demand for abrogating Article 370 is totally misplaced. It would only result in the further alienation of the people of Jammu and Kashmir..."

Firstly, subtract people of Jammu: they would welcome the full integration with India, either through the abrogation of Article 370 of through separate statehood for itself and Union Territory status for Ladakh. Secondly, subtract Hindus of Kashmir: they would gladly welcome full accession to India. But then, they have already fled to areas that are really India. Thirdly, why would the people of Kashmir feel alienated by integration? That seems a contradiction. It might be more accurate to say that Nehru has treated the Kashmiri Muslims like spoiled children, afraid to refuse them anything, so if you tell them now that they will get equal treatment with the rest, they become very nasty.

The blatant communal discrimination that guarantees the Muslim majority in Kashmir by forbidding non-Kashmiris to settle there is also defended by our Nehruvian:"There is little practical scope for settling any considerable body of outsiders in the valley. What land there is, is already under the plough." By these standards, outsiders should be prevented from settling in Bombay. Moreover,"there would not be many Indians from elsewhere in the country who would wish to actually settle there."

But abrogating communalist Articles is a matter of principle, of upholding the basic constitutional and democratic principle of non-discrimination, and is not dependent on just what number of people it will affect in practice. As BJP spokesman K. L. Sharma said: "Equal status to all states and equal rights to all citizens is the BJP secularism." Moreover, as a political precedent, Article 370 affects millions of people, viz. those in states where separatist movement are encouraged by it and use the demand of the extension of Article 370 to their own state as a propaganda item or bargaining chip ("our ultimate concession short of independence").

Of course, it is not certain that the abrogation of Article 370 will make much of a practical difference for Kashmir itself in the near future. As long as the secessionist terror continues, and even for some time after that, not even the refugees will go back, let alone other. But at least the principle of India's integrity will have been restored. And it will discourage the secessionists in Kashmir and elsewhere, as well as the Pakistani agents, to see that India is reasserting its integrity on at least the level of legislation, that one level where terrorist created ground realities need not be taken into account and where principles can be upheld without compromise.

The argument of the secularists against the allegations of minorityism is that Hindus should be generous, and that they are not entitled to a persecution complex since their very majority makes it impossible for them to become the object of injustice. Moreover, the Muslims are a poor and wretched community who must be suffering a lot of discrimination otherwise they would not be so underrepresented in government jobs, business, the army, and the universities: how can Hindus claim they are put at a disadvantage by this pitiable minority?

As often, the secularists defend their case by confusing issues. There is a difference between suffering legal constitutional discrimination, and being poor. In the Islamic Republic of Malaysia, the Chinese are second-class citizens, legally discriminated against as being non-Muslims, yet they are very successful in business, and considerably wealthier than the Muslim Malays. If the Muslims in India are poor, it is not at all because of discrimination, as should be clear from the record of other minorities. If Sikhs are overrepresented in government services and the security forces, if Christians are overrepresented in education, if Jains are overrepresented in business, it is not because of preferential treatment by the law or by the executive.

In fact, if we drop the false socialist parlance, these communities are not over-represented in the said fields; it is more accurate to say they are great achievers. And the Muslims, unfortunately, are on average poor achievers. That is almost entirely due to one single factor: their poor schooling. This factor in turn may be reduced to Islamic factors like large families, low status of women (keeping them uneducated and thus less able to teach their children and to create an education-friendly atmosphere for them), and stress on Quranic rather than secular studies. Short, the hold of Islamic orthodoxy over the Muslim community is by far the largest factor in Muslim community is by far the largest factor in Muslim backwardness (as well as fostering its ghetto mentality).

By contrast, while Hindus may be doing alright economically etc., they do objectively suffer legal discrimination. They are denied certain constitutional rights and guarantees, as well as many political favours, and that constitutes a real inequality even if it is not impoverishing.

The secularist line that Hindus should bear discrimination without complaining, since there are worse things in life (such as this abysmal poverty which these wretched Muslims have to suffer), presupposes that Hindus have no sense of honour. It assumes Hindus don't mind being second-class citizens, as long as they make a decent living. This presupposition certainly fits the stereotype, created in the centuries when Hindus were sharply discriminated against in the laws laid down by Muslim rulers. But that does not justify continuing legal discrimination. Moreover, on top of this undeniable political and legal discrimination, Hindus perceive a serious threat to the very existence of their culture and society, when they look across the borders and into the future.

Their acute sensitivity to minorityism is strengthened by the perception that the minorities indulge in aggression against the Hindus wherever they get the chance, and that they are also growing stronger by the day. When you consider the population trends in the Indian Subcontinent, it seems inevitable that Muslims will make up 50% of its population in less than eighty years. Extrapolating the trends within India, it will be less than fifty years until the Muslims are again 24% of the population, the percentage which in the forties was enough to enforce Partition.

Add to that the millions-strong illegal Muslim immigration into India, which will only accelerate as population pressure increases in Pakistan and Bangladesh. So, the majority status of the Hindus is by no means guaranteed. Moreover, the so- called minority is in fact the Indian department of a world - wide movement, from which it effectively gets moral and financial support. It is no fable or prejudice that Muslims as a community have the highest birth-rate in practically every country where they co-exist with other communities. In some article that set out to debunk this propaganda, three countries were cited as counter-examples. Unfortunately, the writer had not chosen his concocted examples very well: one of them was Lebanon.

The cause of the civil war there, apart from the legitimate reaction against Palestinian take-over tactics, has been the fast rise in Muslim population, which rendered the earlier power division on a communal basis disproportional. The Muslims, now in the majority, want to abrogate the old power division and freely exert their majoritarian powers. The Christians fear that this will cause a speedy end to their age-old presence in Lebanon. In Pakistan, family planning is a joke. The responsible ministry is at present headed by a fundamentalist Muslim, Saddar Niazi, who boasts of being one of fifteen children. He has declared that the pressure for family planning was a holdover from the liberal secularism of Benazir Bhutto, and that he did not intend to implement the policies of a woman charged with corruption and overwhelmingly voted out in the 1990 election.

His stand is not exceptional; rather it is the rule among Muslim governments. At any rate, Pakistan's birth rate stands at 3.2%, almost the doubt of India's. Bangladesh, the world's most densely populated country and perhaps the only Muslim country that ever seriously considered a family planning policy (apart from the moderate states Egypt and Indonesia, and in contrast to Malaysia, which has actively encouraged a high birth rate among its Muslims), today also has a birth rate markedly higher than India's. Both Pakistan and Bangladesh consciously seek to solve their overpopulation problem at least partly by dumping excess people in India, where they can be useful for the long-term pan-Islamic design. Kashmir has been an eye-opener for the Hindus if one was needed. In the first part of 1990, more than two lakhs of Hindus, practically the entire non-Muslim population, were driven out from the Valley. Refugee Arvind Dhar testifies: "The aggression has been entirely one-sided. All central government employees (generally Hindus) were asked to leave their jobs, and those who did not were placed on a hit-list. One newspaper (Al-Safab) had a headline in March asking all Hindus to vacate within 48 hours of face bullets".

Predictably, secularists and Muslim communalists have joined hands to deny the propaganda that Kashmiri Muslims have unleashed a purely communalist campaign of violence against the Hindus. Some papers declared that it was actually the Hindu refugees who were "creating a communal crisis" by fleeing to Jammu or Delhi. In their Newspeak, which calls terrorists militants, the refugees are called migrants, and it is an interesting illustration of the perversion of India's political parlance to see how even the refugees themselves have sometimes adopted this secularist-imposed usage.

Syed Shahabuddin declared, along with some moderate Kashmiri Muslims, that the Hindus could come back to Kashmir, and that their property was being looked after by their Muslim neighbours. But the first-hand information of refugee Arvind Dhar tells a different story:"All my movable property has been stolen and my house was burnt a month ago. But Mr. Shahabuddin says that migrants' property is being looked after. Bhushan Bazaz, president of the terrorist-sympathizing J&K Democratic Forum pontificates:"As far as the migrants are concerned, they should show boldness in returning to their native land. They committed a great blunder in migration... The migrants should take it for granted that they will not be harmed, physically or emotionally, if they return to the valley immediately". It is worth quoting a reply: "By advising the migrants, many of whom live in squalor in camps mourning the death of their kith and kin, to 'return to the valley boldly, taking it for granted that they will not be harmed...', Mr. Bazaz is mendaciously suggesting that these hapless people have fled the Valley out of an imaginary fear at someone's instance. The naked truth is that the peace- loving and peaceful non-Muslims were forced to flee when they found that the goodwill of their well-disposed but unarmed Muslim neighbours was of no avail to them against the orgies of selective murder, rape and arson perpetrated by armed Pak-trained militants... Considering that even a few gullible migrants, including a lone woman, were recently gunned down within hours of their return, one wonders whether Mr. Bazaz's facile assurance of safety to migrants emanates from his desire to fool the uninformed or to propitiate India-baiters in Pakistan".

The kashmiri militants, Bushan Bazaz, Syed Shahabuddin, the Nehruvian defenders of Article 370, they are all, each in his own way, objectively part of the strategy of the anti-Hindu forces on the Kashmir front. The Kashmir Samiti has produced a report titled Riots in Kashmir, listing 85 temples destroyed in the valley, and claiming that 550 Hindus had been killed (630 with security men included; official figure 495) in the Islamic purification campaign in 1990. And one cannot just blame Pakistan, for even a secularist paper admits: "There is no evidence to suggest that the average Kashmiri is fed up with the militants. Everywhere ordinary people are sheltering 'the boys fighting for a cause".

The common Muslims in Kashmir believe in the two-nation theory. After all, Islam itself instills the communal separateness in its followers. It is a communalist ideology through and through, and all the talk of Kashmiriyat as a bond between Hindus and Muslims have proven to be just wind as soon as the call for a separate Dar-ul-Islam was spread. In Pakistan, the dwindling percentage of 1% Hindus ekes out an existence in constant fear of the never-ending harassment and attacks by the Muslim majority (which is untroubled by any minoritism). A secularist paper, prudishly and secularly titling: "Ethnic violence drives Sinhis across the border", lets out the truth in the small print: "According to [refugee Sukh Ram], most of the Hindus are forced to desert their homes because of their religion. We are not allowed to pray peacefully in the temple of celebrate Hindu festival he said". Moreover, at several places in Sindh, cremation grounds had been usurped by Mohajirs, funeral procession was attacked with stones, and women were not safe either. Pakistan Hindu leader Raja Chander Singh, who left Benazir's Pakistan People's Party to form the Pakistan Hindu Party, says that the Hindu migration to India is now (proportionally) bigger than during the Partition day: "The future of Hindus in Pakistan is very bleak. They are leaving because of fear".

So the Hindus flee, and Pakistan likes it that way:"The Pakistani leaders... seem to be encouraging Hindus to leave the country". A 16-year-old boy is quoted saying: "We all think here that Pakistan is a country for Muslims and only Hindusthan is the country for us Hindus". Perhaps this accomplished fact had better be faced: Hindusthan is the homeland and refuge for the Hindus fleeting Muslim states. Since India is not willing to defend the rights of the Hindus in the Muslim neighbour states, it should automatically grant citizenship to Hindu refugees (as Israel does to Jews).

With all this persecution of Hindus by these poor wretched minorities, it is quite understandable that Hindus feel they should reassert their own democratic rights. They have done enough for the minorities by recognizing their democratic rights and religious freedom. Justice for all without any unequal appeasement of any religious community should be enough in a secular democratic state. But here they have to confront the watchdogs of secularism, who know it all better.

A.S. Abraham writes: "The observe side of the coin of 'minoritysim' is that the majority is held is to the victim of discrimination by the state. To indulge the minorities is automatically to discriminate against the majority. On the other hand, 'majoritarianism' cannot, in this scheme, entail discrimination against the minorities because, unlike 'minorityism', which is an unnatural distortion, 'majoritarianism is natural and healthy". The last sentence is merely a scheme attributed to the Hindus by Mr. Abraham, as part of the old rhetorical trick: if you can't beat their argument, attribute to them a weak or stupid argument and attack that instead. The very term 'majoritarianism' is not a

Hindu scheme; it is of the secularists' own making, coined as a swearword for religiously neutral democracy. It is obvious that to "indulge the minorities" automatically means discriminating against the majority. Privileges mean inequality, and if one party is more than equal, the other is less than equal. No-one would object to the minorities' right to open (subsidized) schools, was it not that the majority is denied this right.

Today, this right is a privilege of the minorities and a discrimination against the majority. Of course, there is nothing objectionable or anti-national in this right of the minorities, so the discrimination should be abolished by extending the same right to the majority (incidentally, this discrimination, laid down in Article 30, is glossed over in mr, Abraham's column). For Mr. Abraham's brand of secularists, constitutional guarantees of religious freedom and non-discrimination are not good enough:"The fact is that 'minorityism' inheres in the very idea of secularism." So, he concedes to Mr. Advani that the Indian secularists are indeed champions of minorityism.

However, as a citizen of a fully secular state, I strongly object to Mr.Abrahams minorityist statement. I have never heard of minorityism either as a term or as a concept somehow functional in our secular system. We do not give religious minorities a veto against decisions enacted by a democratic majority. Let us take the example Mr.Abraham himself gives. He concedes that "superficially, the Advani position looks unexceptionable", consisting of "reasonable demands for secularizing our affairs". However, it is not truly secular, for if it were, "then they would also have to stop demanding a ban on cow slaughter, which is a religiously motivated proscription that cannot be endorsed by a secular state".

As usual, out secularists prove their point by mixing things up. There is a difference between the motives for which a state enacts a law (which in a secular democrat is not Scriptural authority but the will of a majority of the people), and the motives that make the people favour the enactment of this law (with which the state has no business: they may be religious motives as well as any other). The nice thing about democracy is that it allows for difference between countries. If a majority of the people in my country favor cow slaughter, then we can practice cow slaughter; and if a majority in India opposes it, then the Indian state can ban it. Both countries adhere to the political form of democracy, but the contents of their policies are different, reflecting the different will of the respective nations. Democracy is a formal concept, it is a procedure of decision making, not concerned with the contents of (nor with the motives for) the decisions. So if a majority of the Indian citizens favour a ban on cow-slaughter, then the secular state does not avail of a Thought Police to check out their religious or other motives or this political choice. A secular democracy merely registers the will of the majority and enacts laws and policies accordingly.

At this point, there might be one limitation: unlike the Islamic republics, who ride roughshod over the religious rights of minorities, a secular state should safeguard the religious community in India that imposes on its adherents the duty to slaughter cows. So, from a secular viewpoint, no compromise whatsoever is needed, and nothing stands in the way of enacting a ban on cow slaughter, provided a majority votes for it. And at any rate, there is nothing objectionable, or threatening to the secular character of the state, in a citizens' initiative to create opinion in favour of such a ban. The Muslim League always objected to a ban on cow slaughter, and demanded a veto right for the Muslim community on every issue. Today, many Hindu politicians have interiorized this demand for a minority veto right, and don't ever dare to suggest a ban on cow slaughter for fear of provoking the Muslim veto. In a secular democracy, the veto right of a religious minority is limited scrupulously to those decisions that directly the exercise of their religious freedom. Banning cow slaughter is not among them, so the democratic secular republic of India can certainly enact a ban on cow- slaughter the day a majority of citizens decides in its favour.

As Mr. Abraham himself writes: "A secular state, such as we are committed to building, is one in which the religious beliefs of its citizens are of no consequence to it. It regards them indiscriminately as equal citizens are of no consequence to it. It regards them indiscriminately as equal citizens under the law." More precisely: the religious beliefs of the citizens are of no consequence to the form (the procedure) of the decision-making, but they may of course be an element in the contents of the decisions, to the extent that the sovereign citizens choose to take them into account.

Minorityism, by contrast, means that you give special legal rights and political favours to citizens on the basis of their professing certain religious beliefs (or rather, on their belonging to certain religious communities with political clout). Minorityism does interfere with the form of democracy. In India, while not overwhelmingly affecting the democratic policy, it does thwart the principle of equality in several domains. Mr. Abraham attributes the wrongs of minorityism to another ideology, invented by his own tribe for the sake of rhetoric, majoritarianism: "Just as 'minorityism' is indispensable to secularism, so 'majoritarianism' is its antithesis. To be 'majoritarian' is to want the religious beliefs of the majority to colour, indeed to determine, the values, goals and institutions... This is an agenda for theocracy masquerading as 'genuine' secularism."

All decisions are determined by beliefs. To adapt an example from Indian tradition: if you believe the rope in the dark room to be a snake, your decision not to go in will have been determined by the belief that it was a snake, not by the reality that it was a rope. Instead of belief, we could better say more neutrally: perception. If a majority of the representatives of the people decide to have a state-run economy, then that decision has its roots in a belief or perception that such an economical system will be best suited to realize national goals (of which the choice again is based on the belief that, for instance, distributive equality is more important than wealth creation etc.). It is for the democracy not important whether this belief is correct. Observers of economical history may believe that the faith in a state-run economy is unfounded, but before this minority belief can democratically influence policy, they will have to persuade a majority to adopt this belief. You cannot get out of this: in a democracy, decisions are made on the (issue-related) belief of the majority. One may deplore that these beliefs are often inadequate but it is beyond the role and the power of the state to help it; the thinkers and educators of the people have to raise the people's consciousness so that its beliefs become more adequate to reality. Non-despotic democracy can only register and translate into policy the actual perception of a majority of the people.

So, by definition, "the beliefs of the majority do colour, indeed determine, the values, goals and institutions" of a secular democratic state. Sometimes, some of these beliefs are codified into a doctrine roughly called a religion. Well, the secular state has no business with that, as long as these beliefs do not interfere with the formal principles of the secular democracy itself. Thus, the Islamic belief that non-Muslims must be treated as third-class citizens and debarred from taking top government jobs, is intrinsically incompatible with secular democracy, and must on that ground be prevented from determining the institutions of the state.

But legislatively acting on the belief that cows are worth protecting against slaughter, is quite compatible with secular democracy, even if a minority doesn't think that highly of cows. After all, imposing the order "Keep off the grass" in city parks does just the same thing as imposing a ban on cow slaughter in India. There exists a minority of people who don't believe parks ought to be equipped with healthy lawns. They don't mind healthy good-looking lawns, just like beef-eaters don't mind unslaughtered cows, but they believe that for themselves the freedom to take a shortcut across the lawn is more valuable. Others may respect the lawn, but they don't feel any duty to respect it themselves. Yet, nobody in a secular democracy objects to the imposition of the majority's respect for nice-looking lawns on this unrespectful minority. This imposition of a uniform behaviour on a population with non-uniform beliefs is unavoidable in government relative to public affairs, and is no way a threat to the secular and democratic character of the polity. It become undemocratic only when a minority imposes its chosen rules of behaviour on a majority, and it becomes unsecular only when a religious authority rather than the will of a majority lays down the rules.

Now, what is the fuss about this majoritarianism effectively about? What possible policies would constitute this threatening phenomenon of majoritarianism; it cannot be the issue of cow slaughter, or the re-adoption of Vande Mataram as the anthem, much less the abolition of the discrimination against Hindus in education or temple-management. Mr. Abraham gives exactly one example, and I don't think he has another:"When the 'majority'... wants to build a temple on a site which the 'majority'... believes is the birthplace of Ram, then the proper course of action for the state is to assist, and certainly not to hinder that project. If it so happens that a mosque stands on the site, then not to allow the temple to be built for that reason is to be guilty of 'minorityism'." this argument deserves some scrutiny.

First of all, the word majority as the term for Hindu society is a creation of the secularists. If Mr. Abraham distances himself from it here, through the quote marks, it is because he is using the term here in another sense, in fact it's proper, democratic sense: a majority of opinion on the specific issue under consideration. By distancing himself from the term in this meaning, he wants to sow doubts that it is really a majority of the Indian people that want the Mandir to be built. Well, that can be ascertained by a referendum, as the BJP has demanded. Secondly, democratic states the world over do have the right to expropriate people or communities when they consider it necessary for the common good- a category to which a concrete meaning is given by the perception of a majority.

Not only are roads built on land expropriated from unwilling landed farmers: sometimes as a matter of social reform policy, poor landless peasants are given lands expropriated from unwilling landed farmers. The majority of poor people can impose harsh measures on the rich minority. Stealing from the rich to give to the poor, you may consider it just or unjust, but it is one of the options in a democracy. And it is sometimes done, and then mostly justified as a corrective measure for past injustices (a case in point: positive discrimination policies like job reservation). So, if a majority decides to take something from a minority, it is not yet fascism, in fact it is more probably socialism.

Nevertheless, the point which Mr. Abraham makes is that in a majoritarian (i. e. democratic) system, no minority is safe from the possible extortions by the majority. For instance, in Bangladesh the property of the Hindus has been threatened by the Enemy Property Act (the democratic caliber of Bangladesh is poor, but it is quite certain that even otherwise, no majority would have come forward to prevent the enactment of this law). In fact, in most countries, democratic or not, minorities are at the mercy of the majority. What protect the minorities are not so much the democratic character of the state, but the effective rule of law and/or the kindness and tolerance of the majority.

Let us narrow the discussion down to the example under consideration: taking over a place of worship. On what ground was it reprehensible that the Soviet government, claiming to be a people's government, claiming to be a people's government (a claim which we will concede here for the sake of the argument), expropriated the places of worship in order to transform them into temples of modernity and socialism (like factories and bureaucratic offices)? The majority of dialectical-materialist peasants and workers took from the minority of feudal and petty-bourgeois obscurantists their places of worship. This was reprehensible because (granting all other claims) it interfered with the exercise of these people's religious freedom.

Taking a single, or let's say three, mosques from the Muslim minority, is less than a denial of their religious freedom. But it is a small factual encroachment on the material exercise of their religious rights. As such, it can be justified as a, merely symbolic, righting of an old wrong. In a juridical sense, the communities that own and use the mosques, or their Waqf boards, can certainly be considered the successors to the rulers that built these mosques and initiated the worship that is continuing there. So, demanding from them these few places as a delayed and merely symbolic compensation for the wrongs inflicted by the erstwhile mosque-builders, while leaving them all the freedom and maybe even financially assisting them to set up alternative mosques nearby, is not at all misplaced, nor unjustifiable, nor in violation of internationally accepted limitations to a government's rights of expropriation.

However, the point about majoritarianism is not so much whether the expropriation of three contentious mosques is justified. The point is that a majority has the power to enact such expropriation regardless of its being justified or not. Conversely, a minority does not have the power to enact a similar expropriation, even if justified. A case in point: the Hindus in Bangladesh have no democratic power to reclaim some of their sacred places which the Muslims laid waste, not in Babar's or Aurangzeb's time, but the last few decades. This separation between justice and power is of course one of the most fundamental political problems that humanity faces. A minority cannot democratically enforce its claims, even if justified; while a majority can, even when its claims are unjustified.

A majority can democratically enact blatantly unjust laws and constitutional provisions (as it effectively does in Pakistan, Malaysia and other Muslim countries). That possibility of the majority riding roughshod over the minorities is indeed present in the democratic system. Yet normally it doesn't happen. Most majoritarian democracies do not oppress their minority communities. The very fact of running a pluralistic democratic polity will condition people to be respectful towards all the different components of their society.

The outright oppression of a minority by the majority almost exclusively happens where other ideological factors condition the majority community to disrespect towards the minorities. The most important such factor in the world today, you guessed it is Islam. So, it is not his system of majoritarian democracy that will make minorities oppressed and reduce their members to second-class citizens. It is the contents that the majority gives to the polity that may have this effect. In Bangladesh and Pakistan, Hindus have been oppressed by the Muslim majority in almost equal measure under dictators as under democratic governments.

Not the political system, but the chauvinistic anti-Kafir attitude of the majority community brought this about. In Hinduism, such fostering of intolerance towards non- Hindu communities, let alone active oppression, is not sanctioned by Scriptures or other sources of doctrine. Even if the continuing Islamic aggression against Hindus, both in the Islamic republics and in India itself, provokes Hindus to an anti-Muslim polarization, this will remain a peripheral and occasional tendency. There is simply no danger at all that the normal majoritarian form of democracy will lead to any oppression of the religious minorities in India.

By contrast, it is already a fact that minorityism, the policies with a bias towards the religious minorities, has effectively led (even within a formal structure of majoritarian democracy) to a number of discriminations against the Hindus on the basis of religion. In most majoritarian democracies in the world (all except the few Islamic republics that know democracy), there are no legal or political discriminations against the minorities (first of all because minorities are only recognized as a relevant category in some very few contexts, otherwise there are merely individuals).

But then, in most majoritarian democracies in the world, there is no minorityism either and the recent claim of some secularists that minorityism is essential to democracy. That Hindus suffer from discrimination favouring the minorities, is not an effect inherent in the prevalent political system. It is a policy followed by Hindu politicians of their own free will. And it can stop the moment these Hindu politicians come to their senses, and stop enacting or maintaining discriminating laws against their own people. This minorityism is not a legislative or constitutional problem (except secondarily), it is primarily a problem of mentality. And it is not so much a problem created by the aggressive minorities; it is at least partly created by the morbid willingness in Hindu politicians to appease minority arrogance.

So, solving the problem of minorityism requires chiefly a change of mentality in Hindu society. It should free itself from the wholly mistaken notion that it owes the minorities anything. It has not done them any injustice (which is more than what at least the Muslim minority can say) even in centuries past, and fully discharges its human and democratic duty by giving members of minority communities full citizen's rights and equality before the law, as well as full religious freedom. Hindus should realize that there is no reason at all for them to co-operate in policies that impose on them an inferior status in matters like education, settling in Kashmir, temple management, or marriage rights. Hindus should shake off the mental chains (nowadays called secularism) that make them tolerate these political and constitutional injustices.

TARGETING A MINORITY

"Majority communalism is far worse than minority communalism, for minority communalism can only lead to secessionism, while majority communalism leads to fascism", so some secularists say, citing Nehru as their guide in this vision of things. It is what the white minority in South Africa has been saying for some time: if we oppress them, it is only oppression, but if they get a chance to oppress us, we will be exterminated. No Indian secularist is known to have come out in support of this reasoning. The comparison with South Africa is fair to this extent that, generally, the problem posed is the same: in how far does democracy (in South Africa called majority rule) have to modify in order to give safety and autonomy to non-territorial sub-units of a nation?

India need not be apologetic about having this problem in common with South Africa: it is one of the main political problems of today's world. It is a fact that majorities can do a lot more harm to minorities, once they really want to, than the reverse. The Germans never could have taken on the Jews the way they did, if the Jews had formed the majority. Then again, it is not the number of heads that counts, but the effective power. When as army invades a country, it is mostly outnumbered by the populations it is out to subdue. The Conquistadores, who committed the final solution on the Native American population of the Caribbean and much of the South American continent, were vastly outnumbered by the population they exterminated.

It is not just numbers and military might that count, but also the unscrupled will to go to such an extreme. Moreover, what is a majority? In Western Armenia in 1915, the Christian Armenians outnumbered the Muslim Turks. But the Turks on Armenia were not left to themselves; they had a support base in Turkey proper. And they exterminated the Armenians in that area. The same thing, minus the genocide, we have seen in Cyprus: the Turkish minority, claiming oppression by the Greek majority, called in big brother Turkey, and imposed its will (Partition) on the helpless majority.

So, calling the Hindus a majority is a statement that must be qualified in different respects. They are fragmented. They are outnumbered by the Muslims worldwide. In the Subcontinent, the Muslims already number one third of the population (in 1981 it was 28% and increasing fast). Most of all, the Hindus don't have the ruthless determination to impose their will, of which the Muslims gave proof when they forced Partition on the country. But going by secularist parlance, and calling the Hindus the majority community, there is still no reason to postulate an imminent re-enactment of the German vs. Jewish story of 1933-45, with the Hindus exterminating the Muslims.

First of all, the relations between the communities concerned are very different in two cases. The Jews had not forced a Partition on Germany. They had no history of Persecuting and massacring the Germans. They were not sending infiltrators from a neighbouring Jewish Republic (they were actually preparing to set up a Jewish state in far-away Palestine). They were not forcibly occupying a piece of German territory. They were not starting riots. The Jews were blamed for all Germany's problems. The economic crisis was because of: "Jewish capitalists".

So was the German defeat in World War I (in which many Jews even outside Germany had in fact supported the German war effort). Decadence was attributed to Jews like Sigmund Freud. The Communist threat was attributed to the Jew Karl Marx (who merely had a Jewish-born, but converted, father). This does not apply to the Muslims in Hindu perception. Poverty, the defeat against China, the non-victory against the Tamil Tigers, corruption, unemployment, India's poor showing in the Olympics, all these are not blamed on the Muslims.

The Muslims are blamed for creating riots (which is at least partly correct), for oppressing and hounding out the Hindus of Bangladesh, Pakistan and Kashmir, for having inflicted Partition on India (all correct, except that it is done by *some* rather than by *the* Muslims, but it is certainly done under the banner of Islam). Then there are some allegations of things that in the short term are not actual problems for the Hindus, such as refusing family planning and a common civil code. But it is absolutely not true that Hindus attribute all their problems to the Muslim hand, the way the Germans (and generally also the Poles and the Russians) used to do with the Jews.

According to M.J. Akbar: *"Just as Hitler had given a frustrated Germany a target and that target was the Jew, so through the Ram Janmabhoomi movement, a frustrated country was given a target and that target was the Muslim"*. Before we analyze this comparison, I would like to point out that Mr. Akbar is in absolutely no position to blame anyone for making people into a target the way Hitler did with the Jews. Mr. Akbar is a Muslim, a congressman, and a Nehru worshipper. Now, the Muslims are still doing what Hitler did: blaming the Jews for all the problems. So many Muslim or Arad resolutions on any topic include condemnations of the Zionist entity.

When someone falls out of favour with a Muslim dictator, he tends to get caught spying for Israel, and hanged. When Khomeini counter-attacked Iraq, he declared his real goal was

Israel. When Muslims made a slander film about Rushdie, he was portrayed as a Zionist playboy. Stereotypes about the influence of the Jewish-controlled press and the Jewish capitalists, which in Europe count as unpermissible expressions of anti-Semitism, are current in Arab and pro-Arab comments on the Arab-Israeli problem.

And don't try to be clever by making a distinction between Jews and Zionists. In Europe quite a few bomb attacks are committed by anti-Zionist Muslims against Jews, including doctors, schoolchildren and citizens who have no plans of settling in Zion. The Islamic terrorists are not making that distinction, and neither are the Islamic governments who plan to destroy the state of Israel. If Israel will be destroyed, it will be with a chemical or nuclear holocaust killing millions of Jews. And then the Congressmen, who have continued Nehru's policy of total support for the anti-Israeli cause, will say: Wir haben das nicht gewusst.

In fact, Nehru himself fluently went from anti-Zionist to anti-Jewish. This is what he wrote: "In practice the Hindu is certainly not tolerant and is more narrow-minded than almost any person in any other country except the Jew". (In practice, Nehru was certainly not tolerant and he was more narrow-minded than almost any other person in any other country except Hitler) So, before Mr. Akbar starts to elaborate comparisons with Hitler's propaganda of blaming everything on the Jews, he should first of all belongs, are reiterating Hitler's propaganda till today. Now, in M.J. Akbar's comparison, Jews were made a target for Germans by the Nazis, and Muslims are made a target for Hindus by the Hindutva organization. At one point, which M. J. Akbar does not mention, the comparison is correct: in both cases, the hatred aroused was nothing new, but a centuries-old animosity with stable historical roots.

While Islamic anti-Judaism (or "anti-Semitism") had three causes:

The belief that the Jews killed Christ (who was himself a Jew, cfr. blaming Hindus for killing Gandhi), which was a lesser factor in the secular Nazi movement, but which till today is a reason for the Russian Orthodox Church to foster anti-Jewish attitudes. The associations of Jews with Muslims during the middle Ages, when many Christian lands had been overrun and forcibly converted to Islam, while in the Mediterranean many Christians were made slaves by the Muslims. By these experiences, Christians decided on a forward strategy known as the Crusades, they started by attacking the non-Christians in their midst: the Jews. The fact that the Jews or at least a conspicuous section among them were rich and powerful. This was a modern phenomenon due to the 18th century Jewish Enlightenment (or Haskala), when the Jews came out of the ghetto and involved those in society at large and yet retained a separate identity. This kind of hatred against successful minorities occurs in many countries, such as against the Chinese in Malaysia and Indonesia, or against Indians in some African countries. In Europe, it got blown up into a suspicion of a Jewish conspiracy to take over the world.

Let us compare this with the Hindu attitude towards the Muslims:

1. The traditional Sikh animus against the Muslims has a lot to do with the murder of the fifth and the ninth guru by the Muslim rulers. Unlike the allegation that the Jews killed Jesus (more probably the Romans did it, but the later Gospel-writers absolved the Romans and blamed the Jews for reasons of mission tactics: blaming the weak and wooing the strong), blaming Muslims for killing these gurus is historically correct. Thousands of sadhus were also killed, thousands of temples demolished, etc. But unlike the killing of God's only-born Son, this was just a huge crime committed by people, not a God-ordained event with cosmic dimension. And unlike the killing of Christ, it was not distant history, but recent history continuing till today in the Muslim parts of the Subcontinent, and the actualization of a doctrine that could any moment give rise to new crimes of the same kind. Jewish Scripture does not say that Christ must be killed, but Islamic Scripture does ordain an all-out struggle against

the unbelievers. So, while the Christian's allegation that the Jews murdered Christ is largely mythical, the Hindu resentment against the Muslims is firmly historical.

2. Hindus have not attacked others (including Jews to avenge the crimes of Islam. Neither have they attacked Muslims to avenge the crimes committed by others (the way the German flare-up against the Jews was partly a reaction against the unjust treaty of Versailles imposed by France and Britain). If they have a dislike for Muslims, it is not by association, it is not because of a general fear or hatred of Non-Hindus, it is a precisely directed reaction to a collective memory of Islamic atrocities heaped upon them as unbelievers.
3. If Hindus dislike Muslims, it is certainly not for their being rich and powerful. In fact, Hindus have not started hating any other minorities for acquiring a disproportionate share of the wealth and the power positions. On the other hand, most Muslims who remained in truncated India are not at all rich, though as a collectivity they are rather powerful. The suspicion of an international conspiracy is in this case not without foundation. The Muslims do have international co-ordinating bodies like the Rabita (the World Islamic League), with huge sums at their disposal for furthering the cause of Islam in any area deemed strategic. Unlike the Jews, the Muslims do have a doctrine of world conquest. Unlike the Jews, they effectively oppress other religions, and they do convert secular countries into Islamic republics (e.g. Malaysia, Libya, Iran, Bangladesh, and Sudan): there is no guarantee that they don't have similar plans for India.

So, these are the suspicions Hindus have against Muslims. It is possible that inflammatory speeches occasionally manage to transform that suspicion into violence. But M.J.Akbar is trying to fool us if he says that it is the BJP/VHP campaign that has created this suspicion and made the Muslims into a targeted group. Firstly, the collective memory of the crimes of Islam is quite established among the Hindu populace, which doesn't need campaigns for knowing about these crimes. Secondly, if there has been a Hindu awaking in recent years, it is not thanks to any campaign, but thanks to reality. It is the stands taken by the Bukharis and Shahabuddins, the plight of the Hindus in Kashmir, Punjab, Bangladesh, and the endless riots started by Muslim criminals that has caused the Hindu masses to stop and think. The BJP/VHP have not created the Hindu wave, they are merely riding it.

It is not entirely impossible that the Hindu-Muslim conflict will further escalate and turn India into a giant Lebanon. As Hindus are afflicted more seriously with more Muslim violence, they may start reacting in kind. It is the secularists, like Tavleen Singh and Madhu Limaye, who are painting this picture of the near future. While I am 100% sure that Hindus will not start a conflict on that scale, they may join it unreservedly once a *minority* really gets it going. It is certainly not the *Hindu communalists* who will create such a situation: they wouldn't know what to do with it; they just don't have the martial character and equipment for it.

AUTHORITARIANISM

It is alleged that the Hindu movement is against democracy:"For the VHP, Ayodhya is not an end but the means to an end. It has become both the justification and the rallying point for a coldly calculated bid to mobilize support under the banner of recalcitrant, vengeful Hinduism. What it is doing is not to defend Hinduism - the very idea that this is necessary in a country where 85% of the population is Hindu is ludicrous - but to hijack the symbols of Hinduism to serve the political end of creating an authoritarian state".

There are not too many facts known that could give rise to this allegation. And in fact, I am sure the allegation has not grown out of interpretation of given facts. It has grown out of the slogan *fascist!* When someone is called fascist, on the basis of whichever aspect of his behavior or thought that the may have in common with historical fascism, the (intended) effect is to associate him with all aspects of fascist thought and behaviour. So, if someone is a fascist because he "singles out a minority for attacks, like Hitler did to the Jews", he thereby also becomes an imperialist, anti- democrat, advocate of violence, genocide-planner, racist, etc. That us the most important reason for the sloganesque allegation of being anti-democratic, which has been levelled against the whole Hindutva movement.

During the Janmabhoomi controversy, the BJP has demanded a referendum. Is this anti-democratic? It is a shortcut to deciding on the will of the people, cutting through the corrupt horse-trading of the political parties, through the perverse arithmetic of the British constituency-based (first-past-the-post) election system, and through the secularist mental inhibitions of Hindu politicians. As demanded in South Africa, democracy will imply that the majority has the freedom to act as the majority.

Another case of implied anti-democratic bias among the secularists was all this nonsense of accusing politicians of building vote banks. Well, that is precisely what the democratic game is all about: pleasing the voter. If the secularists are against this (though they support politicians in building Muslim vote banks), then they should say clearly that they are against rule by the voters. They could take the aristocratic line, like Plato, who pointed out that democracy could only be the rule of the vulgar, the uninformed, the people with no vision, because they are the most numerous. They could say: we are elitist, we advocate the imposition of our own principles as a state policy, and we don't want voters to come in our way.

Of course, it is a fact that far-sighted leaders are often unable to rally a majority, and have to give way to demagogues. That is one of the problems of democracy, and those who decry others as anti-democratic are themselves not sufficiently conscious of the inherent imperfections of democracy. They should admit that democracy as we know it is not the final word in government by the people. At any rate, the solution for this distance between principle and popular support has so far been, to consider this as a challenge to the politicians. They have to convince people of the correctness of certain views and policies. So, rather than imposing principled policies on the people, as aristocrats would do, they should endeavor to make the people a party to the principled policies they propose.

So, far, the Hindutva politicians have not anywhere advocated the abolition of the democratic system (as opposed to the communists, who openly advocate the installment of the Dictatorship [of the Proletariat through its Vanguard Party). The BJP stresses that it wants a common law for all and equality for all regardless of religion, things that are considered evident in all democratic countries in the West. One thing that might be mentioned against the democratic credentials of the Hindutva movement is that Bal Thackeray, the Shiv Sena leader, has made some naughty remarks about dictatorship. In some interview I read, he was asked what he thought of Subhash Chandra Bose's remark that India needed one year of dictatorship to get on the right track.

And he replied with a grin that he fully agreed. But so what? For such remarks, the secularists call Thackeray an unabashed advocate of dictatorship, but they don't do the same thing about Subhash Bose, just mentioned as saying the thing which Thackeray merely confirmed. They don't mention the numerous well-meaning foreign commentators who have opined that India is too vast and complex and backward for democracy to function and to preserve the country's unity. Anti-Hindu anti-fascists of Congress obedience, like M.J. Akbar and M.S.Aiyar also tend to gloss over Indira, who actually practiced dictatorship. They all forget to point out that Marxism-Leninism, a strong component of the secularist front, by definition aims at the establishment of dictatorship.

And they all forget that the point is not what off-hand remarks Mr. Thackeray makes in casual conversation, but what his party offers as a programme. In the Shiv Sena programme, you do not find any demand for the establishment of dictatorship. There have been a few incidents of the Shiv Sena using muscle power against opponents. But this again does not prove authoritarian ambitions, unless you add that other parties, who use large-scale muscle and gun powèr especially at election time, have even stronger ambitions for dictatorship. But the parties I mean have succeeded each other in forming the government at the centre, so they have been in the best possible position to launch dictatorial rule, and yet they stepped down when they lost their majorities. So I don't think their authoritarian thrust is that strong, and the same thing counts for the Shiv Sena.

About the RSS, it has been said that its organizational structure is authoritarian. In an interview, Subramaniam Swamy (an erstwhile Jan Sangh leader, presently Commerce Minister in Chandra Shekhar's cabinet) once said that the RSS could not be called fascist because it did not advocate or organize violence, but that its authoritarian structure as well as its anti-intellectural bias is elements which the RSS has in common with fascism. And the two are related: an anti-intellectual bias inculcated in the rank and file, implies that the leader is doing the thinking for them, and they just obey. The structure of the RSS is at least partly democratic.

The general secretary, or Sarkaryavaha, is elected by the 450 district leaders, who meet twice a year (the Pratinidhi Sabha). The constitution of the central executive (Karyakarini Mandal), with about fifty members, is more intricate, with both elected and nominated members. The really controversial point is that the RSS top man, the Sarsanghchalak, is not elected at all, but appointed by his predecessor, like in a monastic parampara (teacher-pupil lineage.) We may compare this with the Roman Catholic Church where the pure is elected by bishops who themselves have been hierarchically appointed, not elected. The idea is moreover that it is the Holy Spirit who arranges the election result by inspiring the bishops. So, the Church is not a democracy.

Nevertheless, it does not follow that the Church, a nonpolitical organization, intends to reshape the secular polity after its own model. And it doesn't follow that Catholic politicians are anti- democratic and planning to impose the organizational model of the Church on the secular polity. It would only give proof of historical incompetence, if one starts using the typically modern category *fascist* for those pre-modern and pre-democratic types of organization. In the general polity, everybody s entitled to participation in the decision-making process. But in a private organization, the founders may reserve themselves the right to select candidates for leadership functions on the basis not of popularity but of loyalty to the project which the founders had in mind.

They have the right to set up such an undemocratic structure, without being deemed an enemy of the political democracy in society at large. In the Communist Party, they do not allow just anyone to become a member, take part in the decision-making, elect the leadership, and thus perhaps force policies on the party for which it was not created (in which case the party would be helpless against a hostile take-over by a large group who collectively join and claim a majority). There is nothing democratic about the Communist Party, yet it is the communists' democratic right to privately run an undemocratic organization. By being a member of society, you have the right to political participation; but that does not necessarily count for private organizations. So, an organization can follow a Parampara-system of appointment of the leader without being politically anti- democratic. Nevertheless, the leadership of the RSS is partly elected, though not by the mass of ordinary members, but by a group of people who have already climbed several steps on the RSS leader.

In its actual functioning, it seems there is a stable consensus between the different components of the RSS leadership. A Sunday Mail report states that "the titular head, like the pope, remains infallible as far as far as orders go. Never has a single order of the Sarsanghchalak been questioned till date in the Sangh's history. This is not due to any totalitarian dictate, as the Left would believe, but because the Mandal and the Pratinidhi Sabha are like huge counter weights in a balance checking the powers of both the Sarsanghchalak and the Sarkaryavaha." It is therefore not accurate or objective to describe the RSS structure simply as authoritarian, much less as fascist. Nonetheless, it is still quite possible that certain follow the leaders spirit prevails in the RSS rank and file, and that independent thinking is not encouraged. I have been told that the late Guruji Golwalkar got angry when he saw people reading papers or books. He would ask: "Don't you have anything more useful to do for the Sangh?" And when you see the total intellectual output of the RSS people, it is not much. Subramaniam Swamy is probably right when he ascribes an anti-intellectual bias to the RSS.

Now, if they would compensate for this near-absence on the intellectual front with great activity on the street violence and terrorist front, then they would be feared and dangerous, and their role would be comparable to the Nazi squads around 1930. But they are not active on the violent front, in the spite of all the propaganda put out by allegation journalists. Several times, dozens of their people got massacred by the Khalistanis: what violence has ensued? Compare with the massacre of Sikhs that Indira's followers committed after Indira's murder: who is a *fascist* then? They do not even react in kind when they are violently provoked. It is therefore that they are not getting much respect. The secularists despise people who don't take to violence, like the Tibetans, and they support people who take to terrorism, like the Palestinians.

If they replaced thought with muscle, then others would be victims of their anti-intellectual bias. But now, it is they themselves who are paying dearly for their refusal to develop an intellectual dimension and to wage the struggle on the ideological front. There they leave the field entirely to the Leftists and secularists. One cannot even say they are on the defensive. Look at the humiliating consequences which their anti-intellectual bias has had on them. Whenever anything happens, they are accused and spit at, by those who are having the entire debating arena to themselves. In the forties, they opposed Partition, together with the Hindu Mahasabha. Everyone else ended up agreeing to it. Yet, in articles written then and today, you find that they are being accused, without any proof, of "provoking" Partition by "frightening" the Muslims into support for the Muslim League. Unbelievable: the only innocent ones are being made the culprits by the united front of culprits. This shows how weak they are: it is always the week who are being blamed. By contrast, the Communists, who betrayed their compatriots to the British, and who actively worked for Partition, were back on top within a few years, respected and imitated by many other politicians including Jawaharlal Nehru. Why? Because they had a thought system which was widely broadcast and fashionable, and by which everyone was influenced, so that everyone owed them a certain ideological allegiance.

But the Hindutva force were mute cows without an ideology, much less any intellectual or media impact on the general public. Even the millions of refugees from Pakistan, who should have become a reliable popular basis or vote bank, could not be attracted with a political analysis that could pinpoint the causes of their problem and indicate a solution: the Hindutva people had no analysis, merely some emotions and slogans. During the Emergency, many socialists were left untouched by Indira, while the RSS was made to bear the brunt of the repression. But when the Janata government was formed, the same socialists, who had come to power on the blood and sweat of the RSS workers, demanded that the RSS members of the government choose between their seat and their RSS membership. There was no come out in their defense, any front or committee of intellectuals of expose the utter dishonesty and absurdity of the whole dual membership issue.

Everybody thinking was moulded by the Left, and had no affinity or sympathy with RSS thought. Everybody felt some allegiance to socialism and would not go against a socialist demand. And in shame the RSS people were sent into the wilderness. These events prove at least that the RSS is not at all a fascist movement. Hitler would not have been treated like that, and otherwise he would not have borne it without protest (in fact, having made it into the government, he would never have given it up). But more importantly, these events prove that the RSS is totally absent from the debating arena. Their anti-intellectual bias makes them into a passive object of abuse and ideological vilification. They don't have an intellectual apparatus with which they would be able to put their enemies in their proper places. They also don't have a propaganda apparatus to put forward their viewpoint (which would have been the first priority of any fascist, as of any communist party.) Therefore, they are at the mercy of their enemies. *Fascism* should be made of sterner stuff. Even when they got the largest mass movements in Indian history going, the Ram Janmabhoomi campaign, they were not capable of putting the secularist Babarwadis on the defensive. While in the historical Ayodhya debate the secularists had no case at all, still they could get away with depicting the solid Ram Mandir case as distortion of history, myth etc. On the strength of the evidence, the Hindutva leaders should have been capable of instilling a massive confidence in all struggle of truth against falsehood. But no, they resorted to the weaker, anti-intellectual and somewhat dishonorable line that it is faith and not historical evidence that has to decide the issue.

And even among their own followers, they did not wage a campaign to inform them about the hard facts of the matter and the larger issues at stake, assuming that the massive Hindus sentiments were enough. Sentiments are enough to get a Ram Janmabhoomi movement going, they are perhaps enough to make that one-issue movement succeed, but they are utterly insufficient when it comes to building a long-term movement for the defense and development of Hindu society. A purely physical movement, of which the intellectual dimension is limited to rumours and slogans, cannot realize (in fact, not even formulate) its goals. Any movement can only succeed if it has an ideological backbone. So, the point about this unwillingness to develop an intellectual thrust is not that it is fascist: it isn't. The point is that it is a sure formula for not achieving anything in the long run.

L.K. Advani is described by M.J. Akbar as having "an interesting blend of falsification of history and his own cool and convincing personality". What is more: "He and Vajpayee are the careful camouflage of decency' over a nasty, vicious and blood-thirsty movement." Now, I wouldn't dare to say such crass things about a fellow human being, but since Mr. Akbar has said them himself, he will allow me to leave the sentences intact but with himself as the subject: Mr. Akbar has an interesting blend of a convincing personality (he has convinced many that he is an authority on communalism) and shameless falsification of history. Moreover, he is the careful camouflage of decency over a nasty, vicious and blood-thirsty movement.

That M.J. Akbar is a falsifier of history, should be clear from his postulation, in the very same article, of a thousand years of brotherhood and amity between Hindus and Muslims, and "of shared culture, of a shared civilization, a shared vision". In reality, as can Islamic history, Islam in India was "a nasty, vicious and blood-thirsty movement". It is never preached or practiced brotherhood and friendship with the Hindus. It has never shared Hindus society's culture and vision. That one occasion when Emperor Akbar ceased persecuting the Hindus, there was a Sirhindi to reprimand him. That one occasion when Dara Shikoh translated Hindus writings and considered them "the mother of the Book", there was an Aurangzeb to kill him. Islam was out to exterminate the Hindus civilization, as it has exterminated the cultures of Arabia, West and Central Asia.

To this vicious and blood-thirsty movement, M.J. Akbar is giving a camouflage of decency. If fascism is to erupt in India in the sense of organized attempts at extermination of selected minorities, it will be in the pockets where Hindus are the minority, and it will be Hindus who get singled out for massacre. So far, the massacres in Punjab and Kashmir have not been intended as steps towards extermination, merely as a tactic to scare the Hindus into fleeting, which has worked very well in Kashmir, and has not been entirely without results in Punjab. If this gets really out of hand, Hindus may retaliate with mass-slaughter wherever they can. While the minority separatists have the guns, the enraged Hindus will have the numbers.

So, a mass killing of minority people is not excluded as a possibility. However, it will only take place if minority terrorists first go very far in their violence against Hindus. Unlike the entirely unprovoked Nazi terror against the peaceful Jewish minority, Hindus will attack the minority community only after being very heavily provoked. The entire history of jihad in India, of communal riots, and of the Partition story, corroborates it. When M.J. Akbar compares the riots of 1989-90 with those of 1947, he is mistaken as to the magnitude of the riots, but the may be right in the tacit analogy that in each case (1947, Bhagalpur, Aligarh, Hyderabad) the Hindu violence was merely a reaction to *minority* violence. A tendency of fascism taking shape in India exists among the self-proclaimed leaders of a different majority, or pretended majority.

There are attempts to forge an anti- Hindu front including all the minorities, the Scheduled Castes and Tribes, and the Other Backward Castes, against the upper-caste Hindus. One of the embodiments of this drive is V.T.Rajshekar's writing; another is Kanshi Ram's Bahujan Samaj Party. These people claim that all the said groups are the big majority (Bahujan) of India, oppressed by the minority of Aryan invaders. They are finding that many of the groups they are claiming as belonging in their anti-Hindu front are strongly attached to Hinduism. Nevertheless, their ideology claims that the majority is in fact not Hindu and this anti-Hindu majority should remove the upper castes from their positions and seize power.

And they are quite unabashed about favouring ruthless methods to root out *Brahmin rule*. Kanshi Ram is on record as saying about the Khalistanis, that he personally doesn't care for Khalistan, but I like their methods. V.T.Rajshekar announces: "As the 20 the century comes to an end, the Aryan imperialism must also come to end. A bloody revolution is in the offing. Don't miss this historic opportunity". An earlier anti-Brahmin activist, Ramaswamy Naicker, had said that "we will do with the Brahmins what Hitler did with the Jews". Another slogan of his was: "If you see a snake and a Brahmin, kill the Brahmin first". While the comparison of the German anti-Jewish attitude with the Hindu anti-Muslim attitude doesn't hold in most respects, the comparison with the Dalit (including missionary, Dravidian, Ambedkarite etc.) anti-Brahmin attitude is more exact.

Just like the Jews, the Brahmins get depicted as: foreign (Aryan invaders), keeping themselves separate, observing maniacal purity rules, having a large inter-state network employing a common language (Yiddish/Sanskrit), very book-oriented, deceivers, always favouring their own kind, dressed distinctively and ridiculously, cowardly but cunning, rich and keeping the others poor. Most of the things the Nazis said about the Jews, are being said by the anti-Brahmin movements about the Brahmins, including that they are a mere minority, and that they have to be shown their place by the majority, and be deprived of the undeserved power they wield. That may not yet add up to Nazism but when see the potential for violence in this movement, as well as its increasing self-righteousness, I know where in India a kind of fascism may erupt. But in the near future I don't see this budding fascism catch on among the masses. For that, they are all still too Hindu, not inclined to self- righteous fanaticism.

When you are accused of a crime, you are considered innocent until proven guilty. There is one exception: the meta-crime of making false allegations, or slander. When you utter an allegation, you are guilty of slander, while the other party remains innocent. This changes when you furnish proof for your allegation: then the other party is considered guilty and you cease to be a slanderer. By these standards, all the people who postulate an ideological lineage from Hitler to Advani are guilty of slander. For, so far I have not seen this oft-repeated allegation substantiated by any evidence whatsoever.

In an article with the promising title in defense of our dharma, she writes that the BJP, RSS and VHP "display much greater fascination with Hitler's ideas and campaigns than with the Ramayana or other Hindu religious texts". That the ruling secularist dispensation has strongly discouraged the study of Hindu tradition, is a fact of which even the Hindu*tva* movement shows the consequences, and the study of Hindu tradition in Indians schools and other media should be a top priority indeed. But that is not Madhu Kishwar's point. Apart from saying that the Hindutva campaigners are illiterates, she also says that they seek inspiration in Hitler's ideas and campaigns: "Their inspiration comes from Hitler, not from Ram". Now, this is a statement which can easily be checked. First of all, both the Hindu Mahasabha (1906) and the RSS (1925) came into being before anyone in India knew Hitler. Savarkar's Hindutva (1923) was published three years before Hitler's Mein Kampf. Clearly, the inspiration to organize and defend Hinduism at the political level does not stem from Hitler, and it did not need any outside impulse. Secondly, the RSS and the Hindu Mahasabha existed when Hitler came to power. Have they sided with Hitler? Have they even called on its followers to follow Subhash Bose and join the Axis war effort against the British? Subhash Bose's title Netaji was just the Hindi equivalent of the German Fuehrer, Hitler's title, and the Italian Duce, Mussolini's title, yet he is not, for that, accused of being Hitlerian.

But of course, since the Hindutva people are at the receiving end of all the blame, their non-support to Hitler is being turned against them, as collaboration with the British in 1942 and supported them in 1944, and yet they are accused neither of effectively supporting the Axis nor of collaboration with colonialism. The Communists opposed the British in 1940 (under Stalin's pact with Hitler) and supported them after 1941, yet after independence they have not been branded as collaborators with either fascism or colonialism. They can get away with it, while the Hindu parties are covered with abuse regardless of the stand they take. The RSS has not glorified Hitler when he was successful in any larger measure than most Indians at that time (the facts of the extermination camps were not known until 1945, and for the rest most Indian were skeptical about the British propaganda).

It would not even prove genuine fascist convictions, for many non-fascist leaders outside Europe were very impressed with the material success of Hitler's non-colonial empire, and with his formidable challenge to the colonial powers. Whatever the evil inherent in fascism, what outsiders got to see in the thirties, was that Hitler succeeded where democratic republics failed, and in the early forties, that he captured or threatened the centres of several colonial empires. So many leaders outside

Europe, from Argentina's trade-unionist Juan Person to the Multi of Jerusalem, were enthusiastic about the Axis successes. And yet, where is the proof that took inspiration from Hitler, though at the time his name didn't carry the stigma it carries today?

Hitler applied some general principles in order to achieve success. He strengthened discipline in German society. Just like Indira Gandhi during the Emergency. Just like Mao Tse-tung in China: what little positive achievements are to his credit, follow from the fact that the he could actually enforce his laws whereas the previous regime was hampered by chaos. Hitler didn't invent discipline, it was always a formula for effectiveness, and if the RSS believes in cultivating discipline within its organization (and that merely as a matter of character building, not as a model for running society as a whole), then that is just an application of universal principle, not Hitlerian or fascist. Unless and until Madhu Kishwar comes up with proof that the RSS chose its ideology and methods in express imitation of Hitler (and explains why in spite of such borrowing the differences are so big), she is a slanderer.

Hitler had made it perfectly clear where he stood and what he wanted, in his book Mein Kampf (My Struggle), written years before his take-over. His speeches are also available. So, please point out where Mr. Advani and other Hindu leaders have quoted Hitler. Failing that, apologize for the slander. Another case of slander is Mani Shankar Aiyar's article "The Saffron Swastika". Since I don't want to feel like a schoolteacher, I will not bother about the string of mistakes Mr. Aiyar makes about the pre-Nazi German politics and politicians.

It is indeed very difficult to write about some distant country without making mistakes. But saying that Gustav Steersman, a true statesman who had nothing to do with majority-baiting or minority appeasement, was "remarkably like Nehru in his commitment to democracy and his opposition to majority communalism", is of course an unabashed declaration of his intention to distort the German situation any which way so as to make it comparable with the Indian situation. Before we listen to Mr.Aiyar's pontification about the Jews in Germany, we should make it clear that here is yet another Nehruvian with an anti-Israeli bias which sometimes comes close to anti-Jewish bias.

It is of course a plain lie, Mr. Aiyar that Hitler ever campaigned on a platform Appeasement for none, justice for all. It was never the Nazi perception that the Jews were being appeased by the state. It was there perception that the Jews were accumulating wealth and power through violent agitation, etc. There were no appeasement issue miles around. When economic crisis struck, "Hitler blames it all on the Jews. The BJP...blames it all on...our largest minority." This again is simply not true. The economic non-success of India is first of all the handiwork of Soviet-infatuate sleepwalker Jawaharlal Nehru, and more recently things have been made worse by the socialist policies to which most Indian politicians still subscribe (not only V.P.Singh, under whose tenure things suddenly looked critical). But no one is blaming the Muslims for this.

If the Jan Sangh/BJP had been a fascist party, it would have grabbed power long ago, and kept it. Since the fifties, it has had the percentage of votes Hitler had in 1928. The percentage of unemployed youth available for enlistment in Private militias has been continually higher in India than in Germany before Hitler's rise to power. The Jan Sangh formed part of the government in 1977-79: unlike the Nazi party, it did not take the occasion to liquidate democracy altogether. Mani quotes an apocryphal statement attributed to Hitler by Thomas Mann:"I am not an anti-Semite. It is just very regrettable that the Jews have this unfortunate identification with Marxism". And then he equates this with an imaginary statement which he thinks sums up Advani's views: "I am not an anti-Muslim. It is just very regrettable that the Muslims have this unfortunate identification with Babar and Aurangzeb."

Of course, one shouldn't really walk into the trap of replying to Mr. Aiyar's rhetoric. He is a proven liar, and there comparisons are not really meant to inform or to argue a point. They are meant to put Hindus on the defensive and make them waste time on coping with such Hitlerian allegations. Nonetheless, it may be instructive to show up the falsehood to which the secularists have to resort in order to be able to blacken the Hindus. Firstly, while Mr.Aiyar has yet to prove that Mr. Advani is an anti-Muslim, it is clear enough that Hitler lied when (if ever) he said that he was not an anti-Semite. This is not only clear when one has the benefit of hindsight; it is quite clear when one reads Hitler's own big statement Mein Kampf. Hitler did not cultivate a Jewish following, the way the BJP woos the Muslims and counts two Muslims in its leadership.

Even without wooing the Muslims, without organizing minority cells in its party units, and without this rhetoric of Muslims being mohammedi Hindus, the BJP would not be anti- Muslim in any way comparable to Hitler's anti-Jewish stand. The most important ideological difference is that Hitler was against a group of people, the Jewish race, regardless of their behaviour (including their confabulated identification with Marxism); while the Hindutva people are against a particular doctrine and attitude, the anti-Hindu stand of some Muslim leaders, rooted in the anti-Kafir doctrine of Islam. Hitler wanted to exclude the largely well-integrated Jews, while the BJP wants to "draw the minorities (who are kept in the ghetto by their bigoted leaders) into the national mainstream."

Secondly, the Jews' "unfortunate identification with Marxism" is not only a fable; it is also based on the crank racist assumption that Marx remained a Jew even after his father had converted to Protestantism and he himself had become an atheist. By contrast, the Muslims' "unfortunate identification with Babar and Aurangzeb", while never postulated by Advani (except in Mani's slander story), does make sense in the case of a few vocal Muslim leaders, who insist on continuing Babar's and Aurangzeb's occupation of Hindu sacred places even while knowing fully well (in contrast to the common Muslim) that they had built their mosques in Mathura, Varanasi and Ayodhya for the sole reason of terrorizing and humiliating the Kafirs. In that sense, some Muslim leaders are indeed the ideological descendants of Babar and Aurangzeb. Thirdly, Marx did not invent his theories in the name of Judaism, while Babar and Aurangzeb did commit their crimes in the name of Islam. Marx had no *identification with Judaism,* while Babar and Aurangzeb had of course a strong identification with Islam. But I repeat that L.K. Advani has never attributed any identification with Babar and Aurangzeb to the Muslim community in India. It is significant that Mr. Aiyar has to make his case on the strength of imaginary statement of appeasement to strengthen his association of the BJP with Nazism. The BJP uses the word appeasement. It was the hard-line enemy of Nazism (or rather, of the German threat to British hegemony), Winston Churchill, who lambasted the appeasement policy of the soft-line enemy of Nazism, Neville Chamberlain.

Similarly the soft line opponents of Muslim communalism become in effect collaborators with it by conceding its demands and thus whetting its appetite for new concessions. Rajiv Gandhi thought he could appease Islamic agitation by conceding legislation enforcing the strict Shariat rulings concerning alimony to a divorced woman. But Islamic agitation found a new focus in the ban on the Rushdie book, which was also conceded, and in the renewal of Babar's claim ton the Hindu sacred site of Ram Janmabhoomi; so that today' secularists are advising Hindus to appease threats of Muslim youth taking to arms (or of Muslim retaliation against Hindus in Muslim countries) by conceding the Babri Masjid. The term appeasement is quite appropriate.

If at all Mr. Aiyar wants to link the use of this term to the politics of the 1930s, he should infer that the BJP, or whoever accuses the secularists of appeasement of Muslim arrogance, attributes to: the " Muslims (i.e. those Muslims that wrest concession by means of threats) the same arrogance that the democracies perceived in the Nazis". Well, the scale is certainly different, but in both cases the democratic forces are indeed dealing with the same phenomenon: the Nazis demanding territory through force, and Muslim fanatics demanding privileges and indeed territory (first Pakistan, now Kashmir) through force.

It is not Hindu society that will bring forth fascism, not even through this Boy Scouts-like unarmed kind of militantism embodied in the RSS. Hindu society just doesn't provide the necessary cultural basis for fascist politics. But Islam has an effective track record akin to that of fascism, with large-scale acquisitions of territory, extermination of unwanted communities, ruthless oppression and reduction of whole populations to the status of third-class citizens, and most of all, with a similar mind-set: division of humanity into chosen ones, inferior ones and doomed ones, and glorification of war and conquest.

To conclude this chapter about the allegation of Hindu fascism, it deserves mention that most original Western publications dealing with the Hindu Mahasabha, RSS, Jan Sangh or BJP, just don't seem to be aware of the notion that these could be fascist movements, or they reject the allegation explicitly after closer consideration. Objective outsiders are not struck by any traces of fascism in the Hindutva movements, let alone in the general thought current of anti-imperialist Hindu awakening. While one should always be vigilant for traces of totalitarianism in any ideology or movement, the obsession with fascism in the anti-Hindu rhetoric of the secularists is not the product of an analysis of the data, but of their own political compulsions.

10

The Emergence of Hindu Nationalism in India

During the course of fieldwork in a remote part of Chhattisgarh, central India, an incident took place that signified the moment when militant Hindu nationalism became a patently visible force in this mixed, Hindu/Christian Adivasi (tribal) village. It was early evening in September 1998, a time when most people had retired to their homes to prepare for the evening meal. The exception was a group of ten young men belonging to the local Hindu community.

As on most evenings, they were engaging in 'time-pass', an activity that usually consisted of loitering about, ogling local girls, or playing cards. This particular evening, they had congregated along the forest road at the edge of the village to share a bottle of local liquor. As equal portions were being poured into makeshift leaf-cups, the sounds of a vehicle could be heard some distance away. This was unusual, for vehicular traffic was still rare in this part of Chhattisgarh due to impassable roads, and the young men began to speculate about who could be driving through the forest in the growing darkness. Soon, they recognized the jeep belonging to two Catholic fathers who were returning to the parish church in the neighbouring village.

As the vehicle drew nearer, the young men spread across the road, forcing the jeep to come to a halt. One of them, Kailash, ordered two others to 'bring fire' and instructed the rest to surround the vehicle so that they could burn it. Kailash then accused the Fathers of wanting to 'turn all Hindus into Christians, like elsewhere in India'. Because 'local Hindus do not want to become Christians', Kailash argued, the Fathers had instead decided 'to bring the Hindu community down by encouraging local Christians to make and sell liquor to the Hindus'. These accusations were met with vocal agreement from the rest of the group and fierce denials from the Fathers, who insisted that they had no such conversion agenda.

To the contrary, they claimed, they were counselling Christians to avoid liquor production and consumption. Throughout this heated exchange, the Fathers remained seated nervously in their jeep. The two young men who had gone to fetch fuel now stood on either side of the vehicle, wielding cans of kerosene and large pieces of burning wood, waiting for the order to torch the jeep. Nearly an hour later, the Fathers were allowed to proceed, but only after agreeing to employ more stringent tactics against those members of the local Catholic community who continued to produce and sell liquor. This incident occurred during the period of anti-Christian violence that spread across India between 1997 and 2000. It was directly connected to the militant Hindu nationalist movement, which, since the late 1980s, has witnessed an unprecedented rise throughout India.

The long-term ideological and political agenda of this movement is the spread of Hindutva, or 'Hinduness', and the transformation of Hindu culture into an undifferentiated, unified whole, for the purpose of achieving 'one nation, one people, one culture'. This kind of singular Hinduism assumes that India has always been 'fundamentally Hindu', a community united by geographical origin, racial connection, and religious belief. Indeed, the very concept of Hindutva itself equates religious and national identity, where an Indian is defined as a Hindu, and the Hindu faith in turn is defined as the core of Indian nationhood.

Like other nationalist movements that revolve around the promotion of ethnic politics, Hindu nationalist objectives tend towards the instrumentalist kind, with its proponents using a strategy of ethno-religious mobilization to propel primordialist claims that an 'Indian nationhood' should attract everyone who is conceivably classified as a Hindu by blood or descent. According to most analysts, the larger political strategy built around the Hindu nationalist quest for power can only succeed in a context where there exists a perceived threat - real or imagined - to the majority community of Hindus.

Indeed, the perception of the 'threatening Other'-those origins and allegiances apparently lie outside of this community-has been called the 'cornerstone of the Hindu nationalist movement'. This strategy has contributed to the political success of the movement in recent years, most notably in 1997, when the Hindu supremacist political party, the Bharatiya Janata Party (BJP), first came to power as head of India's national coalition government. Within Hindu nationalist discourse, the 'threatening Other' has historically been the Muslim community. Protecting the 'Hindu nation' against conversion to Islam has, in turn, been of central concern to leading Hindu nationalist organizations like the RSS, an 'educational' association that is the most visible face of Hindutva in Chhattisgarh.

Along with other Hindu nationalist organizations such as the BJP and the 'cultural' wing, the Vishwa Hindu Parishad (VHP), the RSS has been engaged in a systematic campaign involving the aggressive propagation of Hindutva sentiment. In 1992 the campaign against Muslims culminated on 2 December in the destruction of the Babri Masjid, an important mosque in Ayodhya, north India, an event that led to thousands of deaths across the country. Even as anti-Muslim sentiment continued to underpin Hindu nationalists' attempts to consolidate the Hindu nation, the attention of such organizations was directed towards Christians across India in the mid-1990s, with a particular focus on Christian Adivasi communities.

The reason for this shift revolved around the view that Christians, as 'foreigners and non-Hindus', pose a threat to the national Hindu majority because they are engaging in 'divisive and subversive' activities, particularly amongst 'backward' Adivasi communities. It was partly in response to this threat that in the 1990s the Hindu nationalist agenda for Adivasi communities came to revolve around a twofold strategy: to bring Adivasis into the Hindu mainstream by revealing to them their 'true' identity as 'Hindus'; and to counteract minority Muslim and Christian cultures which have taken Adivasis away from the Hindu fold.

As demonstrated by this short review, there is an extensive body of academic work within the social and political sciences devoted to the origins and contemporary manifestations of the Hindu nationalist movement. Most of this literature situates the antecedents of Hindu nationalism within historical traditions such as late nineteenth- and early twentieth-century German ideas of the nation and ethnic nationalism, nineteenth-century religious reform movements and Christian missionizing practices, and scouting and the British police. Contemporary manifestations of the Hindu nationalist movement, moreover, are framed against the backdrop of a postcolonial context that has been informed by the struggle between parties, personalities, and ideologies for the political reconstruction of India.

As Ludden (2005: 18-19) acknowledges, this struggle, which is underpinned by the gradual disintegration since the mid-1970s of the Congress party's hold over the Indian state, is principally concerned with the legitimacy of the state and the distribution of state resources and power. Since the early 1990s, this struggle has also been shaped by economic liberalization and an increase in urban, middle-class affluence and consumerism. It is in this context that the BJP and other proponents of the Hindu right have gradually enhanced their power and that, in the 1990s, Hindutva 'emerged as a solid competitor for popular loyalties'.

Alongside this research is a great deal of comparative literature that views Hindu nationalism, together with other 'nationalisms', as a product of modernizing and globalizing forces unfolding throughout much of the contemporary world. This scholarship, finally, belongs to a more general discourse on nationalism that has been produced over the past two decades, largely in response to the growing prominence of nationalist movements across the globe. While a detailed review of this literature would unnecessarily duplicate by now familiar arguments that have sought to explain how and why nationalist movements arise, it is important to note that these accounts together point to the role of several key phenomena: rapid industrialization and the uneven development of capitalism; modernity and (post)colonialism; the mobilization and communalization of communities in response to the impact of interstate warfare; and the politics of ethnic and other group entitlement claims in plural societies.

The purpose of drawing attention to this extensive discourse is to highlight what has generally been ignored: namely, the grass-roots processes that explain precisely how nationalism is manifested and spread at the local level, particularly in rural settings, and how ordinary persons' engagement in nationalist projects evolves. It is true that, with specific respect to India, there is a great deal of attention on the spread of Hindu nationalist sentiment and violence in urban settings.

Available accounts include a focus on urban centres as the site of conflict, on the introduction of new rituals or 'invented traditions' created for political purposes in urban areas, and on personal accounts of the victims of (largely urban) communal violence. While a small number of works cursorily mention the 'social upliftment' strategies being employed by Hindu nationalist organizations in rural areas, detailed ethnography is sparse, and there is no work to date that documents and analyses the precise manner by which Hindu nationalism is being introduced amongst rural Adivasi communities.

There is perhaps reason for the lack of attention to rural, *Adivasi* communities, foremost being the fact that Hindu nationalism has its origins and is still concentrated 'in the heart of India's middle classes'. However, the anti-Christian violence of the sort described at the beginning of this chapter is representative of the fact that this movement has successfully spread from its urban centres into more 'backward', rural regions, seeking popular and electoral support from India's dispersed Adivasi communities.

Specific aims are twofold: to identify the social conditions at the local level that have contributed to the emergence of

Hindu nationalism in one particular rural, Adivasi village, and to explore the process by which nationalist ideology is represented and transmitted to this community. Following previous analyses, I argue that the successful spread of Hindu nationalism to specifically Adivasi areas is dependent on the 'instrumentalist' involvement of self-interested, powerful outsiders, such as proponents of the RSS, who use their positions to communalize social identities and relations by actively promoting the idea of the 'threatening Christian Other'. Here, I find Paul Brass's analysis of ethnic group politics to be constructive, particularly with respect to the importance he gives to the involvement of political organizations in the promotion of ethnic group loyalties to a nationalist agenda.

The rise of Hindu nationalism as a political force during the past decade was not widely predicted and, if for no other reason than this, has commanded much attention from social scientists. It is always tempting to present a vocal and persuasive social movement as though it were the inevitable culmination of one or another set of forces, a major pitfall of sociologists in their search for trends and periodizarions. Both these books, in their different ways, take Hindu nationalism as a starting point for an analysis of the contemporary Indian polity. Both, however, have the merit of avoiding a 'wise after the event' determinist stance and both give the contingent and unpredictable their dues.

Why did India need reinventing as Corbridge and Harriss suggest? The political ideals expressed in the constitution that Nehru helped to draw up and the modernizing, secularist and would be dirigiste policies he pursued have been discredited in the eyes of many people in India. Their decline demands a redefinition of the relationship between state and civil society. The diminishing popularity of the Congress Party also left a hiatus in electoral politics. Disillusion with corrupt politicians at both centre and state level also created the need for a new 'state idea'. Corbridge and Harriss provide an excellent account of the political economy of India post 1947, 'unashamedly unfashionable' in its appeal to theories of class formation.

Drawing on the Gramscian notion of passive revolution,

they show how a weak Indian bourgeoisie had to make allies of the old elites in order to shape a state that was appropriate for the establishment of capitalism. The re-emergence of Hindu nationalism is not to be read as evide nce that the Nehruvian modernizing project was an essentially alien imposition on India, an implant doomed to inevitable failure. Rather, the dirigiste state failed to undermine the privileges of key elites, new and old. The chief of these were the rich farmers who benefited by or were the product of the 'green revolution', the emergent bourgeoisie, and the civil service bureaucrats.

While it can be read as a response to this situation, Hindu nationalism - as Corbridge and Harriss rightly observe - did not emerge fully formed in the late 1980s, having its roots far back in the colonial period. Corbridge and Harriss do not see the resurgence of Hindu nationalism in the late 1980s and 1990s as the product of any automatic or inevitable 'fit' between nationalism and the demands of economic liberalization, though doubtless there is a degree of congruence.

"Nationalism" and "Communalism" are synonymous in an Indian context and are negative concepts. They are identified with the misuse of religion in politics. Worldwide, the first such misuse of religion in politics took place in late 19th century in America when the Conservative Protestants in the face of rationalism and scientific values came up with reassertion of 'fundamentals' of Christianity. Essentially, this was an attempt to re-impose the pre-modern values of birth based hierarchy of gender and class and later in Europe, the Nazi and fascist onslaughts used race for similar reasons. In recent times, we have seen the rise of Islamic or communalism in several countries of the middle-east, typified by Ayatullah Kohemini in the Iran of eighties and nineties. Communalism in India made its major appearance, in the pre-Independence era, in 1886, with the formation of two communal streams – the Muslim League (based on Islam) and the Hindu Mahasabha and the Rashtriya Swayamsevak Sangh (based on Hinduism).

Over the years, these two streams have constantly tried to fan the communal passions of their followers, be it in the

Shah Banoo case or the perennial dispute with regard to the Babri Masjid in Ayodhya. With the emergence of the Hindu right-wing party, the Bharatiya Janata Party (BJP) as a major political force in the country, the proponents of Hindu communalism, better known through its ideology "Hindutva", seem to have gained the upper hand.

HINDUTVA

The fundamental goal of the "Hindutva" ideology is the establishment of a Hindu-Nation state exemplified in the fascist doctrine of "one nation, one culture, one language, one religion". It is a very narrow type of "nationalism" which seeks legitimacy through demonizing other religions and faiths, very specially Islam and Christianity. Whilst it is not representative of the Hindu majority of the country, it makes every attempt to appear to champion the concerns of mainstream Hinduism.

These posturings have created a great deal of disharmony in various parts of the country particularly in the last fifteen years when in 1990 one of the main exponents of the "Hindu Rashtra" namely, Mr. L. K. Advani, (a former Deputy Prime Minister of the country and currently the President of the BJP) went across the country on a "Rath Yatra". This created a great deal of animosity, blood-shed and deepened the divide between the Hindus and Muslims of the country.

In the wake of the demolition of the Babri Masjid on 6th December 1992, India became divided even more, on communal lines. This was followed by several other instances of communal violence which include the bashing up of Christians in Gujarat (North-west India) in 1998 – 99 and the Gujarat Genocide of 2002 (when more than 2000 Muslims were killed in Gujarat); among the other communal incidents were the horrendous murder of the Australian Missionary Graham Staines and his two sons (in January 1999 in Manoharpur, Orissa) and the attack on the Sisters of Mother Teresa in Kerala in October 2004.

Bibliography

A.H. Armstrong, ed., Classical Mediterranean Spirituality, World Spirituality 15, New York: Crossroad, 1989.

Adorno, T., The Culture Industry, London: Routledge, 1972/1991.

Babin, P., The New Era in Religious Communication, Minneapolis, MN: Fortress Press, 1991.

Beckford, J. A., Religion and Advanced Industrial Society, London: Unwin Hyman, 1989.

Bell, C., Ritual Thinking, Ritual Practice, New York: Oxford University Press, 1992.

Carey, J., Preface to the First Edition of the Journal of Media and Religion, Journal of Media and Religion, 1 (1), 1–3, 2002.

Christians, C. G., J. P. Ferré and P. M. Fackler, Good News: Social Ethics and the News, New York: Oxford University Press, 1993.

Coleman Barks, trans. The Essential Rumi, new expanded edition (San Francisco: Harper San Francisco, 2004.

Dawood, N.J., trans. The Koran. New York: Penguin, 2003.

Denise Cush, Catherine Robinson, and Michael York, eds., Encyclopedia of Hinduism, New York: Routledge, 2007.

Eickelman, D. F. and J. W. Anderson, New Media in the Muslim World, Bloomington, IN: Indiana University Press, 1999.

Enroth, Ronald, A Guide to New Religions Movements, Downers Grove: Intervarsity Press, 2005.

Geertz, C., The Interpretation of Cultures, London: Hutchinson, 1975.

Greil, A. and T. Robbins (eds), Between Sacred and Secular: Research and Theory on Quasi-Religion, Greenwich, CT: JAI Press, 1994.

Hoover, S. M. (forthcoming), Religion in the Media Age, London: Routledge.

Hunt, Stephen J., Alternative Religion: A Sociological Introduction, Aldershot: Ashgate, 2003.

Jenkins, H., Textual Poachers: Television Fans and Participatory Culture, London: Routledge, 1992.

Kerrigan, Michael, Alan Lothian, and Piers Vitebsky, Epics of Early Civilization: Myths of the Ancient Near East, Duncan Baird Publishers: London, 1998.

L. S. Clark (eds), Practicing Religion in an Age of Media, New York: Columbia University Press, 2002.

Malise Ruthven, Islam: A Very Short Introduction, New York: Oxford University Press, 2000.

Mark Juergensmeyer, Global Religions: An Introduction, New York: Oxford University Press, 2003.

McDannell, C., Material Christianity: Religion and Popular Culture in America, New Haven, CT: Yale University Press, 1995.

Morgan, D., Religious Visual Culture in Theory and Practice, Berkeley, CA: University of California Press, 2005.

Nouwen, Henri J.M. The Road to Daybreak: A Spiritual Journey. New York: Doubleday, 1988.

O'Flaherty, Wendy Doniger (ed. and trans.), The Rig Veda: An Anthology. Penguin Books, NY, 1981.

Park, R. E., 'Immigrant Community and Immigrant Press', American Review, 3, 143–52, 2005.

Rinpoche, Sogyal. The Tibetan Book of Living and Dying. New York: Harper Collins, 1993.

Roleff, Tamara L., ed. Satanism. San Diego: Greenhaven Press, Inc., 2002.

Rossi, P. J. and P. Soukup (eds) Mass Media and the Moral Imagination, Kansas City, MO: Sheed and Ward, 1994.

Steven Heine and Charles S. Prebish, eds., Buddhism in the Modern World: Adaptations of an Ancient Tradition, New York: Oxford University Press, 2003.

Sushil Mittal & Gene Thursby, eds., The Hindu World, New York: Routledge, 2004.

Takeuchi Yoshinori, ed., Buddhist Spirituality I: Indian, Southeast Asian, Tibetan, and Early Chinese, World Spirituality Series 8, New York: Crossroad Publishing, 1993.

Tu Weiming & Mary Evelyn Tucker, eds., Confucian Spirituality, World Spirituality 11, New York: Herder & Herder, 2002.

Veer, P. van der, 'Transnational Religion', paper presented at the Conference on Transnational Migration: Comparative Perspectives, Princeton, 2001.

Wilkins, W.J., Hindu Mythology: Vedic and Puranic, Rupa and Co.: Calcutta, 1986.

Wise, Michael, Martin Abegg, Jr., Edward Cook, The Dead Sea Scrolls: A New Translation, HarperCollins: NY, 1996.

Wuthnow, R., Rediscovering the Sacred: Perspectives on Religion in Contemporary Society, Grand Rapids, MI: Eerdmans, 1992.

Xinzhong Yao, An Introduction to Confucianism, Cambridge: Cambridge University Press, 2000.

Zaehner, R.C. (translation), Hindu Scriptures, J.M. Dent & Sons: London, 1966.

Zaleski, J., The Soul of Cyberspace: How New Technology is Changing our Spiritual Lives, New York: HarperCollins, 1997.

Index

A

Action of Liturgy, 73, 77, 80.
Action of Mission, 68, 80.
Alimony, 1, 4, 279.
Anushilan Samiti, 160, 161, 162, 165.
Arya and Swastika, 213.
Arya Samaj, 13, 55, 95, 142, 166, 168, 171, 176, 179, 202, 203, 204, 246.
Aryan Invasion, Theory 6, 139.
Aryan Race, 149, 150, 193, 200, 214, 220.
Authoritarianism, 111, 264.

B

Behind Fanaticism, 134.
Brahman Conspiracy, 133.
Brahmo Samaj, 159, 160, 187, 188, 190.

C

Carnage, 30.
Celestial Nationalists, 43.
Class Antagonisms, 2.
Colonial Masters, 173.
Colonial Power, 173, 275.
Colonialism, 48, 49, 54, 56, 72, 102, 169, 170, 174, 175.
Concept of Natural Order, 16.
Cultural Nationalism, 2, 113, 161, 164, 180, 184.

D

Demonizing the Muslim, 41.

E

Evolution of Ideological Terminology, 166.

H

Hindu Communalism, 8, 23, 24, 58, 180, 199, 288.
Hindu Fascist Violence, 136.
Hindu Nation, 1, 4, 15, 24, 25, 26, 27, 28, 29, 30, 37, 38, 39, 40, 48, 49, 54, 58, 64, 70, 73, 74, 79, 110, 140, 144, 145, 146, 148, 149, 152, 157, 160, 164, 165, 166, 184, 187, 188, 189, 190, 195, 234, 281, 282, 283, 284, 285, 286, 287.

Hindu Nationalism, 1, 15, 24, 27, 28, 30, 31, 32, 33, 40, 41, 42, 45, 46, 48, 50, 54, 55, 56, 58, 64, 70, 79, 80, 86, 118, 180, 183, 185, 186, 191, 196, 223, 225, 229, 287, 289.

Hindu Rashtra, 15, 39, 40, 128, 155, 167, 168, 183, 184, 185.

Hindu Renaissance, 158, 159, 161.

Hindu Revivalism, 1, 171, 199.

Hindutva, 1, 2, 3, 4, 5, 6, 7, 8, 15, 16, 17, 19, 20, 21, 22, 33, 39, 40, 41, 42, 45, 48, 51, 52, 53, 54, 55, 56, 58, 69, 70, 71, 73, 77, 78, 84, 85, 86, 87, 92, 93, 94, 95, 124, 125, 146, 163, 166, 167, 168, 169, 178, 234, 236, 261, 274, 275, 279, 280, 284, 285, 288, 289.

Hindutva Movement, 1, 7, 15, 16, 19, 20, 21, 22, 24, 106, 198, 209, 232, 236, 265, 266, 274, 280.

Holy War, 12, 22, 23, 198, 219.

Homogeneous Identity, 48.

I

Idealized Men and Women, 42.

Ideological Power Equation, 146.

Independence Movement, 141, 161, 169.

India House, 162, 163, 164.

Indian National Congress, 3, 4, 10, 11, 31, 95, 136, 151, 161, 163, 164, 165, 166.

International Aggressors, 37.

L

Linguistic Homogeneity, 173.

Linking Fascism, 196.

Liturgy as Dual Loci, 68.

M

Monotheism, 13, 168, 190, 218, 219, 222, 223.

Multiculturalism, 45.

Multiple Cultural Belief, 81.

N

New Experiment, 114.

O

Other Faiths, 4, 91, 117.

P

Partition of India, 27, 145, 166.

Pedigree, 31.

Political Void, 31.

Polytheism, 42, 224.

Post-independence, 169.

Power Retaining Philosophy, 116.

Public Rituals, 42, 43.

R

Ramarajya, 164.
Religio-cultural Entity, 49.
Religio-cultural Roots, 61.
Religious Dogma, 3, 50, 201.
Resistive-liberative Momentum, 64, 68, 80.
Revolutionary Movements, 161.

S

Sadhana, 21.
Saffronization, 150.
Satya, 8, 87, 89, 92, 165, 166, 216.
Secularist Critique, 87.
Shifting Political Winds, 30.
Single Idolater, 5.
Social Anarchy, 2.
Social Justice, 3, 92, 132, 138.
Socio-political Forces, 81.
Somnath Temple Movement, 169.
Swayamsevaks, 183, 184.

T

Targeting a Minority, 258.
Transforming Religion, 133.
Two-nation Theory, 166, 180, 254.

U

Uniform Civil Code, 3, 4, 104, 109, 115.

W

Wooing and Wounding of Minorities, 54.